P9-DFO-009

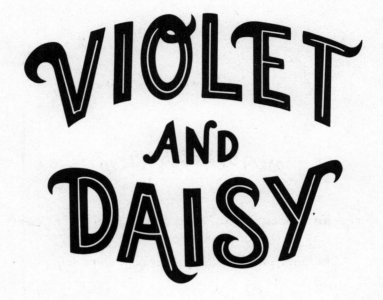

ALSO BY SARAH MILLER

The Borden Murders: Lizzie Borden and the Trial of the Century

The Miracle & Tragedy of the Dionne Quintuplets

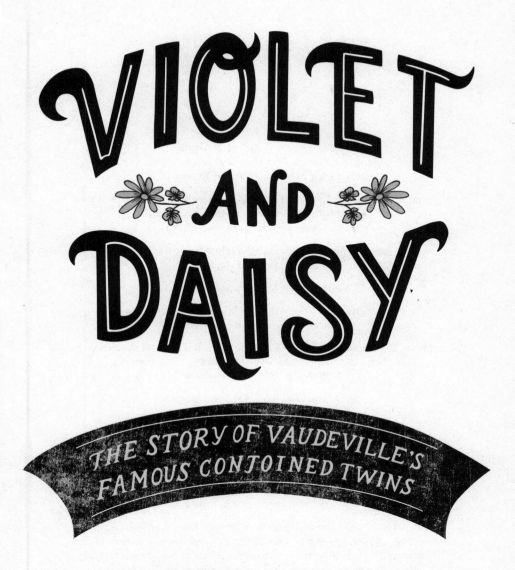

VIOLET AND DAISY

THE STORY OF VAUDEVILLE'S FAMOUS CONJOINED TWINS

SARAH MILLER

schwartz & wade books · new york

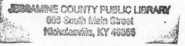
JESSAMINE COUNTY PUBLIC LIBRARY
600 South Main Street
Nicholasville, KY 40356

Text copyright © 2021 by Sarah Miller
Jacket photograph from the collection of the author
Jacket lettering copyright © 2021 by Kimberly Glyder

All rights reserved. Published in the United States by Schwartz & Wade Books,
an imprint of Random House Children's Books,
a division of Penguin Random House LLC, New York.

Schwartz & Wade Books and the colophon are trademarks
of Penguin Random House LLC.

Visit us on the Web! GetUnderlined.com

Educators and librarians, for a variety of teaching tools,
visit us at RHTeachersLibrarians.com

Library of Congress Cataloging-in-Publication Data is available upon request.
ISBN 978-0-593-11972-3 (trade) — ISBN 978-0-593-11973-0 (lib. bdg.) —
ISBN 978-0-593-11974-7 (ebook)

The text of this book is set in 12-point Dante MT Pro.
Book design by Jen Valero

Printed in the United States of America
10 9 8 7 6 5 4 3 2 1
First Edition

Random House Children's Books supports the First Amendment
and celebrates the right to read.

Penguin Random House LLC supports copyright. Copyright fuels creativity,
encourages diverse voices, promotes free speech, and creates a vibrant culture.
Thank you for buying an authorized edition of this book and for complying
with copyright laws by not reproducing, scanning, or distributing any part in any
form without permission. You are supporting writers and allowing
Penguin Random House to publish books for every reader.

TO PETER SIERUTA,
WHO TOLD ME ABOUT VIOLET AND DAISY HILTON,
AND TO MICHAEL WILDE,
WHO MADE SURE I REMEMBERED

CONTENTS

PART TWO

PART ONE

CHAPTER 1

OF COURSE THEIR MOTHER SCREAMED WHEN THEY WERE
born. She screamed so loudly and for so long on February 5, 1908, the
neighbors pounded on the wall to command her to stop. But twenty-
one-year-old Kate Skinner could not help but scream. After fourteen
hours of unrelenting pain, her baby had not come. It had not even
seemed to budge. The midwife, Mary Hilton, began to fear that the
unborn infant had died. She ran downstairs and out of the house to
call for the doctor.

As if impelled by the midwife's alarm, the birth suddenly proceeded. For a few minutes, anyway. When the baby was finally halfway born, everything ground to a halt. Something was in the way.
Twins, the midwife decided. There were already five sets in the family; Kate herself had been a twin. One baby must have been blocking
the path of the other. But how, exactly, Mary Hilton did not know,
until out came a pair of feet that could only belong to a second baby.
It was as if both twins were determined to be born simultaneously—
one headfirst and one feetfirst. The headfirst child prevailed. Then
came a great deal of unusual twisting and turning until at last, two
six-pound baby girls lay squalling on the bed.

That was when the real shrieking began. One look at them, and
Kate Skinner writhed and flailed and howled. She struggled so fiercely

3

that Mary Hilton and her twenty-nine-year-old daughter, Alice, could hardly hold Kate still.

The babies were pretty little girls, each with ten perfect tiny fingers and ten perfect tiny toes, the pair of them as alike as two flower buds on a single stem. Kate was not looking at their faces, however, nor their fingers and toes. Instead, she had seen the base of their spines: a raw-looking swathe of flesh that fused the newborn sisters back-to-back.

Conjoined twins, we call them today—a rare type of identical twinning due entirely to a quirk of timing. Usually, identical twins occur when a single egg cell divides in half sometime during the first two weeks after fertilization. The two halves then grow into a pair of complete and genetically identical bodies. If an egg attempts to divide *after* fourteen days, however, the split will be incomplete, and the resulting bodies remain connected. It may happen at the head, or anywhere along the torso, causing some combination of skin, muscle, bone, and organs to be shared or intertwined.

In 1908, such siblings were better known as Siamese twins, after a pair of world-famous brothers, Eng and Chang Bunker, who were born joined at the chest in 1811 in Thailand, which was then called Siam. As far as most people in the early nineteenth century were concerned, though, the simplest term for such people was *freaks* or *monsters*. And that was why Kate Skinner could not stop screaming. According to the teachings of her church, she had committed a sin by conceiving these children out of wedlock, and Kate had no doubt that God had doled out her punishment in the form of these monster-babies.

• • •

When Dr. James Rooth arrived, he tried to console Kate. More often than not, twins such as these died soon after birth, he told her. Any shared organs usually were not up to the task of supporting two bodies.

Kate was not comforted. Her shame as an unwed mother had been great before. Now it had doubled, then doubled again. In the eyes of the world her babies were not only bastards, but freaks besides. Nothing and no one could compel her to hold her daughters. She certainly would not nurse them. She would not so much as look at them. She turned her face to the wall and waited for them to die.

But Kate Skinner's babies did not die.

CHAPTER 2

CONTRARY TO DR. ROOTH'S PREDICTION, THE FACT THAT THE
Skinner twins were attached to each other affected the newborns'
posture and their movement, but it had almost no effect on the most
critical factor: their bodies' function. The bridge between them was
relatively small—a portion of one twin's left buttock was fused with
a portion of the other twin's right buttock. X-rays would show that
their spines were connected in the most minor way possible, ending in a single shared tailbone. The last inch or so of their intestinal
system was also joined. One twin's colon ended in a sort of pouch,
which jutted a little sideways to link with her sister's. That combined
inch of rectum ended in a single opening. (In other words, just one
extra-long nappy would do for both babies, but it needed changing
twice as often.)

Everyone who saw the twins wondered the same thing: Could
they be separated? Dr. Rooth had grave doubts. There was no telling what sorts of anomalies might be contained within that fusion,
no way to learn how extensively their nervous and circulatory systems might be twined together, for instance. Did they share nerve
endings or blood vessels? Could some portion of one twin's blood
travel through the bridge between them and circulate through the
other twin's body? Were there places on that bridge that both babies

could feel? Dr. Rooth probed here and there, but he could not find a spot that made the sisters respond in tandem. That was promising, but it did not guarantee that their spinal cords were not somehow braided together, or that the vital fluid bathing the cords did not mingle. Rooth knew that in two other cases of twins with similar anatomy, the fusion of the spinal cords was "much more intimate and extreme" than anyone could have guessed. Slicing into them without understanding such things might very well mean death for at least one twin.

From the day they were born, the twins' only physical limitation was that they could not lie on their backs or their bellies. It simply wasn't possible. They had to be placed on their sides. Yet because they were not joined across the full width of their backs, and because the connection was off-center, a small amount of hingelike movement was possible between them; they could lean a little away from each other, into a V shape—very much like a book laid spine up over the arm of a chair.

· · ·

To Kate's dismay, her twins not only lived but proved to be "a very healthy, lusty young pair," who seemed "to possess an uncommonly vigorous life." They took to their bottles of diluted cow's milk with noticeable relish, putting on a full pound by the end of the first week.

Still, she would not feed or hold them. She herself would not even eat. At the very least she should give them names, Kate's mother insisted. Days passed before Kate finally surrendered to her mother's pleas. As they lay facing her, she labeled the baby on her left-hand side Violet, the right-hand baby Daisy.

Violet and Daisy. A sweet pair of names from a mother who was not willing or able to give them anything else. All Kate wanted was to be rid of them. But how? Orphanages did not welcome illegitimate children, believing they were fated to be as "immoral" as their parents. Adoption seemed Kate's only hope. But who on earth could be persuaded to adopt a set of "double babies"?

Mary Hilton, of all people, came to Kate's rescue. It was not the first time, either. After Kate had lost her job at a local greengrocer, Mary Hilton engaged the visibly pregnant young woman to wait tables at her pub, the Queen's Arms, when no one else would hire her. Never mind that Kate had not worked for pay. She had worked—and gratefully—solely in return for Mary's promise to deliver her baby free of charge. It was an uneven trade, but Kate did not dare complain. Women in such straits were desperate, and Mary knew it. That was why her bar was so often staffed with young, pregnant women. She used that desperation to extort free labor and long, hard hours from her barmaids, even in the final months of their pregnancies. Raising four daughters of her own despite having been widowed twice before turning forty may have forged Mary into a formidable, resourceful businesswoman, but it had not made her especially sympathetic to others' suffering.

Now, though, what seemed to be a kindlier side of Mary Hilton was showing itself. Sometime during the first week after the birth, Mary began appearing regularly at the Skinner flat, often with her youngest daughter, Edith, to look in on the babies. Mary and Edith lent a hand in the feedings and diaper changes, providing Kate's mother and sister with welcome breaks. While Mary sat at Kate's bedside listening to her woes, Edith doted on Violet and Daisy. For the rest of her life, in fact, Edith would remember the first time those five-day-old babies were placed in her arms. She, more than anyone else, began opening her heart to them.

All of these circumstances make it impossible to say for certain who was most thrilled by Mary Hilton's offer to adopt Violet and Daisy. Despite Edith's blossoming sense of responsibility and affection for the babies, Kate Skinner remains the most likely candidate.

As Edith would remember it decades later, Kate threw her arms around Mary and sobbed, "Take my babies and care for them as a mother. Tell them you are their aunt and never tell them who their real mother is."

In that era, nothing more than a verbal agreement was necessary to transfer custody. No adoption laws or regulations would exist in England until 1926. Mary Hilton could have scooped up the two three-week-old babies and taken them home right then and there. Instead, Mary did something unusual—she took Kate Skinner to see a lawyer.

On February 25, a formal adoption agreement was drawn up and signed at the office of J. G. Bramhall. Under its terms Mary Hilton assumed complete custody of and financial responsibility for Violet and Daisy, guaranteeing that Kate would bear no further obligation or liability for their care, support, or education. She was free. To Kate Skinner, it must have seemed a godsend. Not only was Mary Hilton willing to adopt her babies, but she was willing—eager, even—to legally vow never to foist them back onto Kate. A more traditional, informal arrangement would have provided no such assurance.

The adoption papers granted Mary Hilton several protections as well. Kate Skinner had made it abundantly clear that she harbored not the slightest twinge of affection toward her daughters. Nevertheless, the agreement also carefully guarded Mary against any change of heart, any sudden swell of maternal tenderness or second thoughts that might unexpectedly overtake the birth mother. By signing, Kate agreed never to make any attempt to "regain the care, custody, or control" of Violet and Daisy nor "at any time hereafter molest or in any way annoy" Mary Hilton. If she violated that promise, the agreement required Kate to repay Mary Hilton ten shillings for every week that the children had spent under Mary's care.

Kate Skinner signed. So far as anyone knows, it was a decision she never regretted.

CHAPTER 3

ALMOST SIMULTANEOUSLY–AND CERTAINLY NOT COINCIDENTALLY–
news of the unusual birth appeared for the first time in the *Brighton
Herald* on February 22, 1908. Now that Violet and Daisy were legally
hers, Mary Hilton was as eager for the world to know all about these
extraordinary twins as Kate Skinner had been to forget them.

To hear the newspaper tell it, that "motherly lady" who had helped
to deliver them was as good as a saint, taking in two such extraordinary babies. Mary Hilton admitted to the *Herald* that at the moment
of their birth, "her emotions were very perturbed when she saw what
had come into the world." Three weeks later, though, her excitement
over her two little foster daughters was as plain as day. Never had she
seen two finer babies, she said, perfectly delighted over their progress.
Well before Violet and Daisy were two months old, Mary had them
photographed, nestled tightly in a wicker pram with their long white
dresses draped over the handle.

They wore those same white dresses to their christening. It was
a private affair, attended only by Mary Hilton; her husband, Henry;
Edith; and, surprisingly, Kate Skinner. Edith whisked the babies, who
were already becoming "tolerably well known" in Brighton, from the
cab and into the church without attracting an iota of public atten-

tion. They were wrapped in "white robes, fastened at the sleeves with dainty white silk ribbon, and enveloped in a soft ample white woollen shawl." As the group waited in the vestry for Reverend Gould, Violet dropped off to sleep. Daisy kicked up a fuss and was quickly hushed with a "comfy" to suck. *Smack, smack, smack* went her vigorous little lips as the reverend carefully cradled the pair of sisters on his left arm, as Mary had taught him beforehand, and sprinkled their identical foreheads with water. Violet slumbered on, oblivious.

After Mary and Kate had signed the register and the reverend had offered "the kindliest words" to the children's mother, Mary Hilton presented Reverend Gould with a picture postcard of the babies "as a souvenir of the most extraordinary Christening he is ever likely to perform." Then the twins were bundled out of the church and back into the waiting cab as inconspicuously as they had come in.

As soon as it was over, however, Mary told the *Herald* all about the christening in minute, satisfying detail. She had shrewdly guaranteed the paper's interest by inviting reporters into her home earlier in the week, to admire Violet and Daisy firsthand.

"They are as comely a little pair of babies as one could wish to see," the newspaper observed, "with large dark blue eyes, and a goodly crop of fluffy brown hair."

At seven weeks old, Daisy had already captured the reputation of being the prettier one. Her chin was just a fraction narrower than Violet's, lending her face an especially fetching heart shape. "Violet is not quite so bonny," the *Herald* decided. Her coloring was not as vivid, her features somehow less irresistible. "Still," said the *Herald*, "as she lies sucking her bottle, with her large deep blue eyes looking out wondrously into the world, she is quite a winsome and appealing little lady." She had a habit of tucking her head against Daisy's neck, and the two of them would nuzzle each other that way until they wore each other's hair off. Violet's "air of serene contentment" as she lay there next to her sister was so complete that she could make you believe that "one of the finest things in the world was to be a 'Siamese Twin.'"

Daisy was another matter. "When she is awake, she is very much awake," the *Herald* reported, noting that Mary Hilton had dubbed her "a little terror." Though the way Mary said it, it sounded "as if she were calling her an angel."

"I suppose you're getting quite fond of them?" the *Herald* reporter asked.

"Fond of them!" Mary replied. "Why, I wouldn't part with them for anything."

She kept them beautifully dressed, in little lace-fronted frocks with lace sleeves woven through with narrow pink or blue ribbon. The dresses could not be fastened up the back as usual, a problem solved by a simple alteration: one side seam of each skirt was opened and fitted with hooks and eyes. That way the skirts could be fastened both above and below the bridge between the babies. (Eventually Edith would contrive a special undergarment, "a covering which resembled in shape the . . . connection between the girls," to keep their skin from peeking between the seams of their dresses.)

All these intimate facts stoked the public's interest, and Mary Hilton welcomed the town's inevitable curiosity with open arms. "The twins are not really on public view, but Mrs. Hilton is prepared to let interested persons see them," the *Herald* article concluded, assuring the squeamish that apprehensions about encountering "anything unpleasant" at the Queen's Arms were altogether unwarranted. Violet and Daisy were as ordinary-looking as could be, despite their status as "the most wonderful little couple in the world."

For a woman who claimed that she was not exhibiting her foster daughters, Mary Hilton was more than accommodating to such visitors, welcoming the curious seven days a week, between eleven and seven o'clock. There was no charge specifically to see the babies, but it was understood that anyone who bought a pint was invited to step back into the parlor and have a peek at the two little girls in their pram. All summer long the customers came, buying the requisite pints and often spending an extra few pennies to indulge in souvenir postcards just like the one Mary had given to Reverend Gould.

This was almost certainly what Mary Hilton had had in mind from the very beginning.

CHAPTER 4

PERCHED ALONG THE NORTHERN SHORE OF THE ENGLISH Channel, the town of Brighton bustled with tourists during the warm months of the year. Its seaside hotels, restaurants, theaters, and piers had been attracting holidaymakers for well over a century by the time Violet and Daisy were born. With no effort at all, those two babies quickly changed the Queen's Arms from just another pub to a popular destination. They were so good for business, in fact, that by the time Violet and Daisy were a year old, the Hiltons were operating a larger pub several blocks away, the Evening Star, where business continued to flourish.

Though the girls were hardly old enough to form memories, the constant traffic left an indelible impression on Violet's and Daisy's senses. "Our earliest and only recollections," Daisy would reveal years later, "are the penetrating smell of brown ale, cigars, and pipes, and the movements of the visitors' hands, which were for ever lifting up our baby clothes to see just how we were attached to each other." The babies were so pretty and their clothes were so cleverly made that many people did not believe the sisters were truly joined. Up went their skirts and down came their nappy, again and again and again. "The first thing I remember about my early childhood that I remember clearly," said Violet, "and Daisy says she remembers it, too, was that everybody stared at us so much and old women used to poke their fingers at the spot where we were joined."

The public remained fascinated by the Brighton United Twins, as Mary had dubbed them, and on the occasion of their first birthday, the *Herald* obliged by reporting on their weight (thirty-two pounds combined), how many teeth each had (three for Daisy and four for Violet), and the amusing details of their out-of-sync bout with bronchitis. Daisy had fallen ill first, making Violet envious. Every time Daisy received a spoonful of medicine, Violet raised a fuss, "convinced that favouritism was being shown to her sister—that Daisy was having some little luxury that was being denied to her."

No longer was Violet the quiet, contented one. A complete reversal in temperament had taken place. "Possibly it was the extra petting Violet received, on account of her delicacy," the *Herald* supposed. Now she was the little terror, "the more irritable and the more fractious."

. . .

The idea that they could differ that drastically from each other so early in life strained the very limits of the public's comprehension. For the rest of their lives, the world would debate time and again whether Violet and Daisy were one person, or two. Were they made up of two bodies joined together, or a single shared body?

No one but Violet and Daisy themselves seemed able to grasp the possibility that they could exist simultaneously as distinct individuals *and* members of an indivisible unit. In their own minds they were not one or the other, but both.

From a very young age, Violet and Daisy understood that they were unique. Yet at the same time, being joined together felt to them entirely normal. They harbored neither resentment toward each other nor envy toward those who were not similarly joined. Quite the contrary. "We were never permitted to play with other children," they said, "and when we looked over the sill of our window and saw little girls walking alone we felt quite sorry for them because they were not as we were."

Their first awareness that they were different from other children had come when they'd learned to crawl. In the beginning it was an advantage to be joined. Together they moved faster, propelling each other across the room. "Then something happened!" Violet and Daisy recalled. "We discovered to our dismay that we could not pass when the leg of the bed, or table, was between us!" They tried over and over again, until they frustrated themselves to tears. Defeated, they turned to their building blocks, only to be thwarted anew when they inadvertently knocked down each other's towers with a stray knee or elbow. Spurred by exasperation, their minds sparked into action in a way they hadn't before, and Violet and Daisy experienced their first conscious thought as they came to a simultaneous realization: "One of us would have to be allowed to build her house alone while the other remained motionless. Which one? Why, the one who wanted more to build."

The one who wanted it more. That simple precept would govern the rest of their lives. Violet and Daisy did not yet know the word for compromise, but before they learned to stand up, it had become as vital and intuitive as breathing, a process so elemental, it did not require a name. "The thought did not take such clear form until later years," they explained. By the time it did become clear enough to articulate, their tearful fits of frustration were a distant memory and the concept was permanently ingrained: Take turns giving in, or give up altogether.

IT WOULD SEEM THAT BY MID– TO LATE 1910, MARY HILTON had stopped showing off Violet and Daisy at home and turned to exhibiting the toddlers across the British Isles. Perhaps in Brighton the novelty of the United Twins had finally worn thin after two years. After all, Brighton had no shortage of theaters and piers full of other amusements to lure tourists away from the Hiltons' pubs. Or, perhaps, Mary Hilton did not want to blatantly exhibit her foster daughters for cash in the town where she had so carefully cultivated her image as Violet and Daisy's rescuer.

The truth was that Mary Hilton was not at all what she seemed. Under her care, Violet and Daisy had grown plump and happy-looking—"as good and lovable as they are pretty." Watching them play pat-a-cake and coo for *Dadda* and *Mamma* as they banged their brand-new dollies like drums on the tray of their high chair, the *Brighton Herald* could only conclude "that they are treated with the utmost fondness." But the girls' delectable little dresses, the specially made double-wide high chair, and the pairs of dolls and teddy bears were all for show. Behind closed doors, a side of Mary surfaced that was never exposed to the press or the public. This was the side that Violet and Daisy came to know best.

"There was a speech repeated to us daily, over again like a

phonograph record," they remembered. "It was spoken by a big, curly-haired woman who bathed, dressed and fed us. She never petted or kissed us, or even smiled. She just talked."

"Your mother gave you to me," Mary intoned. *"You are not my children. Your mother gave you to me."*

Mary told Violet and Daisy she was their grandmother, though she instructed them to call her Auntie. As they grew, her daily speech become more elaborate.

"Your mother was afraid when you were born and gave you to me when you were two weeks old. You must always do just as I say."

Though she was tall and attractive, with lovely long hair, the sisters' most vivid and lasting memory of Mary Hilton would be her wide leather belt with its large metal buckle. With one quick jerk, she could release that buckle. Her temper was vicious, a volatile thing that could not be calmed by her daughter or her husband. When the two sisters disobeyed, Mary Hilton yanked that ever-present belt loose and flailed Violet and Daisy with the buckle end. Always, the blows landed on their shoulders and backs.

"She'll never hit your faces, girls," Mary's husband, Henry, told them. "The public will not be so glad to pay to look at little Siamese twins with scarred faces."

Henry Hilton was right. If "Auntie" loved anything at all about Violet and Daisy, it was the money they could make for her. The one thing she would never do was jeopardize their earning power. Where money led, Mary Hilton would follow, and whatever the reasons may be, the money led her away from Brighton and toward Scotland in 1910.

• • •

Records of Violet and Daisy's earliest United Kingdom engagements, if they exist at all, have yet to be uncovered, making it impossible to trace their route across the country. For an amateur act working alone, without the benefit of a manager, booking agent, promoter, or advance man, or any show business experience whatsoever, it was sure to be an arduous and haphazard way to earn a living. Violet and Daisy certainly remembered it that way: "We lived in dingy European boarding houses," they said, "traveling at night between exhibitions at bars, fairs, carnivals, and circuses."

Conjoined twins in those days were billed as "freak" acts. All that was required of a so-called freak act was a willingness to be stared at. "A lot of the freaks just stood up and said 'Look at me, here I am,'" longtime sideshow promoter Ward Hall explained. Those who cared to go the extra mile could captivate an audience simply by demonstrating how they carried out everyday tasks. A performer named Prince Randion, born without limbs, famously rolled and lit a cigarette with his lips, for instance. Violet and Daisy's act consisted of no more than playing with their toys, for they had not even learned to walk yet. They could stand only with the help of a little wooden frame for support.

At outdoor venues like carnivals and fairs, people with physical anomalies were generally exhibited in pit shows, which also showcased exotic animals and performers such as sword-swallowers and fire-eaters. For potentially dangerous animals like snakes and alligators, the pits were actual holes dug into the ground and framed with a waist-high railing that acted as a fence. Striped canvas hung from the railings to prevent anyone outside the open-sided tent from sneaking a free peek. Human beings had the added luxury of a six-inch-high stage to raise them off the ground. All day long, carnivalgoers wandered among the pits, peering at the contents for as long as they cared to look.

Did Violet and Daisy feel like freaks when strangers leaned on the railings and stared down at them? They never reflected publicly on their earliest show business engagements and would only barely acknowledge that they had ever appeared in pit shows. Whether this was because they were traumatized by the experience itself or because they were too embarrassed by their lowly beginnings, it is impossible to know.

Only one thing is certain: the two little girls always *appeared* happy. They were so young and had seen so little of the world outside the back room of the Hiltons' pubs that playing within a rectangle of striped canvas under the passing gaze of hundreds might not have felt particularly unusual to them. Strangers' eyes had been a regular feature of their daily lives since earliest infancy. "We were always being looked at," they remembered. Only the surroundings had changed. Starved as they were for affection, it is even possible that Violet and Daisy found some enjoyment in the cooing and exclamations of their audience, for they never failed to delight onlookers. Moreover, as long as they were in public, they were safe from the lashings of Mary Hilton's leather belt.

Nevertheless, Violet and Daisy were hardly more than babies, unable to resist, much less consent to being put on display for hours on end. What Mary Hilton was doing with them was exploitation, plain and simple, and she had no intention of letting up.

. . .

When the seasons changed and the weather became inhospitable, theaters, music halls, museums, and waxworks offered more opportunities for Mary Hilton to turn a hefty profit. The going rate at the turn of the century for such "rare novelties" as Violet and Daisy was £20 a week or better (nearly $3,000 in modern American money), though whether an amateur like Mary Hilton could have commanded such a salary is debatable. Through luck or skill, she managed to get the two-and-a-half-year-olds booked for the holiday season of 1910 in Stewart's Waxwork on Edinburgh's High Street, where they just might have caught the eye of world-renowned magician Harry Houdini.

No one in all of show business was more famous at the turn of the century than Houdini. He was the greatest escape artist of all time—no handcuffs or jail cell could hold him. Strap him into a straightjacket, bind his ankles, and dangle him upside down over a bustling city street, and Houdini would squirm free in as little as three minutes. Padlock him into a box made of wood, plate glass, or metal; wrap it in ropes; and drop it into a river, and just when it seemed he must surely have drowned, a triumphant Houdini would bob to the surface. His fame extended from his childhood home of Appleton, Wisconsin, to the far corners of tsarist Russia and the coasts of Australia.

As the story goes, when Houdini saw the two curly-haired moppets playing at Stewart's, for once it was his turn to be entranced. He, like the rest of the world, must have been familiar with Eng and Chang Bunker of Siam, Millie-Christine McCoy of North Carolina, and Josefa and Rosa Blažek of Bohemia, but never had he seen a set of conjoined twins so darling as Violet and Daisy. He knew just the man to tell all about them, too—the very man who handled Houdini's own European bookings, the talent scout and impresario Ike Rose. When Rose arrived in Scotland, Houdini met him at the train station. Anything that could excite Harry Houdini must have been worth a look, and Ike Rose promptly went to Stewart's to see what all the fuss was about.

Violet and Daisy were apparently everything Houdini had promised, as authentic as they were adorable. Rose would have signed them up right then and there, if only Mary Hilton had been willing to close up her pub back in Brighton to travel the European continent.

On the surface it seems an odd refusal, a veering from the money-making path Mary had so clearly embarked upon—all the more so because of the Houdini connection. To be associated in any way with

Harry Houdini brought tremendous prestige; to be discovered by Houdini would lend Violet and Daisy lifelong bragging rights. And so a story like the Hilton-Houdini connection, which seems to have materialized in 1928, two years after Houdini's death, requires a moment's skepticism. Once he was gone and unable to provide evidence to the contrary, performers of all kinds felt free to concoct serendipitous tales of Houdini encounters in hopes of piggybacking on his fame.

Even so, the Hilton-Houdini story just might be true. Houdini was indeed booked at Edinburgh's Empire Palace Theatre for the six days leading up to Christmas of 1910, and Ike Rose was in fact touring the United Kingdom in late 1910 and early 1911, with none other than the Blažek twins, whose bodies were fused in a fashion similar to the Hiltons'. Violet and Daisy themselves would recall that their first professional appearance had been in Scotland at the age of two and a half, and *Edinburgh Evening News* advertisements confirm that they were breaking records and drawing "enormous crowds daily" at Stewart's Waxwork during the first two weeks of January 1911. Every piece is tantalizingly close to fitting neatly into place. Even Mary Hilton's refusal has a certain logic upon closer inspection. Despite her reputation for unbridled greed, there were several practical as well as emotional ties that might have kept her from jumping at Rose's offer. She and Henry had a new pub to run—a larger, presumably more lucrative pub that they had owned for less than a year. That pub was also providing shelter and support for Mary's seventy-six-year-old father, as well as for Edith. Henry Hilton, who coincidentally was also seventy-six, was not in the finest of health and possibly not up to managing the business on his own. Grandchildren were beginning to arrive on the scene, too, thanks to Edith's three elder sisters.

Regardless of how he first came to encounter Violet and Daisy, Ike Rose was determined to have them. The Blažek sisters were already making him so much money, he needed a suitcase to carry it home each night and a secretary just to count it; adding another set of twins to his troupe promised to double his riches. Thus it was that the summer of 1911 found him in Brighton, enjoying a pint and a look at the Brighton United Twins at the Evening Star. This time, Mary accepted Rose's offer. As Violet and Daisy would later tell it, Mary "rented" them to Rose for a paltry weekly sum of £4, allowing him to tote the three-year-old girls from one country to another while she stayed behind to tend her pub. That was not the case. Ike Rose paid a reported $60 a week (about $1,600 today) for the chance to exhibit Violet and Daisy in Europe. Rose also invited Mary; her husband, Henry; and her daughter, Edith, to accompany the girls on what he promised would be an all-expenses-paid tour of the Continent. They departed for Germany by sea in July or August 1911.

. . .

The voyage was anything but glamorous. "Our earliest lessons in getting along were taught to us in the tiny cabin of a ship," the sisters remembered. Mary and Henry spent a good deal of the voyage quarreling, and the most popular topic seems to have been Violet and Daisy. If Mary had had her way, she would have kept the children shut inside the cabin for the length of the trip. Henry Hilton thought the toddlers should "be taken into the air" above decks to enjoy the sun and the sky and the sea and the wind like any other passenger. He also believed they ought to attend religious services. Mary disagreed. Letting people so much as glimpse the Brighton United Twins for free, she argued, would undermine their moneymaking potential. Mary always prevailed, leaving Henry's anger and frustration to fester within.

The Hiltons' disputes and the animosity that lingered afterward made a lifelong impression on Violet and Daisy. "We decided early that a grudge was the lowest form of emotion," they said. At three years old, they already understood the price of physical opposition with each other. "We soon found that if one wanted to go in one direction, and the other pulled in the different way," Daisy recalled, "nobody got anywhere. That is a lesson a great many people who call themselves normal have not learned yet." They also came to realize that other kinds of hostility would come with a cost even steeper for them than for Mary and Henry. "Mental as well as physical resistance by either of us would prove fatal," they decided; "the other can retaliate with the same policy too easily." Yet total agreement in every little particular was too much to ask of themselves. Harmony, though—blending their different traits and expressions into a balanced whole—became a characteristic Violet and Daisy honed ever after.

· · ·

By late August, Ike Rose had brought the Hiltons to Berlin, with an eye toward exhibiting them at the biggest German fairs in Hamburg, Munich, Dresden, and Leipzig. After that, virtually no news of Violet and Daisy would reach the English-speaking world for the next eighteen months. Later reports would claim they had toured not only Germany but also Italy, Russia, Austria, Belgium, Holland, and Switzerland, and had been presented to the crowned heads of Europe. Though no proof of a royal audience has ever turned up, the prospect is not entirely outside the realm of possibility. The chance to see a single pair of conjoined twins is rare enough; the sight of the Brighton United Twins *and* the Blažeks would perhaps have been an opportunity too unprecedented even for royalty to pass up.

Most of these later reports, it should be said, were carnival ballyhoo—colorful sales pitches laced with exaggerations specifically designed to tempt the curious into parting with their nickels and dimes. How much Violet and Daisy actually traveled or performed with Josefa and Rosa Blažek is in fact something of a mystery, though a formally posed photograph of the two pairs of sisters, said to have been taken in Bavaria in 1912, strongly suggests that they were indeed exhibited together in Europe at least once.

In Germany, Ike Rose put up an innovative venue that sounds tailor-made for just such a double act. It was a two-sided theater, the building itself mirroring a pair of sisters joined together. Each side held an audience of three hundred fifty spectators. When the first half reached capacity, Rose opened the other. How exactly these two sides were utilized during a performance is unclear. Were there two separate stages? One for the Bohemian Twins and one for the Brighton United Twins? Did the two sets of sisters perform simultaneously, then switch stages to entertain the other half of the audience? Rose himself specifically mentions only the Blažek sisters' performance, leaving us to wonder whether Violet and Daisy appeared in the double theater at all. It's difficult to envision what they could have done onstage, at age three, to enrapture an audience of three hundred fifty.

For Josefa and Rosa Blažek, on the other hand, drawing a crowd was almost effortless. Curiosity about the Blažeks had turned lurid in April 1910 when Rosa had reportedly given birth to a son. All the Blažek sisters needed to do was show off baby Franz and let the audience's imagination run wild. If the Blažeks were indeed performing alone, their earning power was formidable. Running sixty to eighty shows daily in his double theater, charging the American equivalent of six to twelve cents per person, Ike Rose reported to *Billboard* that he was collecting $500 to $1,000 a day ($12,500 to $25,000 today). On "ladies' day," when Josefa and Rosa were exhibited in a custom-made set of tights that outlined every contour of the union that linked them, the price of admission was hiked to a quarter apiece, doubling or quadrupling the day's take.

Violet and Daisy could hardly compete with such salacious ploys. As long as the two little girls sat among their toys while Mary Hilton recited facts about their lives, they could not hope to attract any more attention than the typical freak show. Years later, Ike Rose would claim he "positively could not make a dollar" on the toddlers until he teamed them up with the Blažek sisters. But as Violet and Daisy would later recount it, in a tale that, like so many others they often told, flouted reality, this was when they began training for an act of their own—one that could rival Josefa and Rosa Blažek's popularity.

Music would be their ticket out of obscurity. "Teach the girls the hard way, professor," they remembered Mary Hilton telling their instructor. "They're strong and tough, old for their years." Three-year-old Violet was assigned piano, Daisy the violin. Music immediately appealed to them. Not only were the melodies pleasing, but the instruments created unique physical responses as well. When Daisy played her violin, the vibrations of the strings thrummed down her spine and across their connecting bridge to Violet, allowing the sisters to feel every note in tandem. The shared sensation delighted them. Violet's piano notes did not travel in the same way; no matter how hard she banged the keys, the instrument was "too detached" to create the same effect for Daisy. Nevertheless, Violet practiced just as hard as her sister to perfect their routine.

If the music itself had not been a joy, the grueling schedule might have broken them. Violet would remember rehearsing a waltz for two and a half solid hours in preparation for their debut, while Daisy practiced violin and learned to wield a conductor's baton. "It was amazing how much training was crammed into our early lives," the two remembered. "When Auntie discovered that we could stand in a chair, rock until it turned over and flip in the air without falling, she added dancing lessons to our long days of study."

This would have been an entirely different tactic than Ike Rose had taken with Josefa and Rosa. While the Blažek sisters' act revolved around tantalizing people's curiosity about their physical union, it became Violet and Daisy's goal to captivate an audience so completely with their talent and charm that the spectators would forget the sisters were conjoined at all.

. . .

In order to spread the word about his latest set of twin performers, however, Rose fell back on his tried-and-true method: the medical examination. Berlin would forever be associated with doctors in Violet's and Daisy's minds, for Ike Rose could think of no better way to introduce the sisters to the German press than to invite the city's most prominent doctors to study them.

Doctors were nothing new to Violet and Daisy. From the time they were infants, Mary Hilton had allowed medical men into her pub to examine the children. It was not unusual for the two of them to waken and find surgeons or scientists staring down at them. The medical men didn't just peer—they probed, too. Violet remembered them "stuffing candy in our mouths to keep us from crying." Little though they were, Violet and Daisy knew without being told that no one, not even doctors, should have the right to stare between their legs and pass instruments into their bodies against their will. The looking and the touching made the girls half crazy. It happened so often that "the very bedside tone" of a doctor's voice triggered a special kind of loathing. The sound of the first doctor they could recall hearing remained permanently embedded in their minds. "His voice was a cold, sharp blade through our hearts. To this day it symbolizes the aggregate of doctors' voices, begging to experiment with us," they said decades afterward. Every time, Violet and Daisy screamed and scratched and kicked until the doctors finished. When each examination was over at last, Auntie whipped them for misbehaving.

The German exam was worse yet. Never before had Violet and Daisy been confronted by so many doctors all at once. Hundreds of them—the entire Berlin Medical Association—watched as Professor Otto Bockenheimer examined the two little sisters. In those days, such exams were still conducted in semicircular auditoriums called operating theaters, where row upon row of men could peer down at the procedure from tiers of seats. The ordeal was as terrifying as it was degrading. Lying there while Professor Bockenheimer hovered above, instruments in hand, lecturing in a language they did not understand, was a special kind of torture for the girls. All Violet and Daisy could do was wonder what might happen next as Professor Bockenheimer's audience listened to him discuss the various ways they might be carved apart and debated whether or not they might survive such an operation at all. Would this be the time the knife descended? It seemed inevitable, for doctors were always more fascinated by the question of whether the girls could be split in two than by the prospect of learning how their bodies had evolved to function together.

Whatever relief Violet and Daisy felt when they left the examination table in one piece was short-lived. Professor Bockenheimer had concluded that an operation to separate them was probably possible, though it would be best to wait two or three years to allow the girls to become stronger and the bridge between them larger and more flexible. No one appears to have deemed it necessary to ask Violet and Daisy themselves whether they wanted to exist separately, for no singly born person could feel anything but horror at the thought of being permanently joined to another human being. "I can hardly imagine a more blessed operation," Professor Bockenheimer proclaimed, "than the separation by surgical means of two independently thinking, feeling, and functioning beings, whose lasting union with each other is robbing of every joy of life." As with every doctor before and after him, Bockenheimer's own revulsion toward their condition blinded him to the reality of Violet's and Daisy's absolute contentment with their shared body.

Fear of surgeons and their scalpels haunted Violet and Daisy ever after. For them, the very notion of separation was abhorrent. It did not signify freedom, convenience, or independence, but rather a unique physical and psychological violence—a knife piercing the center of their shared identity and slicing it into two incomplete halves.

"We would lie awake, crying silently, holding hands, wondering." At just three years old, they knew perfectly well that Auntie didn't love them, only the money they made. What if Professor Bockenheimer and his associates offered to make Mary Hilton rich in exchange for the chance to experiment upon them—richer even than Ike Rose's contract? She would be able to stop traveling, stop troubling herself over their care and training.

"I will never leave you, even though they say that they can cut us apart," Daisy promised.

"I never want to be away from you," Violet whispered. If they could not live together, they did not want to live at all. "We can hold our breaths until we die."

Better to die together than live apart.

CHAPTER 6

VIOLET AND DAISY'S MONTHS OF REHEARSAL PAID OFF. AT their debut in Berlin, Violet played her waltz flawlessly while Daisy conducted a fourteen-member orchestra. Their act took the audience by storm. "The theater thundered with applause our opening night," they recalled. Cheers filled the auditorium as Auntie and Edith rushed the girls from the stage and into their dressing room, where Auntie refused to open the door to the clamoring hordes of admirers and fellow performers.

That was how Violet and Daisy would tell it three decades later, anyway. Berlin's newspapers are conspicuously silent on the matter. After the medical examination with Professor Bockenheimer, in fact, the Brighton United Twins seem to utterly vanish from the city's notice. Odder yet, newspaper articles and advertisements alike would not begin to mention their musical talents at all for another three years—a striking omission if Violet and Daisy were truly the prodigies they claimed to be.

The truth of the matter may well be that their sensational Berlin debut never took place at all, that the sisters concocted everything, from the punishing rehearsals to the thunderous applause, for the sake of adding drama and garnering sympathy for their life story in the 1940s. Exaggeration, after all, is the bread and butter of the sideshow world. If they had made such a resounding stage triumph at the tender age of three or four, surely Ike Rose would have bragged about his new wonder-children in one of his periodic reports to *Variety* or *Billboard*, where the entertainment industry exchanged news, reviews, and gossip. But those reports instead focus on the Blažek sisters' success, mentioning Violet and Daisy only occasionally as a side note. Consequently, it is far more realistic to presume that they continued trouping from one fairground to another, their routine largely unchanged.

How long they lingered in Berlin and where they spent the first several months of 1912 are unknown. What is certain is that the Hiltons were in Leipzig on May 5, 1912, for it was there that Mary's husband, Henry, died in St. Jacob's Hospital. All his grudges against his wife, it seemed to Violet and Daisy, had slowly but surely rotted Henry from the inside out. Weak and spiteful though he may have been, Henry was the one and only person Violet and Daisy would ever credit with standing up to Mary Hilton, albeit unsuccessfully, on their behalf. Now the only buffer against their foster mother's greed was Edith, a young woman so inconspicuous that she might as well have been invisible.

If Mary took time to grieve Henry's death, it was not for long. By September of that year, Ike Rose reported to *Billboard* magazine that he was exhibiting Violet and Daisy in Milan. Next came the autumn fair in Basel. There, a telegram arrived with an offer for the Hiltons—and only the Hiltons—that forced Ike Rose to rethink his moneymaking strategy. The offer, from amusement titan J. D. Williams, prompted Rose to leave the Blažek sisters in the care of a European manager so that he could take Violet and Daisy to a territory free of competition. In December, Ike Rose and the Hiltons set sail to conquer a new continent: Australia.

• • •

Their destination was Melbourne, where an expansive outdoor amusement ground called Luna Park had just opened along the sunny shores of Port Phillip Bay. Billed as "A Fairyland of Palaces of Pleasure by the Sea," the £40,000 complex was the first of its kind in Australia.

For sixpence, thrill-seekers were admitted through what the *Melbourne Argus* called the "horrifying smile" of the park's mascot, Mr. Moon himself—a thirty-five-foot-wide gate shaped like the man in the moon, with a gaping mouth and electrically illuminated eyes that lolled back and forth. A plethora of amusements, both modern and time-honored, awaited within. Magicians, jugglers, and tightrope walkers. Mechanical fortune-tellers. A Ferris wheel. A subterranean riverboat ride through intricate scenes of famous grottoes around the globe, built at a staggering cost of £5,000. A labyrinth of mirrors called the Crystal Tangle. The Pharaoh's Daughter, where a statue of an Egyptian princess came magically to life. In the American Bowl Slide, passengers whirled down the sides of a monstrous polished wooden bowl like water swirling down a drain. For heart-stopping excitement, there was the Globe of Death, where a trio of motorcyclists risked life and limb to defy gravity as they careened over, around, and under one another within a round cage of steel mesh. The less adventurous could laugh themselves silly at any of the hundred sideshows in the Palais de Folie, marvel at the curiosities in the Palace of Many Wonders, or simply relax in the sea breezes at the Terrace Tea Gardens. Ringing the entire park was the Great Scenic Railway, a sixty-five-foot-high wooden roller coaster whose seven-eighths of a mile of white track was studded with thousands upon thousands of gleaming lightbulbs.

The Hiltons had left Europe in the grip of winter. Now, in the southern hemisphere, summer was at its peak, and Luna Park was flourishing. Violet and Daisy would be the latest jewel in its many-splendored crown. They were not to appear in the Palais de Folie, or the Palace of Many Wonders. No, Luna Park's owner, J. D. Williams, had decided the "Modern Siamese Twins," as they were now being called, merited a pavilion all their own, constructed especially for them. There they would sit in their custom-made double-wide chair and play with their collection of dolls and toys while being interviewed by the audience. They also "walked about," showing the crowd how they coordinated their movements. By this time they may have added singing and dancing on a small platform to their repertoire.

Violet and Daisy's performance was not included in the cost of admission to Luna Park. Anyone who wanted to see it had to part with another sixpence to satisfy their curiosity. Apparently the fee was a bargain. "No other amusement enterprise could afford to let you see them for that price," the park's advertisements bragged to prospective customers.

Before the exhibition began, though, Violet and Daisy had to endure another medical examination for the sake of publicity, this time before an audience of at least fifty surgeons in Melbourne's Masonic Hall. The girls' "wonderful agility" surprised and delighted the medical men as the sisters demonstrated their ability to go up and down stairs and run from one end of the hall to the other. Where a year earlier one sister had had to walk backward when the other went forward—taking great care not to knock their heels together—now the bridge between them had grown flexible enough to allow Violet and Daisy to master the knack of moving "almost side by side." If the doctors had had any instruments capable of measuring the girls' charm, it would have been off the charts. As much as they hated medical men, the two of them were "not slow at making friends with strangers," noted one reporter who was present.

That skill stood them in good stead as Luna Park customers poured into their pavilion on Friday, February 14, 1913, drawn by impossible-to-miss advertisements touting the "Special Engagement of the Modern Siamese Twins." This "Absolute Wonder of a Baffled and Mystified World" had been procured by J. D. Williams at "enormous expense," the ads said, "because the best is none too good for our patrons."

His patrons didn't just take the bait—they gobbled it. Luna Park's notice in the next morning's *Melbourne Herald* announced "THE MODERN SIAMESE TWINS" in giant capital letters, larger even than the park's name, boasting that Violet and Daisy had "captivated all who saw them at play last night." A full-page ad in *Melbourne Punch* magazine followed, announcing "Here They Are!" alongside three photographs of the pretty little pair of "grown-together" sisters. As far as *Melbourne Punch* was concerned, Violet and Daisy instantly became the "principal attraction" at the park, "delighting and astonishing thousands nightly." The *Prahran Telegraph* agreed, reporting, "The modern Siamese Twins, Daisy and Violet Hilton, are a great draw, their pavilion being usually crowded."

Every night from seven o'clock to eleven-thirty, Violet and Daisy appeared before the vast majority of Luna Park's customers. On Saturdays, their day began at one p.m. They had just turned five years old.

• • •

Their engagement at Luna Park lasted a month. In those four weeks, a reported fifty-five thousand to sixty thousand people came to see them—nearly two thousand people each day. At sixpence apiece, Luna Park took in £1,375 to £1,500 at the Hiltons' pavilion alone—the equivalent of between $145,000 and $160,000 today. Ike Rose bragged to *Billboard* magazine that Violet and Daisy were "a revelation and sensation in Australia," where they were "doing 80% of the business at Luna Park."

During the three months that followed, Ike Rose paraded the Hiltons across eastern Australia, proceeding up the coastline to Sydney's

Royal Easter Show and then north toward Brisbane and beyond. Violet and Daisy were hailed as "the greatest attraction at the Sydney Easter Show," drawing more than forty thousand visitors. Their popularity during those early autumn months was so self-evident that their ad in the *Queensland Times* did not even bother to give the location of their pavilion. "Follow the Crowds," it urged instead.

For Violet and Daisy, Australia blurred into a continuous stream of shows and performances. "We were exhibited in different circuses, night carnivals, country fairs, and a number of other places," Daisy recalled. The schedule was merciless. "Our colleagues in the circus were engaged to appear only during a certain part of the day, but we were presented to the public from early morning till late at night." Their act had not changed substantially: the usual interview with the audience, topped off with a song and a dance. Once, though, they found themselves plunked down as the centerpiece in "a circus thriller." While the two little girls stood petrified in the middle of the arena, Daisy remembered, "wild riders galloped round us, shooting as they rode."

. . .

As the Australian winter took hold that June of 1913, a new money-making scheme seized Ike Rose: a "Lilliputian exhibition." Diminutive human beings so fascinated the public that exhibiting them en masse could yield $150,000 (nearly $4 million today) in a single year. Rose could not resist the temptation to capitalize on the latest sideshow craze. Leaving Violet and Daisy (as well as Mary and Edith) in the care of an associate, E. S. Eisermann, he set off in July to scour Europe for little people to populate his show. The Hiltons carried on, working their way back down the coast and swinging west in time to make their seaside Christmas booking in Adelaide.

Somewhere along that long and curving path across Australia's southeastern tip, the Hiltons made the acquaintance of a man who would permanently and irrevocably alter the course of their lives. Violet and Daisy would remember him as a peripheral member of a circus—a balloon and candy seller. If so, he was a man whose talents were vastly underutilized.

Born Myer Rothbaum, the bright and enterprising twenty-three-year-old had kept a shop in Perth until he'd fled east and reinvented himself as Myer Myers after being found guilty of auction fraud in 1912. For the most part he was an ordinary-looking fellow, short, a bit on the stout side, with a smooth face and dark, close-set eyes that were perhaps smaller than most. Violet and Daisy decided at once that those eyes were cruel.

Edith Hilton saw Myers in an entirely different light. After a life of near invisibility, Edith, at thirty-two, found herself the center of Myer Myers's attention. "We were not allowed to have friends," Violet and Daisy pointed out, but the rules were different for Edith. While the sisters were busy performing, Edith "received her beau in our crowded room." All signs indicated a budding romance. But Myers's courtship of Edith, the two perceptive youngsters suspected, had an ulterior motive. To hear Violet and Daisy tell it, Myer Myers was attracted to Edith for one reason and one reason only. "She was fortunate enough to inherit a dowry," Violet said. "Us."

Though outwardly kind to Edith, Myers made no attempt to win the affection of his sweetheart's foster sisters. He instead intimidated the girls by telling them "how a brute had raised him"; as far as Myers was concerned, a beating was standard punishment for disobedience, and so Mary Hilton's abusive discipline tactics did not faze him. Violet and Daisy were instructed to call him *Sir*.

Whether his true motivation was romantic or financial, the fact remained that a future with Edith Hilton was inextricably bound up with Violet and Daisy, and it would seem that Myer Myers was eager to take an active role in managing that future. What ideas, plans, or suggestions did he discuss with Edith and her mother? What formidable gifts of persuasion did this sometime swindler possess?

Either Mary Hilton was fooled or she recognized some untapped potential in Myers. Perhaps an element of both came into play, for by 1914, the Hiltons had broken off their business partnership with Ike Rose—an internationally recognized impresario—and placed Violet and Daisy's career in the hands of an unknown balloon man.

CHAPTER 7

THE NOTICES WERE TINY AT FIRST. A HALF DOZEN OF THEM, each perhaps a quarter inch tall, scattered like a chain of whispers throughout three columns of the *Dunedin Evening Star*'s want ads:

"Daisy and Violet, Modern Siamese Twins, will be on show in a few days."

"Daisy can sleep, Violet be awake. Modern Siamese Twins."

"Violet can laugh, Daisy can cry. Modern Siamese Twins."

"The United Sisters, Daisy and Violet. Modern Siamese Twins."

"They are two beautiful children, Daisy and Violet, Modern Siamese Twins."

"Daisy and Violet. They have won beauty competitions all over the world. Modern Siamese Twins."

Not a hint of where or when these marvelous children would appear—just a handful of tantalizing snippets, wedged in between advertisements for Lee's wallpapers, Gillette razor blades, and notices of lost kittens and retrievers. A similar set of advertisements was sprinkled throughout a page of the *Otago Daily Times*. Myer Myers had set the first stage of his plan in motion.

. . .

During his auction fraud days, Myers had demonstrated an ability to convince one bidder after another to "buy a lot of rubbish." Now, with Violet and Daisy, he had a genuine article to promote, something so rare and authentic, it promised him the chance to reach his full potential as a salesman.

Nevertheless, Myers firmly believed there was more to worth than a number on a price tag. He'd watched it happen in that auction house back in Perth: tell a man a watch was made of gold, and he'd pay ten times its actual value to keep another fellow from winning it, even if his eyes ought to have informed him it was plain brass gilt.

"Not over one-fifth of what anything costs is represented in actual value; four-fifths are in the mind," Myers would profess years later. "In the case of the Hilton Sisters it is more than nine-tenths created value. It takes imagination and enthusiasm to create those intangible values and convert them into realities. That is showmanship in its highest sphere. It is salesmanship in its highest phase."

And so Myers set about contriving the perfect setting to make Mary Hilton's two little gems sparkle like never before. The only people he had to answer to were himself and Mary and Edith. Upon returning to Australia, Ike Rose had retaliated against Myer Myers by taking out an injunction to prevent Violet and Daisy from performing in the state of Victoria. Rather than tangle with Rose, Myers moved on to fresh territory: New Zealand.

Myer Myers took a fresh approach, too. In one town after another, he rented a storefront for a stretch of several weeks—often next door to or across the street from a theater—which he then "fitted up like a nursery." Surrounded by their playthings, Violet and Daisy would "chatter away to the audience," just as they had always done.

He changed virtually nothing about the act itself. All Myers did was tweak the presentation. It was nothing less than a small stroke of genius. By displaying the girls in a nursery-like setting, he changed the whole tenor of the experience. Curiosity-seekers weren't gawking at a freak show—they were visiting two charming little hostesses named Violet and Daisy Hilton. "The twins will be 'at home,'" the advertisements said, not onstage, but in their "parlour," where they entertained their guests during "hours of reception."

Clever though it was, Myers's strategy took some time to catch on. The public was long accustomed to being duped by such advertisements. Sideshows were famous for luring customers in with spectacular promises, only to deliver a lackluster or downright revolting experience. More often than not, what was billed as a mermaid in a sideshow turned out to be a desiccated monkey head and torso sewn to the hind end of a fish. Ersatz conjoined twins could be created in a number of similarly abhorrent ways. Authentic or not, specimens of conjoined twins were more likely to be mummified or skeletal remains than living, breathing people. If indeed they were alive, many presumed Violet and Daisy would be "maimed or invalid children," as the *Wanganui Chronicle* put it.

Myer Myers countered the public's fears and doubts with bold-print reassurances. "ALIVE! ALIVE! ALIVE!" his advertisements trumpeted. Some of them offered a reward of £100 (over $9,000 today) to anyone who could disprove Violet and Daisy's authenticity. Half-price children's matinees on Saturdays provided further enticement.

His ploys worked. When skeptical newspaper reporters hazarded a visit, Violet and Daisy won them over instantly. "One would expect to see two imbecile or half-witted children," the *New Zealand Free Lance* admitted, "but, instead, you see two healthy, rosy-faced children." The *Auckland Star* agreed. "The show can be recommended as one that does not contain any of the repellent features that are sometimes associated with these matters." Once people began venturing in to see Violet and Daisy, word of their guests' satisfaction spread rapidly. "Fourteen Hundred People have visited us in Three Days," Myers announced in the *Otago Daily Times*. By the end of the week, the number had more than doubled, to three thousand.

There was no need to bother traipsing across the country on the coattails of small-town circuses and carnivals now. Myer Myers only booked the girls into big annual shows like the Auckland Exposition, the Taranaki Winter Show, and expositions hosted by agricultural and pastoral associations. In between, the Hiltons could settle in for weeks at a time at their storefront exhibits.

For a year and a half, they toured New Zealand and Tasmania to general acclaim. This was when Violet's and Daisy's musical training truly began. Myer Myers had seen the rewards that came from innovation. Run-of-the-mill curiosity was reliable but fleeting. A glance, and it was over. Quality and presentation, however, could hold an audience in thrall. The key was to give customers more than what was expected. If Violet and Daisy could be taught to entertain their audience, the revenue they could draw would only increase.

In January 1915, the newspapers suddenly began taking note of their developing skill on the piano and violin. By the end of that year, Violet could play a waltz "with easy grace that would do credit to a child many years her elder," and Daisy "displayed considerable ability" on her violin.

Their manners, too, were drawing admiration. Mary Hilton had meticulously cultivated the girls' behavior to impress, achieving a delicate balance of friendliness and modesty. "There is nothing either bashful or forward about them," noted the *North Western Advocate and the Emu Bay Times*. Violet and Daisy were also so rarely around other children that they spoke like miniaturized adults. The combination of charm, graciousness, intelligence, and "wit worthy of anyone much older" delighted spectators. "The show is a cut above the average show-yard exhibition," Tasmania's *North West Post* praised.

For the girls themselves, however, things were not so different from the carnivals and pit shows. What Myers termed a parlor was in fact a square pen roped off from the rest of the room in the manner of a boxing ring. Before showtime, Myer Myers stood in the doorway calling to passersby like a "raucous-voiced" carnival talker while Mary Hilton gave a lecture on the girls' lives to the accumulating audience. When enough people had gathered, Mary took Violet and Daisy on her knee and undid their underclothes, exposing the ligature between them to the crowd.

It was the Queen's Arms and the Evening Star all over again, with the lifted skirts and the probing eyes—not dozens this time but hundreds of them. That part of the routine was something Violet and Daisy never became accustomed to, a memory whose sting never faded. "They had to lean over and this woman would part their dress and show the place where they were joined, to prove . . . that they were not fakes," a friend confided over sixty years later. "That used to just hack the hell out of them." Medical men were also offered "opportunities for private examination of the children."

Instead of being continuously on display for four and a half hours each weekday, as they had been in Luna Park, Violet and Daisy performed in three sets daily, lasting from ninety minutes to three hours apiece. The schedule sounded more bearable, but in fact the performances added up to five or six and a half hours a day. At least there were two-hour breaks between the sets. Theoretically, at least. It is not difficult to suppose that Mary Hilton and Myer Myers were more likely to prioritize music lessons and other training over meals and rest.

• • •

Violet and Daisy were nearly eight years old before anyone seems to have taken offense at their treatment at the hands of Mary Hilton and Myer Myers. On December 11, 1915, a scathing editorial entitled "The Siamese Twins: A Revolting Exhibition," appeared in *Truth*, a Melbourne tabloid.

"The pressing need for legislation to prevent unscrupulous and heartless people from making money out of the misfortunes of others has within the past week been strikingly illustrated by a side show located at the corner of Bourke and Russell streets," it announced.

The column derided the exhibit as a whole, with particular outrage aimed at Mary Hilton's habit of undressing the girls to expose the site of their union to the audience. "Apart from the indecency of the spectacle there arises the question of the children's ill-treatment, for such it surely is, just as much as though the ill-treatment were physical."

Everything about the performance sickened *Truth*'s reporter, from its "indecent posters" down to the audience itself. "One hurried glance" at the spectators was enough to turn the reporter's stomach. "In their faces is seen the same evil gloating air which is to be noticed on the countenances of these degraded creatures who pack the public galleries of the Criminal Court when a trial for rape or some other abominable offence is in progress."

Moreover, the article insinuated that Myers was taking advantage of a legal loophole by keeping the girls off the stage, where child labor was closely scrutinized by "vigilant inspectors [who] are ever ready to pounce down and prosecute for what they may consider an infringement of the law." Since Myers's impromptu venue was not a theater, nobody with the power to enforce these protective regulations seemed to be paying attention. "Either the Act of Parliament in question does not apply to the degrading spectacle in Bourke-street," *Truth* scolded, "or else the authorities are napping." Somehow the paper also came under the impression that the girls were being forced to remain linked unnecessarily, purely for the sake of profit, adding further fuel to the indignation.

"In the interest of public decency, no less than in the interest of the poor children so callously exhibited to the public gaze," *Truth* demanded, "action should be taken by the police to put a stop to the exhibition."

Truth was a newspaper that thrived on salacious stories and sensationalized reporting, yet the complaint sparked action in the state of Victoria's Legislative Assembly almost immediately. Just as the premier moved that the lower house adjourn its December 14 session, Henry Bailey, the member from Port Fairy, 175 miles west of Melbourne, interrupted.

"I want to bring under the notice of the Government what I consider to be a degrading, indecent, and inhuman exhibition which is going on in the city," Mr. Bailey announced. Didn't the government have any power, he asked, to come to the rescue of two unfortunate little girls being victimized by the shameless greed that was being demonstrated in Bourke Street? "I understand that from early morning until late at night they are on view in a pen in the same way that we exhibit sheep," he said, and proceeded to read *Truth*'s entire article into the record.

The chief secretary volunteered to "make inquiries," and the legislature moved to investigate.

All the concern was well-meaning, and well-founded, but it went one step too far. As was nearly always the case, both *Truth* and Mr. Bailey made the assumption that Violet's and Daisy's lives would be inherently better if they were not only removed from exhibition but also surgically separated. Speaking under the mistaken assumption that such an operation would consist of a simple snip of the ligature between them, Bailey declared that to compel the two sisters to remain bound to each other was in and of itself a "degrading" condition. To Bailey, it was just as important that Violet and Daisy be able to attend "to the calls of nature" separately as it was for them to attend school and "enjoy life in the same way that others do." None of those who so passionately wanted to improve circumstances for the "poor little kids" understood that Violet and Daisy were perfectly capable of enjoying themselves exactly as they were. "We find life very joyous," Daisy would explain in her teens, "and we are sure we have just as good a time as do any girls we know, even if they go freely about alone."

Whether Violet and Daisy ever learned that someone had come to their defense is unknown. If they noticed any change in their lives as a result of this solitary intervention, odds are it was for the worse. Mary Hilton's temper was no less caustic than it had ever been, and Myer Myers was not a man who took kindly to any sort of meddling in his business affairs. Worse still, Myers and Edith were due to be married on Christmas Eve, making the public denouncement doubly inconvenient. It's safe to assume that Myer Myers was none too pleased to appear before the district court in the new year.

And then the whole *Truth* affair abruptly fizzled when the authorities realized that Myers did not hold the lease on his exhibition space in Bourke Street. Since he was not the official tenant, obtaining a permit from the Board of Health—which presumably would have overseen the girls' treatment—was not his responsibility. He was off the hook.

Violet and Daisy's Australian sojourn lasted just six more months after the dust settled. Myer Myers may have felt that the legalities of exhibiting in Australia were becoming too burdensome. Or perhaps he had simply exhausted Violet and Daisy's novelty Down Under. Western Australia was unofficially off-limits to Myers, given his criminal record in Perth.

On June 21, 1916, Violet and Daisy, along with Mary Hilton and newlyweds Myer and Edith Myers, boarded the steamship *Sonoma*, bound for San Francisco.

THE THREE-WEEK VOYAGE ACROSS THE SOUTH PACIFIC turned out to be far more pleasant than the one that had carried Violet and Daisy from England to Germany. For the first time, they were allowed the speck of freedom Henry Hilton had tried to win for them five years earlier. "The little girls have very sunny dispositions and all during the voyage from Australia romped about the decks and made friends with everyone," reported the *Honolulu Star-Bulletin*. It's tempting to picture them attending the onboard Red Cross benefit; playing with the chimpanzees, parrots, and cockatoos in the cargo hold; practicing duets and trios with a fellow child violinist; or enjoying slices of the huge surprise birthday cake baked for the ship's chief steward, but that may be too great a stretch. At any rate, the change is inexplicable—unless Myer Myers had managed to convince Mary Hilton that Violet and Daisy needed to be glimpsed out in the open now and then, if only for the sake of free publicity.

· · ·

The *Sonoma* docked at Angel Island, just outside San Francisco, on July 10, 1916. Immigration inspectors boarded the ship and, dumbfounded by the sight of conjoined twins, snatched Violet and Daisy off to a medical examination as the girls fought and cried all the way down the gangplank.

According to Myers's account, Violet and Daisy were declared "physically and biologically inferior" and therefore unfit to enter the United States. Federal law, he was informed, prohibited the entry of "any alien who has a physical deformity affecting his ability to earn a living."

"This means, sir, that you never should have tried bringing them freak girls here," the immigration official said. "America is not a dumping ground for foreigners with deformities that could make them liabilities to the government."

It was true. The Immigration Act of 1882 specified that "any convict, lunatic, idiot, or any person unable to take care of himself or herself without becoming a public charge . . . shall not be permitted to land." Unable to conceive of how conjoined twins could prove to be anything but a burden to the American economy, the inspectors marked Violet and Daisy's record L.P.C.—"likely public charge"—and relegated the eight-year-olds to the women's detention center on the island until their case could be reviewed by the quarantine surgeon, Dr. Adrian Drew. Processing detainees routinely took anywhere from two weeks to six months.

But Violet and Daisy got out, and quickly, too. How? The answer is tricky to untangle. Twenty years afterward, Myer Myers told a story of a canny plan Mary Hilton concocted on the spot to leverage public opinion. Armed with her hickory cane and a heap of scrapbooks, Mary took the first ferry to the mainland, in hopes of convincing the *San Francisco Chronicle* to print an article on Violet and Daisy's heartbreaking predicament. Myers, relating the story secondhand, two decades later, painted a picture of a woeful Mary Hilton thumbing through her clippings as she lamented to the paper's editor, "They're so, *so* lovely, they are. They're so, *so* talented," wooing the *Chronicle* with her grandmotherly demeanor just as she had wooed the *Brighton Herald* into publicizing the sisters' christening years before.

Meanwhile, Edith, to her horror, was dispatched to the detention barracks to soothe Violet and Daisy. "No, no, no!" she begged as she sobbed in protest, but her mother and her husband would not budge. Mary had her mission to the mainland, and Myers could not be admitted into the women's barracks. As a child, attending the Brighton and Hove Girls' Industrial Home for Training Servants, Edith had doubtless been schooled in submission and obedience. Now she calmed herself as best she could and did what was demanded of her.

In the time it took to set the plan in motion, the ordeal had already taken its toll on Violet and Daisy. They'd been stripped and prodded and stared at before being deposited in a barracks filled with detainees they could not communicate with. (Angel Island's primary objective was to turn away immigrants who did not meet the racist qualifications of the Chinese Exclusion Act of 1882, which was specifically designed to block Chinese laborers from entering the country.) When Edith arrived, she found the two girls sitting on a bunk surrounded by a crowd of curious Asian women and children, the sisters so silent and motionless, it was as though they'd pulled an invisible curtain between themselves and the world. Edith did not detect a flicker of relief on their faces at the sight of her.

. . .

Violet and Daisy and Edith did not have to hold out long. Myer Myers recalled with great satisfaction how the *Chronicle*'s article, proclaiming "Tie That Binds Them Seems No Bar to 'Earning a Living,'" appeared in the paper the very next day. The result was almost instantaneous. Dr. Drew bowed to public censure and reviewed Violet and Daisy's case immediately. News of Dr. Drew's decision to release the girls appeared in both the *Chronicle* and the *San Francisco Examiner* on Monday, July 17, Myers remembered.

It would have been a triumph of public sympathy over bureaucracy—an entire city uniting for the freedom of two helpless little girls—if only we could be sure it was true. But there is a gaping hole in Myer Myers's story. No article on Violet and Daisy's sad internment appeared in the *San Francisco Chronicle* the day following the *Sonoma's* arrival, as Myers claimed. Nor the next day, nor the day after that. In fact, no article bearing the slightest resemblance to what Myers described is to be found in the *Chronicle* during the entire week of the *Sonoma's* arrival. In its Maritime News section on July 11, the newspaper noted only that "Daisy and Vilton [*sic*] Hilton, 8 years old, Siamese twins, who are making a tour of this country, were among the passengers." The *San Francisco Examiner* is likewise silent on the issue. Nor did either paper print an update on Violet and Daisy's happy ending the following Monday.

Another piece of the puzzle doesn't hold up to close scrutiny, either. Angel Island's "Record of Aliens Held for Special Inquiry" reveals that only Violet, Daisy, and Mary Hilton were detained upon arrival—not Edith. Could Mary have extricated herself and sent Edith to watch over the girls in her place so that she could sweet-talk a newspaper editor? Perhaps. Mary's detention record lists her only as an "accompanying alien," possibly giving her the right to leave if she pleased.

Either Myer Myers entirely misidentified the newspapers that carried the articles, or his account of Mary Hilton's scheme to rescue Violet and Daisy from the detainment center at the Angel Island immigration station was a piece of 24-karat-gold ballyhoo.

Looking at Violet and Daisy's detention record today gives the impression that they are still on Angel Island, awaiting Dr. Drew's verdict. It bears no stamp reading "Released by U.S. Medical Inspector," as those before and after theirs do. The release date column is also conspicuously empty.

Amid all this uncertainty, one indisputable fact remains: Violet and Daisy had several advantages over the typical Angel Island detainee. They were white, English-speaking, and healthy. They were also accompanied by three adults dedicated to securing their freedom—albeit for selfish reasons—and thanks to Violet and Daisy themselves, Mary Hilton and the Myerses were presumably not short on cash. Some interplay of these factors came to their rescue. If Myer Myers had kept records of the profits he'd already accumulated, it would have been a simple matter to demonstrate exactly how much money these two children were capable of earning.

. . .

Hazy though the story may be in many respects, one aspect of it is true: Myer Myers was a man who grasped the matchless value of publicity, making his partnership with the equally savvy Mary Hilton a formidable one. Within days of arriving in San Francisco, he'd placed two advertisements in *Billboard* magazine, which at that time catered to the entire entertainment industry, including fairs, carnivals, circuses, and theaters.

"Now Booking High-Class Engagements for Parks and Fairs or Any Good Proposition," read the tall bold print alongside a fetching photo of Violet and Daisy posing with their piano and violin. "There is not a suspicion of repulsiveness about this great curiosity," a second notice in the same issue assured *Billboard*'s readers.

Another eye-catching photo of Violet and Daisy appeared simultaneously in newspapers from Vicksburg, Mississippi, to Pittsburgh, Pennsylvania, that week. They smiled out from under colossal hair bows—Violet's grin broad and bright, Daisy's more bashful and demure—their knobby knees showing beneath a pair of dainty white skirts edged in eyelet lace. "Little Girls, Modern Siamese Twins, Enjoying Tour of World," the headline announced, as though the two youngsters were traveling the globe solely for pleasure. Myers knew that winsome image would be sparking conversations at kitchen tables, barbershops, and park benches from one side of the country to the other. With any luck, Violet and Daisy would pique the curiosity of an entire nation without budging from San Francisco.

While he waited for booking agents to call with offers to hire the Hiltons, Myer Myers opened up a "store show" on Market Street, partnering with another entrepreneur fresh off the *Sonoma* who owned two performing chimpanzees. There, Violet and Daisy almost immediately caught the eye of a press agent from the Great Wortham Shows who promised Myer Myers exactly what he wanted: "a dignified presentation of the girls in the show world."

. . .

Clarence A. Wortham, "Carnival King of the World," owned two successful traveling carnivals and was preparing to launch a third that season. A small man affectionately known as "the Little Giant," Wortham proclaimed as his motto "Decency first"—something that set his shows apart from many others.

Carnivals in the mid-1910s were on the verge of a metamorphosis. "For years the object of every sort of attack . . . hampered and perpetually dragged into the gutter by the grifters and panderers to indecency," these traveling playgrounds had plunged into disfavor by the turn of the century. Most of the midway shows were disappointing, misleading, or downright deceptive, with the exhibit inside the tent bearing little or no resemblance to the banner overhead, much less the outrageous promises shouted by the talker out front. Others were sleazy "hoochie-coochie" performances. At game counters, seedy-looking employees swindled carnival-goers out of their nickels and dimes so skillfully, they lost dollar after dollar without realizing it was happening. "It is no wonder that communities rose up in arms against these roving bands of marauders, who, masquerading as carnival companies, poisoned the minds of all with whom they came in contact," wrote *Billboard* magazine in 1921.

At the time of Violet and Daisy's arrival in America, a few impresarios like Clarence Wortham had inaugurated "the reconstruction period of the carnival business." Everything about shows like Wortham's was squeaky-clean and fair and square, from the well-swept grounds to the bright new canvas big tops. Within the tents, shabby trappings like board seats and flimsy drapes were being scrapped in favor of plush curtains, elaborate stage sets, and silk-shaded 100-watt lamps that projected the air of "a metropolitan theater de luxe." Polite, smartly dressed ladies and gentlemen operated game counters where customers stood a genuine chance (however slim) of winning a prize. "The days of the oldtime ballyhoo, with everything on the front and nothing inside, are becoming a thing of the past," said *Billboard* in praise of the change.

One problem remained: what to put *inside* the tents. Earning the patronage of a respectable clientele required "new and meritorious attractions to take the place of those which were degrading."

Violet and Daisy were poised to enter the American carnival scene at precisely the right moment. Strange though it sounds today, an act like Violet and Daisy's was not then considered degrading by the majority of Americans. Wholesomeness was what counted, and so long as Mary Hilton stopped offering peeks under their dresses, there was nothing the least bit tawdry about a pair of identical sisters in white dresses and puffy hair bows playing piano and violin. (The fact that their mother had been unwed, on the other hand? Myer Myers would have to sweep that inconvenient detail straight under the rug, lest it tarnish the image he was so carefully polishing.)

Wortham's other vital motto was "Something new," and Violet and Daisy fit that bill just as neatly. Only two other sets of conjoined twins were touring the world at that time: the Blažek sisters and four-year-old Guadalupe and Josefina Hinojosa of Cuba. Hiring Violet and Daisy was such an exciting prospect that Wortham wanted them immediately, smack in the middle of the season, and so the Hilton clan set out to rendezvous with the Great Wortham Shows in Great Falls, Montana.

The spectacle that greeted them could have rivaled, if not surpassed, any amusement park west of Coney Island, New York. "Something Doing Every Minute," Wortham's advertisements promised without a whiff of hyperbole. Four hundred performers and employees ran one hundred "distinct amusement features." His train alone was a sight to behold; the unloading of its "25 Carloads of Glittering Equipment" could mesmerize a town for a full afternoon.

The Great Wortham Show featured not a midway but a "Gladway," which hosted a smorgasbord of entertainment: an ostrich farm; a simulated submarine ride; the Trip to Mars; Booger Red's Wild West show; a troupe of little people from the Philippines; an athletic show; a motordrome; an entire arena of trained wild animals; the Torpedo Dip; the Whip; two carousels and Ferris wheels; and the so-called "freak museum," a ten-act sideshow known as Wonderland; to name but a few. "Not one of them a bad one," *Billboard* applauded, "not one of them a disgusting attraction that leaves a bad taste in the mouth."

That summer of 1916, the biggest draw on the Wortham carnival lot was Rice & Wortham's Wonder Water Circus, a $50,000 "marine spectacle." At every town on its route, the Great Wortham Shows excavated a giant pit beneath the biggest big top and installed a 200,000-gallon tank filled with "honest-to-goodness water." During the "aquatic extravaganza" that followed, water clowns, divers, and mermaids delighted the audience with underwater comedy, acrobatics, stunts, and illusions galore. A magical fisherman reeled live dogs from the pool. In the disappearing ballet, a troupe of water nymphs followed Father Neptune "to the caverns deep of the oceans cold, remaining there for an impossible period" before vanishing from the tank without a trace. "The most thrilling and blood-curdling sensation" of all, the Daredevil Knight, leapt forty feet on a bicycle through a ring of flames before plunging headfirst into the water.

"It may be said and without exaggeration that the Wortham shows are by far, the best carnival shows which have been seen here for many moons," raved the *Great Falls Tribune.*

. . .

As had been the case in Luna Park, Violet and Daisy were not to be exhibited as part of the pit shows in Wonderland. Though considered freaks of nature in the literal sense, conjoined twins enjoyed a much higher status than other performers with physical anomalies. A hierarchy existed within the carnival, based primarily on rarity. "Born freaks" like Violet and Daisy were considered sideshow royalty, as opposed to the "made freaks"—people who had intentionally altered their bodies through techniques such as extensive tattooing, or stunt performances.

"Those were the people that drew the customers to the carnival," sideshow promotor Ward Hall said of the people he knew as "legitimate" freaks. "They were our stars."

Among this elite class of sideshow performers, conjoined twins were the rarest of them all. Hirsutism, a condition that can cause a woman to grow facial hair, for instance, affects as many as three million Americans every year—very slightly less than 1 percent of the population. More often than not it's a minor case, making a bearded lady with a full beard a legitimate rarity. The odds of being born a conjoined twin, on the other hand, are at the very highest 1 in 50,000 worldwide, or .00002 percent. On top of that, only 40 to 60 percent of conjoined twins are born living, and a third of those who do survive birth die within twenty-four hours. Violet and Daisy truly were living wonders, and every inch of their tent announced that fact for anyone who walked by to see.

A vast banner across the entrance proclaimed them "The Modern Siamese Twins" in letters nearly two feet high—a nod to Eng and Chang Bunker, the first conjoined twins to achieve international fame. By billing them this way, Myer Myers was presenting Violet and Daisy to the public as the heirs to the Bunkers' legacy. At either corner of the entrance hung a poster-sized photograph of the girls in eyelet lace dresses at eighteen months old. Above, a stretch of canvas approximately as big as an elephant depicted them at the center of a brightly colored mural featuring British flags and curling streamers painted with their names. "Two English Girls—Alive—Grown Together," said the billowing banner to the left. "The World's Greatest Living Wonder," said the one on the right. Over it all, a Union Jack waved alongside two Australian flags at the tip-top of the pavilion.

Some combination of travel and preparation conspired to delay their American debut, for Violet and Daisy's show was not up and running in time for the opening night of the Great Falls engagement. Nevertheless, their tent caught the eye of the *Great Falls Tribune*. "A new feature, which will not be ready until this evening, is Daisy and Violet, two pretty children from far away Australia, who will surely prove of great interest, insomuch as they were born joined together by a small ligament that makes them rivals of the once famous Siamese twins," the newspaper reassured its readers the next day.

Violet and Daisy made good on the *Tribune*'s promise, attracting "Big Attention" from the very moment their tent opened. The paper lauded them as "one of the most interesting human phenomena ever seen in these parts." Little more than a week later they'd earned their place in the top tier of the Gladway. When asked to name the carnival's feature attraction, the manager of the Great Wortham Show replied, "Well, that is a hard question to answer, as we have many sterling features, but it is my opinion that anyone who misses paying the modern Siamese twins a visit is actually doing himself an injustice."

People came flocking. At Kalispell, Idaho, and Nampa, Montana; at the Baker City Fair in Oregon; and at the Interstate Fair in Spokane, Washington, the Modern Siamese Twins were pulling in "top money," at nearly every venue, rivaled only by the Wonder Water Circus. At the Interstate Fair, the *Spokane Daily Chronicle* noted, Violet and Daisy were "especial favorites and their little tent is forever crowded with interested visitors who never seem to tire of watching the children play with their ample supply of doll babies and other toys."

In less than a month's time, *Billboard* reported that Violet and Daisy were "breaking all pit show records on the midway." The show business world was also taking notice of the man behind this extraordinary success. "Newcomer" Myer Myers, said *Billboard*, was proving himself "a bright and energetic showman and a believer in publicity and the press agent. That he will make good in this country is certain," the magazine predicted.

. . .

With this great success came the opportunity for Myer Myers to set aside comparisons to the conjoined twins of the past and fabricate a unique persona tailored specifically to Violet and Daisy. By October, they had metamorphosed from the Modern Siamese Twins to the Royal English United Twins. Emphasizing their British heritage was a particularly sly move. Inventing a royal connection lent their ballyhoo an air of glamour and prestige without making the girls sound *too* foreign—a critical balance to achieve with immigration on the rise and a world war raging on the other side of the Atlantic.

Image had always been important to Mary Hilton and Myer Myers, and now it mattered more than ever. Clarence Wortham's standards for respectability made it absolutely crucial that no whisper of Violet and Daisy's illegitimate birth leak out. Thus, they became the most tragic of orphans: their mother dead in childbirth, their father an English army officer killed in Belgium during the Great War. This imaginary "Captain Hilton" was the man Violet and Daisy themselves came to regard as their father, either because they heard the story dozens of times a day or because as children they had never been told the truth. Even in adulthood, after they'd learned otherwise, they clung to their heroic soldier-father in their own versions of their history. (Their father's identity has never been proven. The few available clues point toward Frederick Andress, the married son of a wealthy newspaper publisher in Brighton.)

There's no telling what other ballyhoo Violet and Daisy came to regard as true. Morning, noon, and night, a talker stood outside their tent, stretching and pulling the truth like taffy until it was sweeter, smoother, and more enticing than anything real life could offer. Every day they heard about their royal heritage, the dozens of countries they'd visited, the virtuous relatives who had taken them in, their musical prowess and dazzling good looks. "Auntie" Mary Hilton was billed as their grandmother. Edith, whom Violet and Daisy had been taught to regard as their cousin, and who had been previously identified in the papers only as their nurse or governess, became their aunt, and Myer Myers their uncle—when he wasn't Dr. Myers, "a famous Australian physician," that is.

Violet and Daisy were eight years old now, and no doubt secretly giggled at some of the whoppers their talker spun out of thin air. But some of those fanciful details—like Captain Hilton—must have seeped into their consciousnesses and lodged there until the details felt no different from the truth. Either that or Violet and Daisy came to believe that the facts of their lives were theirs to do with as they pleased, for the stories they would one day tell of their childhood were heartily seasoned with exaggeration, too.

In keeping with this virtuous fictional history, Mary Hilton continued to dress the sisters as the very picture of old-fashioned little-girl innocence. Beautifully waved masses of hair hung past their shoulders, held away from their faces with bows like mammoth butterfly wings. Their dresses did not reflect the more tailored and practical styles that had come into fashion to accommodate wartime cloth shortages, but hearkened back to Victorian finery with its lace and flounces, its delicate muslin and glossy satin sashes. Knee socks and patent leather Mary Jane shoes finished off the immaculate look. And never once did Violet and Daisy appear in a dress with a single shared skirt, as Josefa and Rosa Blažek or Millie-Christine McCoy always did. A glance at the McCoys or the Blažeks, whose much more substantial physical connections required more elaborate alterations to their wardrobes, resulted in the discomfiting sight of four legs emerging from a single hemline. Violet and Daisy's clothing, by contrast, was always crafted to create the illusion that they were two separate people sitting or standing shoulder to shoulder and hip to hip. Though their livelihood depended on their physical anomaly, the momentary ability to pass as normal was a prized, if contradictory, trophy.

The fact that Violet and Daisy were pretty also mattered to their success. It mattered a great deal, as did the fact that they were white. These two advantages went hand in hand. White audiences, with their narrow standards of beauty, were far more likely to view Asian or African-American twins like Eng and Chang Bunker and Millie-Christine McCoy as "exotic" rather than beautiful or handsome. White conjoined twins were such a novelty that Ike Rose had blatantly announced in a *Billboard* advertisement seeking bookings for both Josefa and Rosa Blažek and Violet and Daisy, "These Freaks Are White." White conjoined twins had verged on nonexistent since the British Biddenden Maids of the twelfth century, in part because at the time of the Hiltons' birth, only people from northern and western Europe were considered white. The Blažek sisters, Violet and

Daisy's only competition in this arena, were from the present-day Czech Republic, which just barely qualified. But the Blažek sisters were not conventionally attractive; some even considered them grotesque. Violet and Daisy, therefore, were the first set of conjoined twins whom white carnival-goers were willing to identify with, and simultaneously take pleasure in looking at.

With help from Edith, Mary Hilton also saw to it that there was more to enjoy about the girls than a pair of pretty faces. "She set about making us 'the smartest Siamese twins alive,'" Violet and Daisy recalled. This was not strictly true. Intelligence was not Mary Hilton's goal. She did not teach the girls how to think, but how to "read, recite, and sing." Everything they learned was for the sole purpose of showing off. Reciting facts and figures was like dancing or playing a duet—a performance to heighten the audience's enjoyment. And it worked flawlessly. "These little girls are as bright as a dollar," the *Daily Inter Lake* gushed. The *Spokane Daily Chronicle* lauded Violet and Daisy as "born entertainers," impressing the audience with their knowledge of English, German, Dutch, French, and Italian, and delighting spectators with tales of their travels across Australia and New Zealand.

. . .

And what of Violet and Daisy themselves? What did they think of their first great American success? They spoke not at all of this period in their lives. Eventually, as traveling carnivals once again fell into disfavor, they would come to regard their stint on the US fairground circuit with a mixture of shame and disdain, but at the time, observation—gauging the reactions and emotions of those around them—was more valuable to their well-being than introspection. "We learned to listen early," they once said of their earliest childhood. "We learned to say little"—a hint that in silence, there was safety.

That protective silence expanded into a lifelong habit between the two sisters: Violet and Daisy never spoke their thoughts aloud to each other. What went on within their individual minds belonged to one person, and one person alone. As the *Dayton Daily News* would observe, " 'Speak when you're spoken to and then make it brief' seems to be their mutual policy."

"Because of our bond we register moods and movements of each other," Violet and Daisy later explained. "We sense thoughts, feel currents and vibrations." It wasn't magic or telepathy—just a matter of familiarity and proximity. "Two good friends may have such experiences," they pointed out. To subject each other to more than that would have been overwhelming, and would have destroyed any semblance of privacy.

· · ·

Being on display for as many as twelve hours a day, every day, Violet and Daisy needed every scrap of privacy they could snatch up, even from each other, for despite their identical appearance and marrow-deep devotion to each other, they were distinct individuals through and through.

As if by mutual agreement, their personalities were developing into two halves of a remarkably balanced whole. Daisy was dreamy and serious, yet quick to speak and quick to move. Violet's thoughts, words, and actions were less impulsive than her sister's, but her emotions were more mercurial, more apt to flare into a temper. Fortunately, she was quick to recover from her anger. Daisy tended to be agreeable, "to avoid a fuss," while Violet, though quieter and less outspoken on the whole, was more likely to stand her ground when she did speak up. "Sometimes I wish I were like Violet," Daisy said. "She doesn't have to do things she doesn't like so much. If someone tells me that something is nice, I say yes whether I think so or not. Violet says what she thinks."

They had different ways of turning loose their excitement and tension, too; situations that Daisy met with laughter often provoked tears from Violet. When Violet smiled, she seemed to hold nothing back—her face tilted upward and her lips and eyes opened big and bright, offering up every ounce of her glee. Daisy did just the opposite. She tended to tuck her chin, gazing almost shyly upward, as though reserving a bit of her happiness solely for herself.

Their tastes coordinated as well. Daisy took pleasure in dolls. Violet had no use for inert playthings. She was more fascinated by mechanical toys, or by climbing and swinging on the furniture. On the occasions when Daisy was in the mood for livelier diversions, Violet invariably wanted to sit quietly, "to read books and to look at nice pictures." Daisy loved flaming shades of red, while Violet was drawn to the soft purples that matched her name. Violet liked chicken; Daisy, pork. Even the sounds of their voices harmonized—Daisy spoke in a higher pitch than Violet, who preferred low tones.

Anyone else might have seen such vast differences in taste and temperament as fertile ground for all manner of clashes and feuds. Not Violet and Daisy. From their point of view, the contrasts in their personalities balanced each other like the two pans of a scale. "It is as though some Power, greater and stronger than ourselves, has given us this inner harmony to compensate for our being forced to live constantly as an entity," they said as adults. "And that harmony has been with us through the years—a harmony that has amazed many who have known us." They had their occasional petty squabbles, of course, as any sisters do—sometimes punctuated with the slap of a hairbrush or two—but from the time they were small, they shared their lives "just as amiably as we shared our childhood toys, without quarreling."

Violet and Daisy shared their love and affection, too, something no one else had ever offered them in a pure, unsullied form. Mary Hilton and the Myerses could be counted upon to keep them well fed, well dressed, and well groomed. Nothing more. Edith's devotion, though genuine, was not strong enough to impel her to insist that her mother and husband treat her foster sisters as anything more than valuable specimens. The girls' success ensured that there would be good food on Edith's table and fine clothes on her back, and most of all, that the baby she was now carrying would never want for anything. And if Violet and Daisy's first few months with the Great Wortham Shows were any indication, Mary Hilton and the Myerses could soon look forward to any luxury that life had to offer.

CHAPTER 9

AT THE CLOSE OF THE 1916 SEASON, EMPLOYEES AND PER-
formers alike headed for "Worthamville," the carnival's winter
quarters in San Antonio, Texas. Violet and Daisy were not among
them. Instead, the Myerses and Hiltons lingered in Phoenix, Arizona,
where Edith gave birth to her first and only child, Theresa Mary, on
the fourth of December. By the time they reached Texas in the first
months of 1917, all the best apartments had been rented to winter
residents. Myers settled for a room-and-a-half "dollhouse" at Millman
and Essex Streets.

If Violet and Daisy had dared to hope for a taste of normal life
in a real neighborhood during those early-winter months of 1917,
they were to be sorely disappointed. Mary Hilton's old policy remained in force. The girls did not go to school, to restaurants, or to
shops. They had no opportunity to make friends. "No neighborhood
children were allowed to visit Daisy and Vi, nor were they allowed
to leave their home to play with other kids," remembered Camille
Rosengren, who also grew up in San Antonio and whose mother was
friends with Edith Myers. "They never had a chance to interact with
any peers. They were prisoners."

At least once, though, Edith took Violet and Daisy along when she
called on her own newly made friends. That was how ten-year-old

Jim Moore managed to get a glimpse of them at the home of his schoolmate, Porter Smith. "Porter, naturally, was bragging about it at school that the Siamese twins were going to come over to their house with this woman, whoever she was," Moore said. (The woman was Edith Myers.) "That's the first time I laid eyes on them."

The next time Jim saw them was in the spring, at the official launch of Wortham's 1917 season, the San Jacinto Fiesta in downtown San Antonio. To Myer Myers's immense gratification, Violet and Daisy's pavilion nabbed "the next prominent corner" on Alamo Plaza—directly across from Texas's most legendary fort.

Jim Moore was among the many thousands who streamed onto Alamo Plaza to see the Royal English United Twins that week. To him, seeing them up onstage was akin to a religious experience. The awe he felt that day remained embedded in his memory for the next six decades. "The girls seemed to be glowing, as if there were auras around them," Moore remembered. "They were bathed by light in a tent that was otherwise dark. I started shivering. . . . I knew my life was not going to be the same again."

Here, at last, were people Jim felt an affinity for. A tall, dapper boy, he was a Fred Astaire trapped in a rugged world of Tom Sawyers and Huck Finns. And here were Violet and Daisy, doing the very thing Jim himself dreamed of: dancing.

Jim could hardly tear himself away from the Royal English United Twins' pavilion. He had to—just *had* to—talk to them. "It was almost impossible to have contact with the girls," he recalled. "They were under strict orders from Myer Myers not to talk to anyone unless he, Edith, or Mary was at their side." Jim lingered in and around their tent every moment he could, waiting for the fleeting opportunities when Edith ducked out, in hopes of speaking to Violet and Daisy alone. There wasn't time to do much more than tell them how much he loved their performances and demonstrate the dance steps he'd learned by watching their act. "I really wanted them to like me," he said.

Much of the difficulty in having a conversation with Violet and Daisy arose from the fact that although the sisters knew how to interact with adults, children mystified them. Only once in their lives had they been given the opportunity to play with anyone their own age—in Germany, when Mary Hilton deliberately exposed them to measles. (Daisy had not caught the disease from Violet, and Mary Hilton was determined to have her catch it from someone to get it over and done with.) Even at the age of three or four, the girls were aware of their own awkwardness and ignorance. "We did not know how to play with children," they remembered. The best Daisy could do was to make funny faces at herself in the mirror for the other girls and boys to laugh at.

They could entertain anyone effortlessly, but to have a real, unscripted chat with a person their own age? Violet and Daisy hardly knew where to begin. Still, Jim Moore sensed that the girls relished his presence just as much as he delighted in theirs. "They liked people, now, don't think they didn't," Moore said; "they loved people, and loved to be around people."

At the end of Fiesta week, Violet and Daisy proved that to him in a gesture more eloquent than words. For the rest of his life Jim would remember standing along the train tracks as the Wortham roustabouts dismantled the show and loaded the tents and rides onto flatcars. It was not even daylight yet, but Jim could not take his eyes off the Royal English United Twins' railcar. He was as desperate to say goodbye as he had been to say hello. As the train pulled away, the curtains parted and two pale, familiar faces peeked through the window. They looked as "unearthly" in the predawn torchlight as they had under the spotlights in their dark tent at that first performance. Violet and Daisy smiled at Jim in unison and blew him two identical kisses.

. . .

From fairground to fairground, Violet and Daisy's climb to fame advanced steadily upward. Newspapers across the Midwest continued to marvel at how refreshingly pleasant their show was. Amid the excitement and hubbub of the midway, their tent became a welcome respite. Making a trip "to the little playhouse of the 'Royal English Twins' is to soothe tired nerves," said the *Omaha World-Herald*.

Myer Myers had nearly as much to do with that as the girls themselves. Never content to rest on his success, Myers continually worked to keep Violet and Daisy's show in the top echelon of carnival attractions. Quality and class were becoming his hallmarks. "The way the show is framed is certainly a credit to the man that gave it birth," *Billboard* praised.

If the Myerses weren't swimming in money by the end of 1917, they were certainly at least knee-deep in it. The near-magic combination of the girls' sparkling personalities and Myers's showmanship was raking in "unprecedented business for a platform show." In September of that year, Myer Myers felt flush enough to dish out $400 to add to the act a Deagan Una-Fon, an electric glockenspiel with a keyboard like a piano and a sound like several dozen finely tuned alarm clock bells. Today that same splurge would cost close to $8,000.

And what did Violet and Daisy have to show for all their success? Exactly seventy-five cents. Violet had a quarter to her name, and Daisy a fifty-cent piece, slipped to them by a sympathetic stagehand. The girls kept the coins—their life savings—hidden in their shoes.

• • •

After a year and a half of uninterrupted prosperity, Myer Myers's allegiance abruptly shifted. "Johnny J. Jones Exposition Makes Another Scoop; Engagement of English Siamese Twins," the *Orlando Sentinel* announced on February 10, 1918. "Mr. Jones is to be congratulated upon securing this marvelous and much sought after attraction," the press release gloated. Myers had severed his ties with carnival king Clarence Wortham and signed Violet and Daisy with up-and-coming impresario Johnny J. Jones.

Why the switch? Any number of factors could have come into play. New territory, for one. Wortham's shows tended to tour west of the Mississippi River. The Johnny J. Jones Exposition's route included the eastern United States and much of Canada, guaranteeing fresh audiences. Its extended season, being the last "big show" to retire to winter quarters and the first to emerge in spring, made the year more lucrative. Like Wortham, Jones ran a clean, family-oriented outfit. "Throughout all the shows there is nothing that could be taken objection to by the most fastidious," said the *Calgary Herald*. Myer Myers would have settled for nothing less, insisting on "high class engagements" from the moment he'd set foot on American soil. Jones's personal reputation was on the rise, too—in 1917, he'd been featured on the covers of *Billboard* and *Optimist*—and prestige always worked like a magnet on Myer Myers. The quality of Jones's attractions may even have ranked a small notch above Wortham's.

Johnny J. Jones, like Clarence Wortham, was not content to have his carnival lot called by the generic name of *midway*. Instead, it was the "Joy Trail" or "Funshine Alley"—a place where "jaded amusement seekers will find a tonic to their liking," the *Edmonton Journal* promised.

In 1918 the Jones Exposition proudly featured two brand-new patented and copyrighted shows: the War of the Clouds and Terrors of the Ocean. Two prior hits, America: The Show Beautiful and the Witching Waves, were newly painted on the outside and updated with fresh surprises inside. The Great War raging across Europe had spurred interest in two military-themed attractions: the World's Fighting Navies, and the British Government War Exhibition, staffed entirely by veterans wounded in the conflict. No carnival was complete without a one-ring circus and accompanying sideshow; Jones's featured a Fat Girls' Congress and Zaza the monkey girl. Dakota Max's Wild West show included buffalo and wild steer, and the wild animal menagerie boasted the largest and smallest elephants in captivity as well as the addition of five new lions. For thrills, Margaret Gast, the Mile-a-Minute Girl, performed in the motordrome, while the Haunted Hotel and the London Ghost Show provided the chills. Tamer offerings included an entire Lilliputian "city" populated exclusively by people with dwarfism, as well as a Monkey Hotel, Krazy House, Bug House, and House of Wonders. An Underground Chinatown replica and a Dixieland Minstrel show were also in the works when Violet and Daisy came aboard.

In addition to live entertainment, Jones had invested heavily in "mechanical attractions." His carousel alone was a $20,000 showpiece with 1,900 electric lights. The Whip and the Ferris wheel, by now carnival staples, were joined by two new rides called Over the Falls and the Cyclonic Helter Skelter.

"There is not a platform or pit show with the organization," *Billboard* applauded.

Perhaps this was the chance Myers had been waiting for—the chance to elevate the Royal English United Twins above the pits and platforms. The fact that Johnny J. Jones considered it such a coup to hire what had heretofore been a pit show is telling. Violet and Daisy's record-breaking earnings had already proved that theirs was no ordinary sideshow. The time had come to see what more they—and Myers—were capable of.

. . .

A trademark of the Jones show was its elaborate "fronts"—the opulent carved and painted facades that greeted patrons at the entrance to each attraction. Many were gilded with silver and gold, their contours outlined with "inlaid" electric lightbulbs that hid their cords from view. For Myer Myers, this provided another opportunity to showcase his knack for presentation. He went to work immediately on "what is going to be a most unique and fascinating front."

Myers understood that the atmosphere of the venue was just as important as the act it contained. Make the place attractive and comfortable, put the audience at ease the moment they step inside, and you amplify their enjoyment. His attention to such details would ensure that spectators left feeling as though they'd attended a "theater" performance rather than a pit show.

By late spring, this "most elaborate" creation was complete. Its appearance is lost to history. Less than two months later, Violet and Daisy's tent and front were whisked from the face of the earth, "entirely blown away" by a tornado in Manitoba. All that remained was the stage floor, a few support posts, and a banner reading "Daisy and Violet."

Myer Myers's determination to have the best-looking show on the Johnny J. Jones lot could not be quashed. That autumn the Spanish influenza pandemic played havoc with the Jones Expo's bookings, causing health officials to cancel state fairs in the Southeast and divert the carnival's train away from infected areas. Instead of heading to its usual winter quarters in Florida, the show was forced to spend four months encamped at the Birmingham, Alabama, state fairgrounds. The upheaval did not slow Myers. "The busy boy" enlisted designer Fred Lewis and got straight to work improving the girls' theater, promising that "his new front and entire equipment for the Siamese Twins attraction will make [rivals] all hustle to compete with them." The result was unveiled in February. No description survives. We know only that out of an entire carnival that was lauded as "resplendent with an abundance of gilt, harmonious color and a lavish display of glittering gold," Violet and Daisy's new front was deemed "positively the most gorgeous and attractive ever seen in this country."

Myer Myers had positioned himself to dominate the Johnny J. Jones midway in 1919, but none of his careful building and planning could anticipate the jolt that was to come.

CHAPTER 10

WHEN THE JOHNNY J. JONES EXPOSITION REACHED ITS SPRING booking in Atlanta, the trajectory of Violet's and Daisy's lives took another unexpected bend for the worse. There, in the earliest hours of Easter Sunday, April 20, 1919, Mary Hilton died of a kidney infection. She was sixty-two years old.

The next day Violet and Daisy sat in Atlanta's Poole chapel, transfixed by the sight of their first corpse, while Edith grieved beside her mother's casket. Violet cried, too.

"Why cry?" Daisy asked. She could not bring herself to care, much less to mourn. "We have hated her forever!"

Yet even Daisy had to agree that something fundamental about "Auntie" was missing now that she was dead. "The cunning and the shrewdness seemed out of her face," softening her, the sisters remembered. In a way, they thought, Mary Hilton had almost been "our first friend." Auntie had been the driving force in their lives since before Violet and Daisy could form memories. With her absence came an unwelcome sense of disorientation.

"I'm afraid without her," Violet confessed. "Now Sir will boss us."

The dire truth of that prediction mustered up a whirl of fear and courage. "Let's run away," they whispered between themselves. All the money they had in the world—Violet's quarter and Daisy's fifty-cent piece—was right there in their shoes. Edith could not see past her tears. Only Myer Myers had to be dodged.

"We'll never have a chance like this again," Violet said, but she did not budge.

"Let's run!" Daisy coaxed. She bolted, pulling Violet with her. For that flicker of a moment, escape seemed possible. A few steps, and Daisy felt a sudden slump in their momentum as Violet lagged. The tremor that passed through Violet then was so intense, Daisy could actually feel the vibration, too. In the same instant, Myer Myers's hand reached out and clamped on to Daisy's, halting both of them.

"Don't touch me!" Violet cried.

Myers took them each by an arm and silently steered them back to their seat.

. . .

The atmosphere in the Myerses' hotel room after the funeral service fairly crackled with hostility. Some kind of reprimand had to be coming, but Edith and Myer just looked at Violet and Daisy without a word.

Violet cried. She perceived a sense of ownership in the stony expressions that confronted her. The same tension that cowed Violet goaded Daisy, who "laughed in their sullen, suspicious faces." Daisy was spoiling for a fight, sure she could stand up to anything the Myerses dished out. Violet's intuition told her they had already been defeated.

Edith broke the long, menacing silence. "Tell them."

"You girls belong to us now! You'll do just as we say," Myers said as he brandished a paper before their noses. "See here—Auntie left you to us—you and her jewelry and furniture are ours. Do you understand?"

The paper was Mary Hilton's will. Daisy argued. Violet only cried more. They were trapped, just as she'd feared.

Mary Hilton, as Violet and Daisy's legal guardian, had had every right to specify who should assume the girls' care in the event of her death. And Edith was the one person in the world who might have harbored some genuine affection for Violet and Daisy. On paper, it has all the appearance of an obvious and compassionate solution.

But Mary Hilton's history of exploiting her two wards nonstop since infancy speaks more loudly. She had left to Edith not only Violet and Daisy but also $5,000 and two small homes in San Antonio. At the absolute minimum, her exploitation of the children she had dubbed the Brighton United Twins had earned her what would amount to $103,000 today, and her will saw to it that nothing would stand in the way of Edith's opportunity to continue cashing in on her foster sisters.

No one batted an eye. Newspapers from Kentucky to Louisiana; New York; Washington, DC; and Kansas carried the story of Edith's unusual inheritance without a twinge of consternation. It was no more than a bemusing tidbit to fill an inch or two of column space.

The world's indifference was not lost on Violet and Daisy. Thousands of people looked at them every day, but no one peered hard enough past the bright facade to see their unhappiness. "During the ten years following the death of Auntie . . . our hearts were scarred," they would later remember. "But our minds grew strong and our Siamese bond of flesh and bone became one of real understanding between us. Our desire to harmonize with each other was, indeed, our real salvation."

. . .

For the next six years, the pattern of Violet's and Daisy's lives would hardly vary. Forty-some weeks each year of fairgrounds, railroads, and carnival tents, followed by winter sequestered behind closed doors. Fewer newspaper stories singled them out for special attention, softening the glare of the spotlight. Nevertheless, money rolled steadily in.

If Violet and Daisy's success seemed to plateau, Myer Myers's did not. Fueled by the girls' earnings, Myer Myers was becoming an entertainment entrepreneur. He invested in a ranch and a horticulture farm outside San Antonio, as well as a $7,400 lot on Vance-Jackson Road. He also expanded his carnival offerings, hiring the six-person, 3,127-pound Karn family to put on a show he dubbed the Fat Folks' Chautauqua. True to form, Myers upgraded the Karns' display into something a cut above the average sideshow offering, shunning the usual "rag banners" and "dinky platform" to earn himself another "hats off" from *Billboard* in praise of his knack for presentation. By 1920, he'd become the owner of the Johnny J. Jones Exposition Side-Show, which put him in charge of a 170-foot tent featuring mind readers, glassblowers, and anything and everything in between. The next season, he teamed up with two other showmen to create the Johnny J. Jones' Big Circus Side-Show and Birdland Side-Show, filling two 220-foot tents with "a tremendous aggregation of strange and marvelous people and birds from all parts of the earth." Violet and Daisy took a liking to the birds and soon began to train a flock of cockatoos to join their act.

At the end of that same season, just as Myers's own career seemed to be cresting a new peak, he left the Jones Exposition and booked Violet and Daisy with Clarence Wortham for 1922. We can only speculate why. A better contract? More money? Or perhaps Myer and Edith Myers wanted to make their permanent home in San Antonio, where the Wortham shows wintered and where their own investments were blossoming.

• • •

The Myerses were at their ranch in San Antonio on March 30, 1922—the day Josefa Blažek died in Chicago at age forty-four. Her sister, Rosa, followed twelve minutes later. Fresh fascination with conjoined twins erupted as the news spread across the country. Myer Myers saw an opportunity to boost Violet and Daisy's prominence to its earlier height. He blanketed the nation with a story and photograph of the Hilton sisters, proclaiming them successors to the Blažeks as well as to Eng and Chang Bunker, the original Siamese twins.

Essentially an understated advertisement, the article painted an idyllic picture of a charmed life. Five months' rest every year in sunny San Antonio. A limousine, a maid, a private tutor. A flock of pet chickens and a troupe of trained birds. Devoted foster parents and a darling little foster sister from whom they were "inseparable," the *San Antonio Evening News* said without a hint of irony or sarcasm. Such a "winsome" pair of sisters with "pleasing personality and sweetness of manner" deserved every luxury their adoptive parents could bestow, of course. Their worldwide travels, according to the paper, had served to grace the girls with "the sophistication of age with the charm of girlhood." None of this was strictly untrue, but as the story made its way out of Texas and into the wider world, the impression it gave veered further and further from the reality of Violet and Daisy's daily life.

A lifetime of pub, amusement park, and carnival appearances vanished from their history without a trace, replaced by fictional friends and frequent trips to the picture show. According to the *New York Herald*, Violet and Daisy were "much sought after as playmates by the other young girls of the neighborhood." The *Herald*'s version, conveniently leaving out the fact that the sisters had been on display since they were three weeks old, even went so far as to claim that Violet and Daisy "repeatedly begged their parents to permit them to accept some of the many offers to exhibit them" but the Myerses "will not permit the two girls to become 'public freaks.'"

Violet and Daisy were fourteen years old, yet the accompanying photograph showed them in long ringlets, big hair bows, and knee-length dresses, as though they were still little girls of eight or ten. Their short stature—neither of them would ever grow above five feet tall—made the illusion all the more convincing. Any other young ladies would have been on the verge of pinning up their hair (or even bobbing it) and reveling in their first long skirts. As long as their perpetual innocence continued to sell tickets, Violet and Daisy would not be permitted to grow up.

One aspect of their image did change, though. For the previous eight years, Myer Myers had consistently emphasized the girls' English heritage, lending an exaggerated air of sophistication and romance to their show. It was not an original tactic. Ever since Eng and Chang Bunker had arrived in America from Siam in 1829, the fashion had been to refer to conjoined twins according to their origin: Siamese Twins, Carolina Twins, Bohemian Twins, Brighton United Twins. With the Blažeks gone, Violet and Daisy suddenly began to metamorphose once again, into San Antonio's Siamese Twins. The girls were "American, and proud of it," one newspaper article declared within three weeks of Josefa and Rosa Blažek's death. The publicity seemed to be asking the United States to embrace Violet and Daisy Hilton as its own.

It was an easy leap for Americans to make. The sisters had been crisscrossing the nation long enough now that they'd become great favorites throughout the Midwest. "It seems the fair would not be the fair unless the girls were here," said the *Sioux City Journal*. It's pleasant to think that Violet and Daisy might have had their favorites, too—people they recognized and looked forward to seeing at each stop along the carnival's route. The newspaper's special note of their "remarkable memories" suggests this could be the case. If so, it would be as close as the girls could come to making friends.

A real conversation with anyone besides the Myerses remained a rare treat for Violet and Daisy. "Except for the people who entered their tent, Daisy and Vi had no chance to relate with anybody from the outside world," San Antonio native Camille Rosengren said.

Back during their 1919 tour with the Johnny J. Jones Expo, Myers had occasionally permitted Violet and Daisy to invite six-year-old Percilla Lauther to visit on Sunday mornings before the show opened. Percilla, known in the show world as the Monkey Girl, had been born in Puerto Rico; due to a condition called hypertrichosis, fine dark hair grew on nearly every inch of her body. The three of them had tea parties together, with Percilla's pet chimp, Joanna, rounding out the guest list. In sixteen years, they had been the Hilton sisters' only playmates.

To Percilla, whose manager doubled as her adoptive father, Myer Myers's tight control over Violet and Daisy seemed perfectly ordinary. "Carl Lauther, my manager, also kept constant watch over me and had the same rule," she explained as an adult. "I'm sure the twins' manager was only trying to protect them. Probably he was worried that someone might try to kidnap them. There were a lot of crazy people on the outside, do-gooders who felt they had a religious mission to rescue the children of the sideshow." But Violet and Daisy did not feel protected by Myer Myers. Unlike Percilla, who never had an unkind word for her manager-father, they felt valuable, rather than valued.

Their fellow performers on the Wortham lot silently sympathized with Violet and Daisy. Most of the other show folk had developed a soft spot for the sisters. Those two girls brought so much enjoyment to others, it only seemed fair that they should enjoy some pleasures outside their tent for once. Together, Wortham's employees hatched an extravagant plan to show Violet and Daisy just how much they were appreciated—"something never before done in the outdoor show world."

When the show reached Hammond, Indiana, in early July, the

plan unfolded. The entire midway would shut its gates to the public for a full afternoon, leaving Myer Myers with no excuse to keep Violet and Daisy sequestered in their tent.

The *Lake County Times* called it a "professional matinee." The carnival's employees always put on their shows simultaneously, the paper explained, and consequently the entertainers never had the opportunity to enjoy one another's performances. "Violet and Daisy Hilton, San Antonio's famous grown-together girls, have been with the Wortham shows for several years, and have yet to see every performance on the big midway." In fact, they had yet to see *any* performance on the midway. Eight years had passed since they'd entered the American carnival scene, and they had never missed a single day's work.

For the first time in their lives, Violet and Daisy were free to see any show and ride any ride they pleased: the Monkey Circus, the Wild West show, Jungleland, Reckless Bob's motordrome, the Bughouse, the Caterpillar, the Ferris wheel, the merry-go-round, and the Whip. Even the great headliner, the Water Show, which culminated in a diver lighting himself on fire and diving eighty feet to extinguish himself in the tank, was theirs to enjoy. For that one day, their invisible shackles were unlocked.

CHAPTER 11

HIS OWN SIDESHOW—"THE BIGGEST ATTRACTION ON THE ground." His name in newspapers, *Billboard,* and *Variety.* A ranch in Texas. An $1,800 custom-built "traveling home" aboard the Wortham train with three rooms, eight-foot ceilings, a bathtub, and electricity. A limousine, unloaded from the train at every stop on the carnival route, so the Myerses could leave the fairgrounds and explore at their leisure. And Violet and Daisy had funded it all.

But still, Myer Myers wanted more. "Big-time," that was what he wanted.

In the 1920s, the big time meant vaudeville. Chains of vaudeville theaters stretched from one end of the United States to the other, theaters with blazing marquees that could put Violet's and Daisy's names in lights.

Vaudeville theaters featured an ever-changing array of live performances. A single ticket entitled a patron to sit down to a dozen different acts in a single show. Singers, dancers, musicians, hypnotists, magicians, jugglers, comedians, lecturers, trained animals—anything, really, so long as it could entice people to hand over their money at the box office. A few days later, the entire lineup, called the bill, would be different. Small-time vaudeville houses ran six shows a day for as little as a dime a show. Those were the theaters where future Hollywood legends like Judy Garland and Bob Hope were just making their start in entertainment. In the big-time houses, luminaries as famous and as unalike as Harry Houdini and Helen Keller performed just two shows a day for $2 per ticket (around $30 today).

Myer Myers aimed for the biggest of the big-time chains: the Keith-Albee circuit. In the late fall of 1924, he packed up Violet and Daisy—sporting fresh permanent waves in their elbow-length hair and carrying the two shining new saxophones they'd recently mastered—and headed to New York City to procure an audition.

How exactly Myers managed to capture the attention of the most sought-after bookers in vaudeville is anyone's guess. "Freak" acts were considered far inferior to the usual fare offered by the big-time theaters. Publicity may have goaded Keith-Albee into taking a chance on the San Antonio Siamese Twins; three different photos of Violet and Daisy appeared in newspapers across the nation between Thanksgiving and New Year's, prematurely crowning the soon-to-be seventeen-year-olds "the first 'Siamese twins' of an English-speaking race to arrive at maturity." Many of the captions also mentioned that the girls were "having the time of their lives" on their first visit to "Gotham." They may even have appeared in a silent newsreel film.

Whatever trick Myers had up his sleeve worked. Sometime near the turn of the year, Violet and Daisy arrived at New York's famed Hippodrome, one of the largest theaters in the world, to show off their talent. They stood petrified in the center of a stage bigger than a baseball diamond, dwarfed by the cavernous scale of the place. Five thousand, one hundred and ninety-seven empty seats stared back at them.

Violet and Daisy did not know how to play to such a vast, hollow room. They were accustomed to feeding off an audience's warmth and excitement—the nearest thing they had to genuine affection—and responding with an unbridled joy that was sorely lacking in their daily lives. This theater was dark and cold, with just Myers and two skeptical spectators watching.

For the first time in their lives, the San Antonio Siamese Twins' act flopped. They had not even finished before the Keith-Albee bookers advised Myer Myers to "take them back to a carnival where they belonged."

Violet and Daisy stood on the stage and cried.

· · ·

All was not lost. Theater gossip quickly carried word of the Hiltons' disastrous audition to Terry Turner, publicity director for the Loew's theater chain, where his job was "to ferret out novelties that would prove to be a box office magnet." He'd hired everything from mind readers to flagpole sitters, but never a set of conjoined twins. Intrigued, Turner sought Violet and Daisy out at the "dowdy New York boarding house" where they'd retreated to lick their wounds.

"I found them a rather dejected lot when first introduced," Terry Turner remembered. The Hippodrome flop had quashed the girls' confidence and stifled the natural vivacity that made them so appealing. Yet he was mightily encouraged by their talent, looks, and ambition. And something more than that, too. "Despite their carnival experience they possessed an innate sense of refinement and dignity that could never be downed," he said. Turner immediately deduced the role that the ambience of the audition had played in their failure and set about convincing Violet and Daisy that they were not the problem. "After considerable coaxing and pleading and assurances that I would not have them do anything on the stage that would make me appear ridiculous in the eyes of other theatrical producers, I managed to get a peep out of them about the volume of a canary."

Over the next weeks, Turner committed himself to tailoring and rehearsing a brand-new act for Violet and Daisy with comedic banter, three saxophone numbers, and as a grand finale, a double fox-trot with a set of twin brothers as dance partners. By early 1925, he was confident that the girls had adapted to the vaudeville stage.

"Now that they were ready, the biggest and most herculean task was at hand," he said. "That of convincing vaudeville bookers that [the Hiltons] would prove a drawing card in their theaters and that mothers and children would not leave the theater horrified."

Turner's own boss recoiled at the very idea of putting conjoined twins on his stages. As far as Marcus Loew himself was concerned, all people like Violet and Daisy were "monstrosities."

Terry Turner bristled at that. "Well, God made the Siamese twins, but you're too high class to let the public see them," he challenged.

Loew was chastened but still couldn't bear to venture a look. He was "too soft hearted," he claimed, "and would feel too sorry for them."

Undaunted, Turner argued with everyone and anyone on Loew's staff, all of whom took to "politely informing me that I had a screw loose somewhere in my system." The vaudeville stage was no place for "physical monstrosities," they said, echoing Mr. Loew's verdict. The chief booker "set his foot down" and refused to schedule a try-out. Even the legal staff were curious enough to lift their noses from their fat law books "long enough to butt in."

Turner riled everyone up so badly that finally, twenty of his colleagues scheduled a meeting "to thresh the matter out." Marcus Loew was out of town. The decision fell to general manager Nicholas M. Schenck, a man Turner characterized as "a great listener" who "weighs both sides of a discussion before attempting to render a decision." Schenck "came to my rescue," Turner said, and gave the San Antonio Siamese Twins an audition.

The rehearsals and encouragement Turner had invested in Violet and Daisy paid off. Their performance convinced general booking manager Jake Lubin to take a risk and make a tentative offer. If Myer Myers would take a gamble on the act, so would he. Lubin was willing to hire the Hilton sisters on a trial basis at $1,000 a week for a four-week tour of New Jersey, Massachusetts, Ohio, and New York. If Violet and Daisy managed to "get over" (vaudeville slang for connecting with the audience) within a month, he'd have the option of extending their contract for as long as he pleased. Myers agreed.

Violet and Daisy's vaudeville debut was set for mid-February, in Newark, New Jersey.

CHAPTER 12

THE LINES AT LOEW'S STATE THEATRE'S NEWARK BOX OFFICE on Monday, February 16, 1925, blocked traffic. The crush for tickets was so thick, a call went out for police reserves to handle the crowds. From the look of the street, everyone in the city clamored to see the San Antonio Siamese Twins perform onstage.

Most of the ticket buyers swarming the box office had been lured in by a flurry of newspaper stories. "Siamese Twin Ill, Other is O.K.," papers from New Jersey, Delaware, Pennsylvania, and Maryland had announced the week before. Daisy, doubled over and yelping with stomach cramps, had been rushed from a Baltimore-bound train to the Newark City Hospital by ambulance, the articles claimed. Photos showed Violet sitting up in the hospital bed beside Daisy, reading aloud to comfort her sister as Daisy recovered. The idea of one twin writhing with indigestion while the other suffered not the slightest twinge roused the public imagination up and down the Atlantic coast.

It was surely a hoax—a clever publicity stunt dreamed up to call attention to the Hilton sisters' vaudeville debut. Follow-up stories even claimed the girls had taken to the stage "as a lark," as though the idea of performing in vaudeville had never occurred to them until they'd glimpsed the awning of Loew's State Theatre from the Newark hotel room where Daisy was recuperating. These articles turned the truth upside down, reporting that the Hiltons "could not be persuaded to make any stage appearance" during their tour of New York City, and that Loew's had practically begged to hire them. That was first-rate nonsense.

Nonsense or not, it worked. When the curtain lifted on a "clean-cut youth" standing in the spotlight, the State Theatre was crammed to the back row of the balcony. The young man, Ray Traynor, began with an announcement to the thousands of spectators that the Hiltons' act "isn't presented for sympathetic approval." In a speech "flecked with as many attempts for laughs as possible," Traynor put the audience at ease, emphasizing the girls' health and contentedness.

Then the curtain behind him parted, showcasing Violet and Daisy's entrance. Just the sight of them walking across the stage together, "as easy and natural as two people strolling arm in arm," transfixed the audience. Behind them, the set was all done up in rose and white to look like "a drawing room gracefully arranged." Traynor went to the piano, where he accompanied the opening number, a saxophone and clarinet duet. Two more saxophone numbers followed, "dotted with bits of crossfire" between the three. As Violet and Daisy bantered with Traynor, the audience's fixation on the girls' physical union receded until people began to sit back and enjoy the show for its own sake. "The comedy angle is a corking stand-off to get away from the freak classification," *Variety* noticed.

The finale, when a pair of dapper twin boys stepped from the wings to dance a double fox-trot with Violet and Daisy, left the audience thunderstruck. "The finish is a wow and a real novelty," *Variety* gushed. Astonished applause filled the theater for a solid sixty seconds. When the applause lasted that long—so long that it interrupted the act—vaudeville folks called it *stopping the show*. And Violet and Daisy stopped the show time after time, three shows a day.

Critics' praise was every bit as enthusiastic. Overnight, the San Antonio Siamese Twins became "the greatest draw attraction and business getter that has hit vaudeville in the past decade." *Variety's* assessment of the act's prospects was blindingly bright. "It's one of those draws which happen once in a lifetime. . . . It could be played in any vaudeville theater in the country regardless of the clientele and will duplicate its pulling power in any spot on any bill in America."

This in spite of the fact that Violet's and Daisy's musical performances were by no means extraordinary. *Variety* called their opening saxophone-clarinet number "very fair" and acknowledged that their voices were "somewhat weak," though still audible from front to back and top to bottom of the theater. Nevertheless, their songs did have enough real merit for both *Variety* and *Billboard* to agree that their talent elevated them above the usual freak act. "Daisy and Violet Hilton cannot be truthfully classed merely as 'freaks,'" *Billboard's* critic said. "The youthful, refreshing appearances they make would succeed in making them pleasing as a sister act were they not 'Siamese Twins.'"

Charisma was the true magic of the Hiltons' act. *Billboard* called them "the most appealing personalities we've seen in any type of young girl artiste in years." Their particular combination of beauty, modesty, enthusiasm, and vivacity created an elusive alchemy no audience could resist. The demand for tickets was so monumental, Loew's immediately scheduled the girls for four shows a day rather than the customary three. Even then, it was just barely enough. "Each show had the house packed," noted *Billboard*.

Packed was exactly the word for it. In their first week at Loew's in Newark, Violet and Daisy smashed the former box office record, held by heavyweight boxing champion Jack Dempsey, by a whopping $5,000. That week alone, Loew's took in the modern equivalent of over half a million dollars. Before the week was out, Mr. Lubin signed Violet and Daisy for the rest of the season, and more than doubled their pay. Their $2,500 weekly salary was a fortune, over $35,000 in today's money. Basking simultaneously in the unparalleled success,

Myers and Lubin competed over who could be more magnanimous— Lubin for leaping to offer the raise the sisters so clearly deserved, or Myers for insisting on sticking to the original salary for the first month.

Even at that steep rate, booking Violet and Daisy was a triumph for Loew's. For the next month, the San Antonio Siamese Twins demolished box office records everywhere they went. The girls were so popular that Loew's theaters could have hiked ticket prices just to force a record to break, but none did. Lent arrived, and while other theater chains had to cope with the lull in attendance that the solemn religious season caused every year, Loew's venues were still selling tickets to see the Hiltons as fast as they could print them. Every seat and more continued to sell out. SRO signs—Standing Room Only— were displayed each and every evening in Boston, and at "practically every performance" in Buffalo. People would rather cram together, craning on tiptoe at the back of the theater, than miss the chance to glimpse Violet and Daisy's show.

In Cleveland, audiences "bent the walls of the theater," causing *Variety* to joke that if Loew's hoped to accommodate everyone, they'd have to sell coat hooks instead of tickets and hang the extra people from the walls. Customers clamoring for the next performance kept the lobby so jammed that the management stationed three musical acts throughout the long lines to ease the tedious wait and keep the crowd in good humor. Four shows a day were still not enough, and the girls were "held over," with Loew's extending their booking to meet demand for more performances. All this, even with the great magician Houdini performing to his own sellout crowds at the Keith-Albee Palace Theatre right next door.

The list of the Hiltons' earnings read "like a report from the Director of the Mint," *Variety* marveled: Newark, $36,000; Boston, $30,000; Cleveland, $32,500; Buffalo, $34,000. Tens of thousands of dollars every week like clockwork, and at ticket prices ranging from just ten to sixty cents apiece.

The story of how Keith-Albee's bookers had summarily rejected Violet and Daisy tickled the press no end. "The 'big time' vaudeville bookers guessed wrong on the Hilton twins and now must sit back and gnaw their nails in envy," gloated the *Sioux City Journal*. *Billboard* and *Variety* watched with bated breath as the Hiltons' tour approached New York City, vaudeville's headquarters. Insiders predicted their act had the potential to earn as much as $50,000—over $700,000 today—in a single week at Loew's State Theatre on Broadway. If the San Antonio Siamese Twins shattered the box office record in the city that had initially turned them down, that would be as satisfying as shouting *I told you so!* at Keith-Albee from the middle of Times Square.

For the most part, Loew's had sat back and relied on the extraordinary velocity of Violet and Daisy's rise in popularity to drive ticket sales. Now the publicity department began shoveling thousands of dollars a week into an effort to propel the girls into breaking Jack Dempsey's $43,000 Manhattan record. "Never in the history of the Loew vaudeville circuit has that organization spent as much money in exploiting an act as it is spending on the Siamese Twins," *Billboard* magazine observed. Letters ten feet high spelled out their names on billboards. Vans plastered with advertisements cruised New York's streets. No one in the city could enter a subway or elevated train station without passing a poster for the Hilton sisters. Broadway itself blazed with illuminated signs heralding their arrival, and a stilt-walker tramped the sidewalk, hollering ballyhoo and clutching at awnings for balance in the stiff March wind. A Hilton coloring contest in the *New York Mirror* offered children under thirteen the chance to win one of 150 coveted tickets to the show, as well as a pair of joined-together Genuine Effanbee Dolls "too cute to describe." Loew's topped it off by hosting an extravagant birthday luncheon for the sisters at the posh Hotel Astor, complete with two joined-together birthday cakes decorated in pink icing and showered with sugar roses, violets, and daisies. (Daisy's cake had one extra, half-inch-high candle, to mark her as the elder by four minutes.) Over one hundred journalists attended the gala, then followed Violet and Daisy to Loew's State Theatre to see their opening matinee.

"The Loew circuit officials state that they never will have any regrets for the money being spent on exploitation," *Billboard* reported, "as the girls are earning every cent of it and bringing it back to the box office in every theater they play." In some cases, Violet and Daisy were nearly doubling theaters' typical weekly earnings.

Fifteen thousand tickets sold daily at Loew's State Theatre in Manhattan, to standing-room-only crowds so thick, they put theater fire codes in peril. Even vaudeville artists themselves could not resist the Hiltons' magnetism. Marcus Loew received so many hundreds of requests from other stage performers who could not attend during regular showtimes that he scheduled an 11:30 p.m. performance especially for three thousand of the city's actors and actresses.

Manhattan did indeed prove to be the San Antonio Siamese Twins' best week yet by almost $4,000, totaling $39,780. In spite of all the hoopla and excitement, Dempsey's record dangled just out of the Hiltons' reach. *Billboard* was quick to point out, though, that the prizefighter had had an advantage: he'd made $11,000 of his $43,000 on Election Day alone, at holiday prices with every state employee in New York off work.

If Loew's expressed any disappointment over the figures, it never reached the press. There was hardly time for disappointment—Violet and Daisy went on to Loew's Metropolitan Theatre in Brooklyn, where their $38,000 week topped Dempsey's take at that venue by $4,000. Loew's promptly booked the Hiltons' one-of-a-kind sister act for a full week at every last venue on its massive circuit, movie theaters and all—the first contract of its kind in Loew's history.

. . .

Throughout 1925, Violet and Daisy's success never dimmed, never so much as flickered. No matter the city, people came flocking to see them. " 'Weather-Proof' and a Sure-Fire Draw," a full-page ad in *Variety* bragged. Rain or shine, or even snow, police officers were summoned to manage blocks-long lines for tickets that often sold out by early afternoon. Theaters begged patrons to attend matinees, despite the lower admission rate, for the sake of relieving the overwhelming crush of evening performances. In Milwaukee, such a crowd was anticipated that the Hiltons were booked at the 3,500-seat movie theater instead of the smaller vaudeville stage. Violet and Daisy broke "all attendance records in Milwaukee's theatrical annals," packing the Wisconsin Theatre to the brim at least once a day. When they returned to Buffalo in November, just seven months after their record-breaking engagement there, the San Antonio Siamese Twins brought in another $25,000. With the help of the Hiltons, Loew's raked in more profits by May 1925 than it had in the entire previous season—$3,234,278, or over $47 million today.

Keith-Albee would never live it down. In December, *Billboard* and *Variety* were both still reminding the entire entertainment industry that the big-time bookers had let the Hilton sisters slip through their fingers. "At that time," *Variety* speculated, "the act . . . could have been signed for probably $500." Now, with a switch from Loew's to the Orpheum circuit for the 1926 season, Violet and Daisy's weekly salary leapt to $3,000, with another $1,000 to pay for extras like their pianist, press agent, maid, and transportation. The big-timers would have to wait an excruciating two years to get "the sensation of vaudeville" into Keith-Albee theaters.

CHAPTER 13

IN A SINGLE, STRATOSPHERIC SEASON, THE SAN ANTONIO Siamese Twins had become superstars. Their fame was due in no small part to the promotion and advertising Loew's lavished on the act—a media push *Billboard* called "the greatest campaign in the history of the circuit."

Everywhere Violet and Daisy went, a flood of publicity preceded them. And while their stage performances downplayed their twinship, the advertisements and newspaper articles did just the opposite, focusing on the sisters' physical union and the conundrums it caused. How many movie tickets did they need? One train fare or two? What about insurance policies? Income taxes? Could they both enter a voting booth at the same time? How did the census account for them?

The depth of the public's fascination stemmed from ignorance of the purest kind. Scientists in the mid-1920s were only on the verge of discovering how conjoined twins were formed. The possibility that Violet and Daisy had begun as a single body that partially split in the womb was just as plausible as the notion of their two bodies somehow fusing together before birth.

The Hiltons' publicity capitalized on the confusion, intriguing and teasing newspaper readers with the puzzle of whether conjoined twins were one person or two. The contradictory reality, that two people inhabiting a shared body could be simultaneously identical *and* individual, remained nearly beyond belief.

Years before, the Blažek sisters had staged an argument over their railroad fare in one European city after another, always ending in a fake arrest that guaranteed a few inches of column space in local papers. Violet and Daisy's standard stunt was tamer, more in keeping with their wholesome image: they visited police stations to have their fingerprints taken as proof that they were not entirely identical. Newspaper reports almost always claimed that the sisters' fingerprints demonstrated "remarkable contrast" and "hardly a point of similarity." That was true looking only at the second fingers on their right hands; in fact, their complete set of prints was rife with similarities, scoring only half as many differences as fraternal twins. (For a change of pace, they sometimes submitted handwriting samples to the newspapers, claiming their writing was identical. It was a bald-faced lie; anyone could distinguish Violet's handwriting from Daisy's at a glance, so Daisy wrote them both. The true similarity, which stunned handwriting experts, was their "absolutely identical" pressure of pen to paper—"an amazing feature" far more significant than matching the shapes of the letters, but almost impossible for the untrained eye to spot.)

Only once did the Hiltons stage a stunt that ended in a faked arrest, in Cleveland, where they sat beside their driver in a motorcar, apparently violating an ordinance that prohibited more than two people from squeezing into the front seat of an automobile. "It was lots of fun," Violet said. "People who meet us on the streets usually stop and say how cute we are, but when we were arrested, right in front of a large department store . . . everybody else glared at us."

In case anyone missed these stories, there were also two-page spreads of advertisements and endorsements. Special twin sales drew even more attention to the Hiltons' impending arrival. Shoe stores, drugstores, restaurants, laundries, printers, department stores, dentists, and chiropractors all wanted their businesses associated with Violet and Daisy Hilton, and they used the girls' faces to sell everything from twin beds to hot baked ham sandwiches.

> "Daisy and Violet Hilton Internationally known Siamese Twins always call a Yellow Cab."

> "Siamese Twin Special: Two Tickets to the Orpheum FREE—will be given to the first 5 customers purchasing one pair of our Special Hose."

> "Why Are Daisy and Violet Hilton Happy and Contented? Because they eat regularly such food as we prepare in our Famous Kitchens."

For twins, there were extra-special enticements. Newspapers ran twin photo contests in the days leading up to Violet and Daisy's arrival, offering prizes of up to $50 (almost $750 today) for the most popular twins. The girls themselves hosted twin parties, with free matinee admission for twins of any age. (One small Ohio boy who requested a single ticket and informed the perplexed attendant, "Brother died this winter," was warmly welcomed, too.) Everyone who attended received an autographed photo and posed for the big group picture with the Hilton sisters grinning in the center. Every twin in every city was encouraged to sign their names and paste their picture into the souvenir Album of Twins that accompanied Violet and Daisy on their tour.

In return, eager admirers often showed their devotion by bringing the girls gifts of grown-together fruits and vegetables. Violet graciously called the double melons, turnips, and cucumbers "interesting, and showing kindness of heart," but they were not what she and Daisy most wanted. "We would much more prefer to have a live 'twin' pet," Violet admitted—a living creature just like themselves. "We have traveled through many lands," Daisy agreed, "but we have not yet found the particular type of pet for which we are searching."

Fan letters poured in, too, some addressed to "The Right Hand Lady" or "The Twin on the Left." Everyone wanted to know how they did things—eat, sleep, walk, dance. More often than not, the answer was *Just the same as anyone else.*

Reporters came to interviews ablaze with curiosity and self-consciousness, unsure how to bring up the topics that most interested their readers. Violet and Daisy were adept at handling these conversations—they'd been answering the same questions since they were tots. "Tactful and bright little creatures that they are, they always try to put their interviewers at ease," a grateful *Calgary Herald* reporter explained. "They do this by starting the conversation talking about themselves and just the other things which interviewers might want to know but don't dare ask."

Nevertheless, it took a bit for the awe to wear off. Simply seeing Daisy lean down to retrieve a dropped handkerchief while Violet remained upright could leave a reporter slack-jawed. "We don't get in each other's way," Daisy patiently explained. "We have to walk together and sit down at the same time, but I can bend about and Violet won't pay the slightest bit of attention to it."

They could do much more than "bend about." Together they could swim, box, and play tennis, golf, and handball. They also enjoyed archery. But *how?*

For Violet and Daisy, moving in tandem was second nature. They could walk either in a synchronized left-right, left-right rhythm or by stepping out with both outer legs at once, followed by both inner legs. They gave this no more thought than any two people who find themselves unconsciously matching each other's pace and stride.

As for dancing, it isn't clear whether the girls or their partners led—accounts vary. Either way, leading and following were the usual matters of learning to interpret subtle cues of momentum and pressure. A gentle push or pull by Violet (or her partner) would signal Daisy (and her partner) to move accordingly, and vice versa.

Reading and responding to just those kinds of movements—the pushes and pulls, the leaning, bending, and reaching—formed the key to their ability to move through the physical world together with grace and agility. "Until we learned to dance with separate partners, we never knew what to tell them," Daisy said of people who couldn't understand how the two sisters could stand up and sit down at the same time without a whisper passing between them. "Now we know how to explain it. . . . We've been dancing together ever since we were born."

Consider: When the path suddenly narrows before two people walking side by side, they rarely come to a halt and debate who should go first. One person makes a faintly perceptible move to lead, perhaps by picking up speed or shifting slightly ahead, and the other falls into step behind. The other way around works just as well—one person can slow or step aside so the other may go first. It happens in a second or two at most, usually without a word. So it was with Violet and Daisy.

Each sister also possessed a spatial awareness of the other's body. Just as anyone riding a bicycle or driving a car allows for the extra space their vehicle needs to maneuver safely, Violet and Daisy understood their bodies' combined range of motion, the space they occupied and required. When they swung golf clubs or tennis racquets, that dual awareness kept them from injuring each other, much in the way that teammates playing on the same court or field are mindful of one another's presence.

That's not to say that Violet and Daisy actually *felt* each other's bodies. Few sensations were shared, though a prolonged headache would eventually pass from one sister to the other, for reasons no one could explain. A scant handful of the thousands of articles about them ever mentioned that their colons merged; of those, only one, in a British medical journal, detailed precisely when and where the function and sensation of their joint organs mingled. That information was considered too intimate, or too vulgar, to publish more widely. In consequence, the vast majority of newspapers and magazines spread the misinformation that the Hiltons' ligature consisted only of cartilage, muscle, and blood vessels.

One fact the sisters more readily acknowledged was that aches in the region of their connecting bridge could be experienced simultaneously. That tended to happen when they were both sick. Sickness, incidentally, came with an unusual benefit: a double immune system. The girls did not necessarily fall ill at the same time; if Daisy caught a cold first, Violet could count on a milder bout (if she caught it at all), presumably because Daisy's immune system had gotten a head start and weakened the virus for her sister.

Illness was among their least-favorite things to share. When one was sick, the other ended up confined to bed as well and, as often as not, became more restless and miserable than the invalid. "When I notice the draft from a window first and it isn't hitting me at all, don't you think I tell Daisy in a hurry?" Violet asked. "I certainly do!" For the most part, though, Violet and Daisy took such inconveniences in stride, dividing up the good and the bad with remarkable amiability. (The one thing they never shared was their toilet articles. Though the identical pairs of hairbrushes, combs, and hand mirrors were indistinguishable to anyone else, the Hiltons knew whose was whose and never mixed them up, even if someone tried to switch them around.)

Being forced to share had ignited a fight just once in their lives— over a visit from Edith's daughter. Theresa Myers boarded at the Bonn-Avon School for Girls in San Antonio while Violet and Daisy traveled the vaudeville circuit, making the chance to dote on their little foster cousin a rare treat. "She seemed to take more of a fancy to me than Daisy," Violet confessed. "Daisy got jealous and we quarreled—but that was a long time ago."

Aside from illness, just a few situations placed genuine constraints on the girls. Violet could not drive, because the steering wheel was on the wrong side of American cars. Daisy always had to play the lower notes of piano duets, and Violet the upper octaves. Theater seats with armrests required a special double cushion that turned two seats into one. Both girls could write with either hand, but Daisy tended to use her left, where she had ample elbow room. Violet favored her right hand for the same reason.

Sleeping posed minor difficulties. Like most people, they slept on their sides, though out of necessity rather than choice. When Daisy slept on her right side, Violet slept on her left, and vice versa. The sole inconvenience was turning over. One had to wait for the other to awaken so they could execute the necessary "barrel roll." The only time they reliably annoyed each other was first thing in the morning, for they rarely awakened in tandem. If Violet woke first, she nudged a reluctant Daisy awake. When Daisy woke first, she tugged her sister's hair. "I'm afraid I don't like that," Violet admitted.

Their synchronization and their separateness were equally striking. They often chimed *How do you do?* in unison, taking new acquaintances aback. "Then they are sure that we really are one person with two mouths," Daisy said. They could also finish and begin each other's sentences with uncanny accuracy. Yet if a question was posed specifically to Daisy, Violet silently disengaged herself, thumbing through a detective story "just as though they were sisters sitting on opposite sides of the room." As a reporter from the *Reading Times* watched, Violet tuned herself out so thoroughly, she did not even realize when Daisy had finished speaking. "When you are talking to Daisy, you are talking to Daisy, and when you are talking to Violet, you are talking to Violet," the paper concluded. The same feat of concentration allowed them to practice two different saxophone pieces at the same time without distracting each other, much to the despair of anyone in neighboring hotel rooms or apartments.

All of these tidbits enthralled the reading public. But to those who were fortunate enough to meet the Hilton sisters in person, the most mesmerizing thing about Violet and Daisy was how ordinary the two teenagers turned out to be—their passion for crossword puzzles and detective stories; their love of new shoes, stockings, and handbags; their hatred of hats; and their utter devotion to their darling little dog, a Pekingese named Boy. "It is surprising how they captivate you with their quiet brown eyes, charm in manner and conversation and make you forget the extraordinary nature of their bodies," marveled the *Calgary Herald*. "I had thought that a variety of amazing adjectives would describe them," admitted a writer for *Movie Weekly* magazine, "but never the adjective 'normal,' yet that is what they are in all but the physical aspect."

CHAPTER 14

NORMAL WAS ALWAYS THE SUPERLATIVE COMPLIMENT. IMAGE remained a crucial element of the girls' success, and Myer Myers made it his business to ensure that the Hilton sisters appeared not only normal but exemplary—*perfectly* normal, you might say.

To that end, Myers commissioned a twenty-five-cent booklet entitled *Souvenir and Life Story of San Antonio's Siamese Twins* to be sold in every theater lobby. Its fourteen pages were printed on smooth, glossy paper, with a red, white, and blue cover and two pages of photos at its center. Purporting to contain the "Life Story and Facts" of Violet and Daisy's "climb from the pit of the street carnival . . . to the pinnacle in the amusement world," the booklet peddled fantasy from its very first page.

Myers's version painted a rosy, almost suffocatingly cloying picture of every aspect of the girls' lives. Once again, they had to be orphans of legitimate birth. Once again, their father became a tragic war casualty. Everything that went into Violet's and Daisy's minds and bodies, the *Souvenir* bragged, was spotlessly virtuous. "Very much of their pep, vivaciousness and ambition to achieve is the natural result of their living clean lives, thinking wholesome thoughts and cultivating noble purposes." They did not eat meat. They were sheltered from "sordid stories" of "jazz-crazed" girl criminals "that make such fat fodder for mental morons." Nothing but healthful sports, "good books," and conversations with "cultured people" were worthy of the Hilton sisters.

The result was a sparkling, too-good-to-be-true innocence. Violet and Daisy's phenomenal success was attributed to "the children's willingness to sacrifice, to work, to study and to aspire"—as though they had ever been given a choice. "The girls radiate happiness for they say, 'We have all the good things in life that other girls enjoy, so what more could we ask.'"

Edith and Myer Myers were similarly portrayed in a light so altruistic, it was blinding. Though Myer Myers likely wrote the text himself, he never spoke directly in his own voice. Edith had a single quote, which the unnamed narrator played up to maximum effect: "'We have tried to show the girls every care and devotion, and have been paid back with every ounce of love their little bodies can hold.' Then with a sort of hushed tone she said, 'That in itself is enough.'" The Myerses' "unity in purpose" in bringing up Violet and Daisy properly had even strengthened their marriage and "smoothed the path of life," the booklet said.

Although they were around twenty years old, the text spoke of Violet and Daisy as if they were youngsters, often calling them "children" and "little girls." Hair bows, ringlets, and knee-length skirts dominated the photographs; the captions pretended their sixteenth birthday was still "around the corner." Nevertheless, the *Souvenir* dared to delve into the topic that aroused more curiosity among the sisters' fans than any other: love.

Love, of course, meant *romance* in the public mind. The idea that Violet's and Daisy's love for each other could sustain them as well as or better than a husband-wife romance never entered the conversation. Certainly they were entitled to any kind of love they desired, but the prevailing assumption would always be that they would and should desire wedded bliss most of all. In a section called "Twins Tell Why They Won't Wed," Violet and Daisy came the closest they ever would to voluntarily invoking pity.

"We have thought of love coming to one of us some day," a solemn Violet said, "and we have solved this problem in advance. Perhaps, it is better to say that it was solved for us at birth. At best, love can only complicate the business of living for us, and possibly bring us unhappiness. . . . There is no way for either of us to find happiness that others find in marriage."

· · ·

One part of the booklet was absolutely true: Violet's and Daisy's thoughts on separation. Violet voiced them: "We have never yet wished to be separated and we would not wish to be now, even if the operation were possible—even if it were a very simple one. No, we are in contented agreement about that. We feel that there is a closer spiritual cord between us than between other human beings." The aversion to separation, the booklet acknowledged, was "more potent than the fear of approaching death together."

Refreshingly, the *Souvenir* treated Violet's and Daisy's wishes on this topic with respect and sympathy, pointing out the dangers and stresses—both physical and emotional—of such an operation. "It is no wonder both the twins view separation with horror. Consider how nervous the average individual is about having a tooth pulled, while the amputation of a leg or arm—even though necessary—is viewed with alarm and repugnance." Of course, Myers's motivations for supporting the girls' wishes were largely self-serving. He not only needed them to remain joined; he needed them to *want* to remain joined. Happy, healthy twins sold tickets and fattened the Myerses' bank account.

The illusion of contentment was impeccable. They smiled "nearly all the time," the *Washington Post* noticed, "for they are happy." For six years, Violet and Daisy traveled the vaudeville stages, seen by hundreds of thousands of fans who never suspected what was hidden behind those bright grins.

"So much had happened during those sad years, when the audiences of the world believed us cheerful and carefree," they remembered. "It wasn't easy to laugh while our hearts ached and yearned for freedom and love." Exactly what happened offstage during these years of unhappiness would remain completely sealed away from any outsider's gaze. Even as adults, when they were prone to sensationalizing nearly every other aspect of their history for the sake of publicity, Violet and Daisy never recounted any of the specific incidents that had caused them pain as children and teens. All they would speak of were the most essential rules that governed life under the Myerses' control.

Above all else, Mary Hilton's old edict of keeping the girls sequestered from the public remained in force. Newspaper stories always attributed their seclusion to the intrusion of fame and celebrity. "Naturally, even as children, they did not want to appear often in public, on the street, or in school, where everyone stared, asked questions, and caused other annoyances," one explained. Waiters and train passengers were also prone to staring, so the Hiltons traveled by private sleeper car and whenever possible avoided hotels in favor of renting apartments where Edith could do the cooking. A limousine picked them up at the stage door each night and whisked them back to their lodgings.

Later, Violet and Daisy would liken themselves to prisoners, a description that would have baffled anyone who followed the newspaper reports of the day. In interviews during the late 1920s, the Hiltons provided no shortage of effervescent anecdotes about going to restaurants, about dances and parties given in their honor. The way they relished discussing their favorite film stars could fool anyone into believing they were regular moviegoers. Of course, Myer or Edith Myers was always present during those interviews, listening to every word. The sisters' lively chatter about Westerns and comedies and clumsy dance partners could very well have been as carefully scripted and rehearsed as their vaudeville act. No doubt some, if not all, of Violet and Daisy's public outings were staged for publicity, like their blatantly advertised swim at New Jersey's Palisades Park (captured by newsreel cameras) and the pleasure jaunt to Coney Island that followed.

Regardless of how often they were treated to these moments in the wider world, Violet and Daisy lived every day with the sense of being caged. They craved privacy as much as they craved freedom—though not from each other. In hotels, Myers rented a single room, forcing the girls to sleep under his and Edith's supervision. There wasn't a moment of the day or night when Violet and Daisy weren't aware of the Myerses' presence.

Every appearance in public felt like a performance, if not an outright lie. On- or offstage, the girls gave a flawless show. Their boundless enthusiasm for meeting new people and seeing new places presented itself as vivacity and zest for life, rather than a desperate eagerness born of isolation.

Ironically, the one place where they could be authentic was onstage, where performing felt honest. "In our work we could be natural, unrestrained," Daisy said. "It has been our one great pleasure." There was no mistaking that genuine, infectious delight, which spilled over the edge of the stage and into the audience like an epidemic of gladness. "There was so much love between the people in the seats and Daisy and Violet that you could slice it with a knife," recalled one fellow performer. "People flocked to the theaters thinking they were merely going to see a couple of sideshow freaks. What they really saw, though, were two of the most beautiful and talented girls God ever created."

There was something else, too. Spectators rarely failed to take inspiration from seeing Violet and Daisy perform. "The art of being happy makes them a feature that spreads optimism and causes you to realize that 'Life's worth living,'" one advertisement decreed. If those two girls could be so merry and successful despite being joined together, audiences reasoned, what right had anyone else to be annoyed by the petty inconveniences of everyday life?

It was a backhanded compliment, an admiration muddied with unspoken twinges of pity and relief: *Thank goodness I'm not like them. Thank goodness I'm normal.* "They inspire an emotion of affection from which regret cannot be eliminated," as one of New York's most prominent reviewers put it. This reverence for the idea of different or disabled people triumphing over adversity was and still remains a burdensome notion, one that left Violet and Daisy no place to express an iota of emotion that might have dismayed their guardians or their fans, such as desolation, discontent, or anger.

More and more, those were the kinds of feelings that dominated Violet's and Daisy's waking hours. Where before they had been confined to fenced-off fairgrounds and rail yards on the outskirts of town, they were getting tastes of cities now, big cities with bustling downtowns full of people, shops, restaurants, theaters, and movie houses. The glimpses were fleeting ones, through the window of the car that ferried them from hotels to stage doors and back, but it was enough for them to begin to realize how drastically the Myerses had restricted their lives.

Their sole act of rebellion was a sharp yet subtle jab, disguised as irritation with each other. "I can get rid of you," Daisy would say to

Violet, just to irk Edith and Myer. She could—in her mind, just as Violet could dismiss her. It was a mental trick they had learned to create privacy from each other. Now it served a dual purpose.

"By saying it aloud to each other," Daisy explained, "we let them know that we could dismiss them from our consciousness, too. We could adjust, even to them!" Their message was perfectly clear to Myer and Edith: *You do not exist to us.*

CHAPTER 15

BEHIND THE SCENES, MYER MYERS WAS MAKING LEGAL AR-
rangements to ensure that no matter how the girls' spirits chafed under
his control, his grip on the Hilton sisters' salary would not loosen. On
May 25, 1925, Edith and Myer Myers were officially appointed Violet
and Daisy's guardians by the Bexar County, Texas, probate court. (Mary
Hilton's will, apparently, was not as ironclad as Myers had made the
girls believe.) Myers claimed the value of the seventeen-year-old sisters'
estate at $1,000. Judge McCloskey must have been woefully ignorant of
vaudeville news if he believed that, for by May 1925, the San Antonio
Siamese Twins' $3,000-a-week salary should already have totaled some-
where in the neighborhood of $42,000. Not only that, but thousands
upon thousands of dollars from the girls' nine years on the American
carnival circuit had gone completely unaccounted for, along with everything they'd earned in Europe and Australia. Despite the absurdity of
the figures, the Myerses prevailed. The court's ruling awarded Myer
and Edith complete control of Violet and Daisy's earnings.

Two years later, Myers had the decision reversed. His wards, he
now petitioned the court, though only nineteen years old and techni-
cally minors until age twenty-one, ought to be declared legal adults
and therefore be permitted to manage their own money, contracts,
and other business arrangements. On April 1, 1927, his request was

granted, and Violet and Daisy Hilton were declared legal adults, thus removing the sisters' "disability of minority," as the court termed it. The two young women were completely unaware of these proceedings, however. A single witness had been called, the Myerses' neighbor W. J. Fetzer, who'd told the court, "They are not flappers and are perfectly capable of handling their own business affairs."

No one raised an eyebrow. Newspapers across the country carried the story, commenting only on the novel fact that a single court ruling had been sufficient for two people—those clever Hilton sisters had secured their independence with half the paperwork and half the cost. From the outside, it looked like a generous gesture, a sign of the Myerses' confidence and trust in the girls' maturity and business sense.

Precisely the opposite was true. Myer Myers knew he had Violet and Daisy so thoroughly ensnared in his control that they would sign without question anything he put before them. And the court ruling meant that when they did, they would be granting him permission to swindle them. Myers wasted no time. On April 20, 1927, he laid a contract of his own devising before the nineteen-year-olds. It was a ten-year term, paying them $500 a week. To two young women who had never handled a dollar of their own pay, Myers seems to have assumed, $250 apiece would seem a fortune. Violet and Daisy signed.

It was a staggering mistake. The girls had essentially sold themselves to Myers for a dismal fraction of their earning power. The contract authorized him to schedule the Hilton sisters' bookings, negotiate their salary, and collect their pay—and by now their act could command nearly $4,000 each week—in exchange for $500. At those rates, Myers stood to pocket over 85 percent of their earnings.

But Violet and Daisy were not as ignorant as Myers presumed. "We could have signed a contract with any theater, variety, or vaudeville in America," Violet later acknowledged. "Why did we sign this contract if we knew all this?"

They were powerless to do anything else. Their isolation not only trapped them in a position of complete dependence on the Myerses for basic necessities, but also cut off all avenues toward an honest deal elsewhere. "We had been kept in a condition of slavery for so many years that, to be quite frank, we had not the courage to say a single word against all that they told us," Violet explained. "We had not been human beings. . . . We were merely the property of Mr. and Mrs. Myers just the same as other goods and chattels which they had bought and accumulated, thanks to our efforts."

Violet and Daisy were not permitted to examine their own theater contracts. Instead, Myers read them aloud. "If by any chance he skimmed over any part of the contract too hastily we neither noticed nor understood it," Daisy said. "Even supposing we had understood the contract, what could have happened? Nothing. We were slaves and had to bear the whole burden of slaves." All they saw was the last page, laid out and ready for their signatures, everything but the dotted line covered with a piece of blank paper. "When we hesitated to sign," Violet said, "he would rave and ask us if we thought he was a thief and if we didn't trust him and if we were afraid—we always signed."

Any mention whatsoever of money matters provoked shouting and accusations from Myers. There were threats, too. Violet and Daisy were not American citizens, a fact Myers used to frighten them with the erroneous claim that without his protection, they would be deported to England, where they'd be dumped into an asylum.

"They didn't know what the word *exploited* meant," said Camille Rosengren, whose mother was friends with Edith Myers, "but they knew the feeling."

. . .

Myer Myers had an uncanny knack for disguising his exploitation. He even had the gall to attribute his biggest extravagance of all to Violet and Daisy themselves.

"This Is the Birthday House San Antonio's Siamese Twins Gave Aunt Who Mothered Them," the headline of the full-page story in the *San Antonio Express* gushed in October 1927. "They had always wanted a big house to shelter their uncle and aunt, their cousin Theresa, and themselves."

The article went on to rhapsodize about how the two nineteen-year-olds had pored over architectural books and magazines and toured residential districts in every city they visited, in search of inspiration for a home worthy of their selfless caretakers. What finally caught their fancy was the quarter-million-dollar Dana-Thomas house in Springfield, Illinois, designed by legendary architect Frank Lloyd Wright.

Once they settled on a Wright-inspired design, Violet and Daisy set about furnishing their mansion with the utmost care. "And, too, let it be said in passing, they are keen young businesswomen," the *Express* praised, "who did not haggle over prices as long as a particular piece of statuary or bric-a-brac or chair or lounge was all that it was represented to be." Nothing but the best would do, and the result was an eclectic mix of pieces from America, Europe, and Asia.

Eight big photographs dominated the page, creating a visual fairy tale that began with the C. A. Wortham carnival train and ended with Violet and Daisy grinning in the archway of their palatial new home. "The castle so long pictured by them has become a reality," said the *Express.*

The whole of this pretty tale of generosity and gratitude was pure fantasy, of course, spoon-fed to the paper by Myer Myers. "That was just a big publicity splash I cooked up," he would proudly admit later. "You know, showmanship." Violet and Daisy never had a say in how their money was spent. The article was purely an opportunity for Myers to flaunt his burgeoning wealth, using his wards as cover.

From the roof line to the terraced gate, the entire estate might have symbolized Violet's and Daisy's lives. It was an elaborate counterfeit, beautiful at first glance but built on a foundation as inauthentic as the girls' newspaper-ready smiles. There was no better word for it than *pastiche*—a medley of imitations.

Studded with windows and shaded by great overhanging eaves, the mansion had broad, low lines that blatantly mimicked Frank Lloyd Wright's style, as did the archways of fanned brick and the corners of the roof, which bent upward like a pagoda's. Asian motifs echoed throughout the gardens and yard. A torii gate, used at Japanese Shinto shrines to mark the entrance to a sacred space, was appropriated to adorn the grounds with a flair of exoticism. The teahouse, with porcelain seats shaped like elephants, was a particular point of pride, as was the neighboring goldfish fountain.

Materials of the finest quality embellished the interior. Every inch of woodwork on the first and second floors was of imported Australian red gum, a eucalyptus tree known for its vibrant crimson hues. Electric lightbulbs glowed in fixtures of silvered bronze or wrought iron. Each of the doors was fashioned from a single, beautifully grained slab of wood.

A plate glass front door led into a reception room, with the living room and dining room beyond forming the main artery of the house—just up a few steps and through an archway. In the living room, a Steinway grand piano and a unique fireplace of brick, stone, and tile competed for attention. A breakfast room opened off one side of the dining room, the butler's pantry and kitchen off the other. An electric range and "the very latest in modern refrigeration" ensured that the kitchen would be the envy of cooks throughout the county.

Two massive porches balanced the central structure like a pair of wings. One was open-air, with views extending across the surrounding valley. The other was screened and glazed for all seasons, with an electric fountain burbling in the center. It looked out on the goldfish pond and teahouse.

Four big bedrooms made up the second floor: one for Myer and Edith, one for Violet and Daisy, one for Theresa, and another for guests. Each room boasted closets lined top to bottom with cedar. A sleeping porch opened out of Violet and Daisy's room, with steel casement windows on three sides and a hidden bed that folded out of a closet in the fourth wall. A pink tile bathroom linked Violet and Daisy's bedroom with the Myerses', while Theresa had a soft green tile bathroom to share with the guest room. A built-in bookcase in the upstairs hallway held Violet and Daisy's collection of detective stories, adventure novels, and the works of Dickens and Poe.

A few special modifications were made for Violet and Daisy's comfort, such as an extra-wide bathtub. The living room and dining room also had chairs broad enough to accommodate them. Another vital space was the small upstairs sewing room, where Edith could help the girls make the necessary alterations to their clothing.

"Down in the basement is where Mr. Myers holds forth," the *Express* said, "in a large, combination billiard room and office and den." The basement also housed the least ornate but no less impressive luxuries: the electric hot water heater, the incinerator, and the steam heating system with its automatic oil burner.

Above the three-car garage with its connecting tool room and full bath were ample servants' quarters, with living room, breakfast nook, bedroom, bath, and kitchenette. Together, the two-story garage and servants' apartment was as large and costly as "the average good home."

The mansion and outbuildings, the garden, private well, pump, windmill, tennis court, fountains, and ponds had cost $100,000— almost $1.5 million today. The fine furnishings added another $35,000 to $40,000, or the modern equivalent of half a million dollars.

Fittingly, the house was sturdy as a prison, built of brick and reinforced concrete with a heavy slate roof. A stone fence and wrought iron gate enclosed the entire property. Violet and Daisy seemed to feel the weight of each brick and bar. "We could never enjoy the magnificent and splendid estate, let alone call it our home," they said. Their money had paid for every board and nail, yet nothing in the house felt as though it belonged to them. Even the sight of the sweeping five-acre lawn, "strewn with lights" that transformed the gardens into a virtual fairyland at night, reminded them only of the parties they would never be permitted to give.

While others drove down Vance-Jackson Road just to gaze through the windows and imagine the luxurious life inside the mansion, Violet and Daisy sat behind its gates, dreaming of life outside. That, too, was an impossible fantasy. Where would they run? How would they get there? Their weekly salary was out of reach, put away in a trust fund, Myers told them. If the seventy-five cents hidden in their shoes would stretch as far as a cab ride downtown, they'd be flat broke the moment they stepped out onto the sidewalk.

Money was something they never hoped to lay hands on, so Violet and Daisy devised another way to secretly fund their escape. "Buy us diamond bracelets," they begged Myers. "Not with small stones—big ones." The plea was couched in vanity. "Other stage stars had jewels," they reasoned. Shouldn't the biggest stars in vaudeville have them, too? That kind of logic put Myers in a bind. Image and keeping up proper appearances had formed the backbone of his success from the beginning. But they were asking him to spend thousands of dollars on something that seemed entirely frivolous.

Relentlessly the Hiltons wheedled for diamond jewelry in front of their booking agent, their publicity manager, and "any friend of Sir." They sweetened the proposal by adding that they wanted to buy a diamond pendant for Edith, too. Put on the spot that way, Myers could not find a way to squirm free. He wrote out a check for $7,000, which Violet and Daisy endorsed. A few days later, Myers presented them with a pair of sparkling bracelets. The sight of the diamonds winking up from their wrists—the modern equivalent of $23,000 apiece—lent Violet and Daisy a semblance of the security they craved. If ever the chance to flee the house on Vance-Jackson Road presented itself, they'd run straight to a pawnshop and trade those jewels for cash.

CHAPTER 16

"WHEN WE WERE TWENTY-ONE, WE EXPECTED THINGS TO BE different," Violet and Daisy said. Not only were the sisters still unaware that they had been adults in the eyes of the law for two years, but February 5, 1929, brought no changes either. Adulthood granted them no means of escape. Worse, eight years of their contract with Myer Myers remained, and the small concessions that might have placated them awhile longer dangled out of reach. "We wanted to have friends, to go out once in a while alone, to have a girl chum spend the night occasionally; even these little privileges were denied us." Instead of the freedoms they anticipated, the sisters recalled, "matters got worse."

Myers knew that as far as the law was concerned, his term as dictator over Violet and Daisy expired the moment they turned twenty-one. His response was to tighten his grip, lest they realize their rights. That and the sisters' mounting frustration would prove to be a poisonous combination.

Only the subtlest hints of the sisters' festering discontent leaked out. "The Hilton twins . . . are looking forward to the time when they will look as though they are 18 years old, not 14," the *Akron Beacon Journal* noted offhandedly in May. These trifling complaints were easy enough to overlook. In the public's mind, Violet and Daisy were still teenagers—indeed, their publicity had been shaving two to three years off their age since at least 1928, making them appear to be just eighteen or nineteen in 1929—and didn't all young people lament about how unfair it was that their parents wouldn't let them wear more sophisticated clothes?

. . .

No one knows what spurred the Hiltons to wrest some of the truth of their past out of the Myerses. One newspaper account claims that the young women ran across a scrapbook filled with clippings that contradicted the familiar version of their life story. A more feasible explanation is hard to imagine. Yet the very same article also declares that up until the moment when they read the scrapbook, Violet and Daisy had believed Myer and Edith were their true parents. That was a lie the sisters never would have fallen for, thanks to Mary Hilton's daily speech about their mother's abandonment. However their suspicions were aroused, Violet and Daisy realized that something in their past did not align, and by the time they were twenty-one, they felt entitled to answers.

Armed with their suspicions, Violet and Daisy confronted Edith, demanding the facts about their heritage. Edith was reluctant. "I asked them if they really wished to know," she later remembered. They insisted. The revelations went over as poorly as Edith had feared. "When the girls learned that their mother was a single woman, they said such bitter things about her I can't repeat them." They were as shocked and dismayed to learn that their father's identity was a mystery. "They told me they had always been under the impression that their father was a British army officer. Where they got this idea, I don't know," Edith said, as though she herself had not recited that bit of fiction to carnival-goers dozens of times a day during the girls' childhood.

That was how Edith remembered the confrontation, anyway. She conveniently left out the sisters' reaction to the truth about her. The woman they had believed to be their aunt—their only living relative— was not related to them in the least. All their lives they had been root- less, shunted from one venue to the next, forty-some weeks a year. Now their family tree was reduced to a bare stump.

. . .

Emboldened by the revelation of Myerses' lies, Violet and Daisy began lashing out at their foster parents. "At times they were affec- tionate toward me and at other times very bitter," Edith said. Myer Myers took the brunt of the girls' anger. "They grew very unkind toward my husband and cursed and abused him on every occasion." Myers retaliated financially, first violating their contract by reduc- ing their salary to $300 per week in January 1930, and then to $200 in April. Likely Violet and Daisy were unaware of this punishment. They never received more than an occasional ten dollars. The rest, they were told, was deposited into a trust fund.

Inch by inch, Violet and Daisy pushed at their narrow boundaries. Whatever sense of family loyalty or obligation they might have har- bored toward Edith, and by extension toward Myer Myers, was gone now. They snuck newspapers and smuggled them out to the green- house to read, so they could learn something of the world beyond theaters and hotels. What they learned about other people's lives in those columns and photographs made them bolder still.

"Why can't we go out and have some fun?" they dared to ask. "We've never smoked a cigarette, tasted a cocktail—had our hair cut. We—"

The answer never varied: "You are not other girls! You are Sia- mese twins!"

Myers's reply read like a textbook example of emotional abuse— deflecting the blame for the misery he'd created back onto Violet and

Daisy themselves, onto their very identity. If his ploy had worked, they might have been duped into hating themselves more than they hated their captor. But somehow Violet and Daisy managed to keep sight of the fact that Myers was wrong. They *were* just like other young women. Unique though their bodies were, they had the same capabilities, the same thoughts and desires as any two separate individuals. "We can hate, we can be happy, we can love just as anybody else, and we can solve our problems in this condition of permanent attachment," Violet said. The older they grew, the more apparent that became.

"In the wings of theaters, across footlights, men looked at us," Violet and Daisy recalled, "not as unusual performers, but in the way they look at girls they long to know." As hungry as the sisters were for companionship, any friendly or flirtatious overtures bowled them over completely. A bandleader named Blue Steele had made a seemingly instantaneous inroads into Violet's heart by dedicating performances of his song "You Darlin'!" to her whenever their acts appeared in the same theater. Daisy, meanwhile, had eyes only for Don Galvan, a young singer who'd broken into vaudeville with a winning smile and a Spanish accent, strumming the guitar and banjo.

One night Daisy watched him from the wings as she and Violet waited for their turn on the stage. Don looked back at her as he sang. "Every word of his song seemed meant for me," Daisy said. After taking his bow, Galvan paused a moment behind the curtains with Daisy. "Our hands clasped for a throbbing second—and I heard my sister gasp for me." The tremor of Daisy's excitement had been strong enough for Violet to feel, too.

A single sparkling instant of delight, and then the moment shattered. Edith elbowed Galvan out of the way and trundled the girls off to their dressing room. A bouquet of yellow roses—a traditional symbol of friendship, and perhaps a nod to the old folk song "The Yellow Rose of Texas" as well—lay outside the door. Myers kicked the flowers aside and forbade either of the girls to pick them up. Myers displayed no more of his temper in public. Punishment awaited behind the closed door of their hotel room.

• • •

Memories of Mary Hilton's leather strap loomed large in Daisy's mind as Myer Myers approached her that night. But the fresh, sweet memory of Don Galvan's voice as he sang to her, and the feeling of his hand clasping hers, overtook her.

Daisy turned her back to Myers, speaking words that transformed an act of submission into one of defiance. "Go on," she goaded him. "You won't kill us. You wouldn't destroy your meal tickets!"

An expression like black flames flared behind Myers's eyes, but he did not strike them.

Something had flared up in Daisy, too. Fear had kept her and Violet from ever challenging Mary Hilton, for Auntie's whippings had been as reliable as breakfast, lunch, and dinner. "We had accepted them along with our daily irritations, struggles, and monotonies," Daisy remembered, "for love of each other. We tried, within our minds, to turn each quarrel and bickering and nagging incident into some kind of lesson for our own harmony." This was different. Don Galvan's kindness and Myers's callousness had ignited a new and volatile mixture of courage and anger in Daisy.

"We've made thousands for you—but we never received a dollar of our earnings!" she raged. "You still keep us caged up like animals in a circus!" That was over, Daisy declared. She and Violet were adults and would not tolerate another moment of being treated like children. "Don't you strike either of us or we'll yell like wildcats! And get us a separate room. We're grown ladies and you should be ashamed to force us to share your and Edith's room!"

To the sisters' astonishment, Myer Myers was cowed by Daisy's outburst. The argument ceased. Edith silently handed them their usual mugs of hot chocolate. No scolding, not a peep in defense of her husband. The Myerses' subdued reaction allowed a tiny seed of courage to take root in Violet and Daisy. "After all," the two realized, "they depended on our well-being more than we did on theirs."

From then on, they got the separate hotel room Daisy had demanded—but not for long. In a victory neither of the sisters could have anticipated, Myer and Edith stopped traveling with them and re-tired to the house on Vance-Jackson Road. Margaret Moore, the Hil-tons' accompanist, became their chaperone. Violet and Daisy adored her and would come to regard Miss Moore as manager, guardian, and mother rolled into one.

Myers also consented to put some of the young women's money into their hands. Compared to what they were earning, it was a pit-tance at $50 a month. Still, they had little opportunity to spend it. "When we went shopping there always was a crowd following us," they lamented. "Our publicity man saw to that." But the allowance was something they could squirrel away, at least.

. . .

The unofficial truce between Myers and the Hiltons held out until December 1930.

"Just look at this!" Myers exclaimed, flinging down the Sunday edition of the *San Antonio Light* in front of Violet and Daisy. The headline read: "Says Her Husband Fell in Love with Both Siamese Twins." Photos of the Hiltons and the mansion on Vance-Jackson Road ringed an image of a woman neither of them recognized.

"What have you done?" Myers demanded. "Bill Oliver's wife has named you in her divorce suit."

Violet and Daisy were aghast. William Oliver was a member of their staff, the advance man for the San Antonio Siamese Twins act.

Mrs. Oliver was demanding a quarter of a million dollars (nearly four million in modern currency) in damages for the Hiltons' alienation of her husband's affection.

The suit had spawned a full-page illustrated article in *American Weekly*—a splashy magazine-style Sunday supplement carried in newspapers across the country. "They both loved him—both of them," Mrs. Oliver would also tell the *Kansas City Times*. "They showered him with lavish gifts—jewelry, a Reo motor car and clothes. William had so many clothes they filled up all the closet space." The two sisters were so smitten with her husband, she claimed, they sometimes went for days without speaking to each other offstage out of pure jealousy.

"We don't love Bill Oliver!" Daisy told Myer Myers. "You know that!"

"Why did you write 'love' on that picture you autographed for him to send to his wife?" Myers challenged.

"Too stunned to reply," the sisters gawked at the paper. The photo occupied the entire upper right corner of the article. Violet and Daisy both remembered it, and Bill's request. "I often tell her about you," he'd said. "Autograph a picture for me to send to her."

Violet had inscribed the photo *"To our pal, Bill, with love and best wishes from your pals, Daisy and Violet Hilton, June 24, 1929,"* and both of them had signed it. "'With love' didn't mean that we loved Bill Oliver," the sisters explained. "It was just the way we had observed other showfolk autograph pictures."

Nevertheless, Mrs. Oliver staked her case almost entirely on that image. Her charges against the sisters were equally dubious. William Oliver's position as advance man meant he did just that—traveled in advance of the Hiltons, rather than with them. His job was "keeping one jump ahead" to schedule interviews, meet-and-greets, and photo opportunities; secure advertising and publicity; and provide theaters with promotional material several days before Violet and Daisy's arrival in each city on their itinerary. By the time they checked into their hotel, he was presumably on his way to the next stop on the tour.

According to the newspaper, though, Oliver was not always running ahead of schedule. "Occasionally he would jump back and spend a day discussing business with his pretty united bosses," the story said. He also allegedly visited them in San Antonio on business for days at a time. "All of this was, or at least might have been, strictly proper and businesslike," the article allowed. But Mildred Oliver's story further claimed that the Hiltons had hired a new advance man and promoted Bill to manager so that he could travel with them. "Mrs. Oliver asserts that soon after this promotion the twins 'fired' their pretty pianist because the young lady had taken a fancy to handsome Mr. Oliver."

That didn't line up with reality, either. Myer Myers had spent the last season in Texas, but he was still very much in charge of the San Antonio Siamese Twins act. William Oliver reported to him, not the Hiltons, on all business matters. Given how closely Violet and Daisy were supervised, the possibility of their carrying on a three-sided love affair right under the Myerses' noses on Vance-Jackson Road is slim at best. And how could they have bought Bill Oliver extravagances like a motorcar, with Myer Myers standing guard over their bank account? "We didn't even buy our own clothes," Violet pointed out later.

The divorce petition stated that William Oliver also denied the allegations, telling his wife "he was not in love with either of the twins, but they were a good meal check for him."

Myer Myers exploded. Publicly, he would scoff and call the suit "a 'shakedown' attempt," but privately, he was rattled enough to enlist one of the best lawyers in San Antonio. Within a week of the story breaking, he and Violet and Daisy sat in the office of Martin Arnold, attorney-at-law.

"The girls have got to fight this," Myers told him again and again.

"We tried to speak," Violet and Daisy remembered of the meeting. "Again and again we tried." They hardly knew how. When had they ever been given a chance to speak for themselves, without a script? The way Myers was carrying on, one wrong word could have dire consequences.

Daisy gripped the arm of the chair and pulled herself up. "Violet balanced me," she remembered, "giving me all her strength, it seemed, so I could raise my voice for all to hear."

"There is something very wrong," she announced. "My sister and I have had only business relations with Bill Oliver—never have we been with him or anyone else alone. We've never been alone in our twenty-three years!"

That odd revelation, combined with Myer Myers's agitated, imperious manner, sent up a red flag in Martin Arnold's mind. "Leave us alone," the lawyer said to Myers, adding that he was to close the door behind him. "I want to ask the girls about this without your being present."

"You can't send me out," Myers protested. "I'm their guardian!"

"They are over twenty-one, aren't they?" Arnold countered. "They don't need a guardian. Now, will you leave us?" Myers had no choice but to back down.

"You are two frightened girls," Arnold said after the door was shut firmly behind Myer Myers. "Isn't something else wrong?" he coaxed. "Do you want to tell me?"

Violet and Daisy had been waiting their whole lives for a moment like this. They did not waste one precious second. "We're practically slaves!" they exclaimed.

The outburst took Arnold aback. "Slavery hasn't been practiced in this country since the War Between the States," he said.

"No one will believe our story," Violet said, ever cautious. "We've been lonely—rich girls who were really paupers, living in practical 'slavery.' The public doesn't know all this and if we tell a judge he might send us to an institution."

"I'm all for the trial," Daisy cut in, speeding ahead.

"Just talk to me," Arnold said. His Texas drawl had a soothing, encouraging quality. "Walk up and down the floor if that will help."

Violet and Daisy talked for forty-five minutes. Every secret they'd kept hidden behind their sparkling smiles for twenty-three years came tumbling out—how they'd been on display "ever since they were old enough to lie on a circus blanket and kick their feet enough to let people see they were alive," that they'd rarely seen a cent of their own earnings, and most of all, how the Myerses kept them locked away from the world.

"We want to be our own masters," Daisy summed up; "we want to settle our own affairs; we want to enjoy the money we have earned; and, above all, we want to meet people and not be restricted to Mr. and Mrs. Myers."

Their revelations left Martin Arnold dumbfounded. Violet could see the wonder and doubt at war behind his little round-rimmed spectacles as he struggled to wrap his mind around the story. He was trying to believe them, Violet thought.

"I don't understand it," he said, almost scoffing at the absurdity. "Why, you are twenty-three years old! Why don't you just walk out of the door? What can Mr. and Mrs. Myers do against or about you? You can do as you wish. Nobody can stop you."

"Yes, yes," Violet said, "but if we escape, or, rather, leave the Myers [sic], then, according to the American law, we shall be deported to England, our native country, and be put in an asylum." They didn't want to leave the United States, or even the vaudeville circuits. Performing remained their one true joy. "It is only the troubles in our personal lives that we don't like. That is why we do not just walk out the door."

A muffled sob interrupted, startling Violet and Daisy. Unseen behind a screen, Mr. Arnold's secretary had been taking down the conversation for the lawyer's records. The Hiltons' story had left her entirely overcome. Arnold invited Miss Lucille Stotzer to come out, and introduced her to the sisters. For Violet and Daisy, it was a little like a fairy tale. Less than an hour after the door had closed behind Myer Myers, they'd made a friend.

In fact, they'd made two friends. Martin Arnold was won over and vowed to help them. Immediately. Mildred Oliver's divorce suit could wait until he'd addressed what he considered the more urgent matter. "You don't have to go home with this man," he assured his two newest clients. With Miss Stotzer as his accomplice, Arnold devised a plan to whisk Violet and Daisy out from under Myer Myers's nose that very day.

At the end of the appointment, Myers drove the sisters directly to their usual music lesson. The minute his car disappeared around the corner, they phoned Martin Arnold's office with the news that the coast was clear. They had a single hour to make their escape. Soon after they hung up, a taxi stopped outside. The Hiltons kissed their music teacher goodbye, took a furtive peek up one side of the street and down the other, then dashed into the cab, where Miss Stotzer sat waiting.

The driver let all three of them out at the St. Anthony Hotel in downtown San Antonio. When Violet and Daisy opened the door of their room, they saw at once just how moved Martin Arnold had been by their plight. He and Miss Stotzer had booked them a suite and stocked it with flowers, candy, a radio, magazines, and newspapers. "Girls," Miss Stotzer said, "you're Mr. Arnold's guests—order anything you like. Telephone your friends—see if you can't enjoy yourselves."

"It was like a dream during the next few days," Violet and Daisy remembered. Together they reveled in the forbidden grown-up indulgences that would have wrecked their carefully cultivated little-girl image: a cigarette for Daisy, a cocktail for Violet. The freedom was more intoxicating than the liquor and tobacco. "For the first time we could order something on a menu which we wanted," they marveled. Making any kind of choice was the height of luxury. They called a department store and had a selection of dresses sent up, savoring the opportunity of picking out "no two alike." Off came their long-hated sausage curls and in went permanent waves and hairpins. "We could dress and act our age, and no longer be made up as children with bows in our hair."

Those first days were not quite as carefree as Violet and Daisy remembered them, however. The way they'd deceived Myer Myers was sure to anger him, and Martin Arnold immediately took precautions for the sisters' safety, enlisting his secretary as well as the hotel staff to keep an eye out for trouble around the clock. "We were put under protective custody by the hotel," Lucille Stotzer said years later, "and I stayed with them until we could get a companion."

. . .

Back on Vance-Jackson Road, Myer Myers rumbled with fury. All of San Antonio—all of the country—now knew that the Hilton sisters were accusing him of years of flagrant mistreatment. Martin Arnold had petitioned the Bexar County District Court for three things on behalf of Violet and Daisy: an accounting of the money they had made in the past, a receiver to intercept their future pay before it reached Myer Myers's hands, and the nullification of their ten-year contract with Myers, which otherwise would not expire for seven more years, in 1937. The petition also revealed to the public for the first time how an unmarried barmaid named Kate Skinner had "sold" her babies to Mary Hilton, who in turn had willed them to Edith and Myer Myers. Headlines from San Francisco to Indianapolis and beyond announced the story in dramatic terms of "Bondage," "Owners," and "Slavery."

In interviews, Myer Myers masked his anger with a mixture of condescension and outright lies, telling the papers that Violet and

Daisy only wanted control of their money so they could waste it on the kinds of frivolous extravagances and ostentatious parties that had been all the rage in the 1920s. "The girls must have had the idea that they can make 'whoopee' like other young people, but they can't do it," he told the *San Antonio Light*. "They would appear obnoxious and out of place. My wife and I have tried for 14 years to take the girls all places possible, constantly taking them to theaters, dances and other places, but they can't fit in with that kind of life and should realize it." Their steady diet of detective and crime magazines, he insinuated, had corrupted them, despite his best efforts to acquaint Violet and Daisy with "the sweet side of life." He dismissed the idea that they'd been held in virtual bondage, pointing out that the sisters had been "left alone in the house frequently," where any one of the household's three telephones would have allowed them to "call for aid at any time if they felt they were being illegally restrained."

As far as he was concerned, all this fuss was due to someone else's meddling. "The girls are easily led by other people," the *San Antonio Light* reported, "and will probably not realize 'their mistake' for quite a time, Myers said."

While Myer Myers blustered, Edith Myers lamented. From the time they were five days old, she had "tried every way in the world to make the girls happy," she told the *San Antonio Light*. Their apparent high spirits the week before had made their abrupt departure all the more bewildering to Edith. The day they'd left, she had been making clothes for them; they had come into her room and kissed her good-bye. Their betrayal seemed to her the height of unfairness. "They don't seem to be making any allowances for the time I have spent with them, constantly caring for them and attending to their wants," Edith said. "I have spent the best part of my life in their interests and now they ignore me. Why, they didn't even send me a Christmas card."

Violet and Daisy's absence had "shattered" the routine of the entire household, right down to the elderly groundskeeper, the *San*

Antonio Express reported. The sisters had been the center of everyone's orbit; without them, everyone seemed curiously suspended around the empty space they had left behind. Together Myer and Edith led reporters through their grandly furnished mansion, "explaining each part of it and citing instances where 'the girls had enjoyed things.'"

"We did everything for them," the Myerses said, "and they left us."

• • •

Violet and Daisy, meanwhile, bided their time in the "toy apartment" on Burr Road that had been rented for them. "Like two little boys playing hookey from school," they were still reveling in every moment of their independence. Being alone was such a sumptuous feeling. Simply gazing around the small rooms that they held complete control over filled their faces with "the utmost contentment."

Speaking freely to reporters was another luxury they took full advantage of. "Always we have had someone prompting us," they revealed to the *San Antonio Express*. Now Violet and Daisy confided their dreams for the future. First, they would seek United States citizenship. Years of Myers's deportation threats had bred a fierce desire to truly belong in the country they had called home for fifteen years. "It will be grand to know we are citizens of America," they said. Once that was properly settled, they would go to England and search out their long-lost family—"if there are any living," they added. "That will be travel for pleasure." Both sisters thrilled at the idea of visiting China. "And we would like to adopt a child to call our very own and give the child the benefit of an education and a real life." They did not say so, but the parallel was clear—Violet and Daisy yearned to give an abandoned youngster the kind of life they themselves had been denied. "Then we will build a little house here which we can call our very own. Nothing big and fancy, but just a little place that will be cozy and comfortable."

Despite their high hopes, they were nervous. "Their high pitched laughter showed the strain they are under awaiting the hearing Friday," the *San Antonio Express* noticed in the final week before their January 16 court date. For almost fifteen years, Violet and Daisy Hilton had performed a lie, and a trusting public had applauded it. Who was to say that the world would now believe such a drastically different truth?

They had little to do in the meantime but read, practice their instruments, and dote on their beloved Pekingese, Boy, who had been rescued from Vance-Jackson Road. He was the only possession they'd bothered to have retrieved from the mansion, Violet said. Nothing else in the house mattered to them. "Boy was the only thing I hated to leave," Daisy agreed.

All their future aspirations were pinned on Martin Arnold. He was the first person to treat Violet and Daisy as thinking, reasoning adults. Such unaccustomed respect and consideration broke their smothered confidence from the Myerses' choke hold. "We actually seemed to grow in stature during our frequent interviews with our lawyer," they said. It was a valuable gift, for they would need every particle of that self-assurance on the witness stand. If the Hiltons lost, the backlash they would face from Myer and Edith Myers after all that had been aired in the press—and everything that was about to be aired in open court—was beyond imagining.

CHAPTER 17

ALL OF BEXAR COUNTY SEEMED TO BE WAITING FOR FRIDAY, January 16, 1931. Everyone, from the press to the court itself, treated the date as though it were the opening of the Hilton sisters' newest vaudeville show. "Court attachés dusted off the 'Standing Room Only' sign and prepared for a rushing business," the *San Antonio Express* reported. Spectators would not be confined to the benches as usual. No one would be turned away until every available inch of space was filled. "They can hang on the rafters if they want to," a spokesperson for the Ninety-Fourth District Court declared. "There will be no restrictions for this hearing. It will be officially just like any other hearing we ever held here."

Officially, perhaps. Unofficially, it was nothing of the sort. When the courthouse elevator dinged and the doors slid open to reveal the arrival of Violet and Daisy on Friday morning, pencils dropped and typewriters stilled as clerks and stenographers sprang up from their desks and flooded the corridors in hopes of catching a glimpse of the world-famous Hilton sisters.

The sight of the two of them, smartly attired in matching sky-blue silk dresses and lushly collared gray fur coats, drew gasps of admiration and surprise from women and men alike. They were so much smaller than everyone had expected. Even their snakeskin shoes commanded attention as people watched them make their way down the aisle of the courtroom.

No fewer than five hundred people packed the room. Some newspapers estimated six hundred, even one thousand. Schoolchildren and women dominated the spectators, "from flippant high school girls to staid grandmothers," filling the room with the sound of "chattering, tittering, giggling." Fifty-some lawyers abandoned their work and wedged themselves in, eager to hear the proceedings. Even Judge McCrory's wife had come, bringing their five-year-old grandson. People leaned over the rail and into the aisle to shake Violet's and Daisy's hands as they passed by. "This is the biggest crowd that ever saw us without having to pay for it," Violet quipped.

Two people were conspicuously absent: Myer and Edith Myers. Much to the spectators' relish, a "crisp exchange" followed Martin Arnold's realization that the defendants were missing.

"Is Myers in the court?" Arnold asked the lawyer at the defense table, Thomas J. Saunders.

"I do not know" was Saunders's bland reply.

"Where is he?"

"I do not know," Saunders said again. The Myerses had not been subpoenaed, he argued. If there was no subpoena, they were not required to appear in court. "I see no reason for the presence of the defendants," Saunders added. "We are here to represent them."

"Do you mean to say that the defendants are trying to dodge these proceedings?" Arnold retorted.

Saunders was on his feet in an instant. "They're not trying to dodge anything," he fired back.

Martin Arnold did not believe that for a second. Arnold began the proceedings by calling Saunders himself to the stand, putting his opponent under oath. "Have you seen Myers this morning?" he asked.

"Yes," Saunders admitted. "I saw him about an hour ago."

"Here?"

"Here in San Antonio."

"Did you see him in your office?"

"Yes."

"Where did he go after he left?"

"I do not know."

"Where is he now?"

"I do not know."

The mutually irritated lawyers conferred with Judge McCrory. Saunders believed the whole issue could be settled through documents and affidavits. That in no way satisfied Arnold, who declared that he intended to call Myer Myers as his first witness and demanded that Edith Myers be present as well.

While Arnold and Saunders sparred, Violet and Daisy sat in an armchair at the plaintiff's table, "wait[ing] for the curtain to go up on the story of their fight for freedom." Unflustered by all the attention, the two sisters scanned the congenial crowd with obvious curiosity, offering bright grins "that left people with the impression of sunny smiles and blue skies."

In ten minutes' time, Arnold and Saunders agreed to delay the hearing until Monday. The Myerses would be present, Saunders promised, bringing with them all the theatrical contracts and financial records that Arnold had requested. And with that, the official proceedings adjourned for the weekend.

The moment the dismissing gavel fell, two dozen spectators darted past the deputies and crossed the rail to the plaintiff's table. An impromptu reception organized itself as reporters, photographers, and spectators flocked to Violet and Daisy, still seated in their armchair. Women and children reached out to shake their hands, patted them on the back, and showered them with smiles.

"We've always been regarded as freaks and couldn't go to Sunday school or anywhere else in public because our manager thought that it would lessen our box office value," Daisy told the assembled crowd. "We couldn't even have girl friends out to the house. We want to live normal lives and be free!"

The spectators cheered.

"How are you enjoying it?" reporters asked.

"Wonderfully," Daisy gushed. "You see, we are accustomed to crowds, but they have always been so far away." This was so much different from gazing out over the footlights at an audience. For the first time, Violet and Daisy felt themselves a part of the world, and the feeling was every bit as delicious as they'd dreamed it would be. "I am sorry it was over so soon," Violet added.

The atmosphere in the courtroom struck Violet and Daisy as something deeper and more heartfelt than ordinary curiosity. Never in their lives had they felt so supported. "We didn't know what to expect," they told reporters, talking at the same time in their excitement. "But everyone has been so kind. We couldn't imagine that people could be so wonderful. All the people seem to be our friends." A tang of bittersweetness, unspoken and invisible to the eye, also flavored the experience. "There in the court-house we felt for the first time how much we had lost by never having been able to meet people," Daisy reflected later.

As Violet and Daisy walked down the aisle to the exit, accompanied by a gallant deputy sheriff dispatched "to do anything that they might want," people unanimously offered wishes of success and happiness. At the doorway stood Judge McCrory himself, hand extended in greeting.

The two of them seemed to shine with appreciation. "Friendliness, awe, wonder—and trust, were found in the large smiling eyes of the two girls."

. . .

The crowd on Monday morning was just as tremendous. Somewhere between six hundred and one thousand people jammed the courtroom itself. Hopeful spectators milled in the halls and overflowed into an adjoining room, where a group of women shoved a table up to the door and climbed on top to peer through the transom window. One of them held her baby over her head so the infant could look down into the courtroom and one day have the right to brag of having seen the San Antonio Siamese Twins.

The entire room watched as Edith Myers, in what appeared to be a remarkable display of goodwill, walked over to the plaintiff's table and with a smile shook hands with Violet and Daisy. "Hello, dear," she said to each of them individually. They even posed for a photo together, with Edith beside Violet, and Myer Myers standing a bit behind Daisy while the sisters grinned broadly for the camera. As the day unfolded, however, the reporter for the *San Antonio Light* noticed Edith "occasionally casting a queer glance at the twins."

The proceedings began with Martin Arnold calling his first witness to the stand: Mr. Myer Rothbaum, known as Myer Myers. Myers could not have failed to notice the fact that the spectators' sympathy lay firmly with Violet and Daisy. It was palpable. "The crowd, quite open in its sentiment, acted as though it was watching a play; even applauding when they felt that the lawyers scored a point on the witness," wrote the *San Antonio Light*. "Outbursts of laughter and sighs of disgust" punctuated the questioning. Perhaps the atmosphere in the room was what raised Myers's hackles and put him on the defensive. Or perhaps barking answers and deflecting questions with jeers constituted his customary demeanor. Whatever the cause, the effect was not the least bit flattering.

The financial figures Arnold presented certainly did nothing to sway the crowd's opinion in Myers's favor, either. Arnold first revealed to the court that when Violet and Daisy had been declared legal adults in 1927, Myers had told the sisters that their earnings totaled $36,142 (over half a million dollars today). And yet, according to a $3,000-a-week contract signed in May 1925, an $118,800 profit should have remained after a single forty-week season. Over $80,000 had vanished in that year alone. The following season, when their act had commanded $3,850 each week, would have yielded another $154,000.

It was not difficult to guess where those tens of thousands of dollars had gone. Although Myers's bank records showed just $150 to $200 in his accounts, that was a thoroughly deceptive figure. He owned the palatial home on Vance-Jackson Road, which he himself valued at $150,000, as well as a 300-acre farm in Atascosa County worth $38,000. Somewhere between $35,000 and $40,000 had been invested in bonds by his New York bookkeeper. Another $5,000 was tied up in General Motors stock, along with $5,000 in the Central of Georgia Railway.

"All this property was bought with money earned by these little girls since you became their manager, was it not?" Arnold asked.

"It was bought with my money," Myers replied. He did not think Violet and Daisy were capable of managing their own finances, he explained. "And they never will be," he added.

Martin Arnold smiled at that. He leaned in and said in a softer, more amiable tone, "Now, Mr. Myers, let us go back to that incident of removal of disabilities of minority. You filed that application, did you not?"

Myers acknowledged that he had indeed petitioned the court to declare Violet and Daisy legal adults, so that, among "several reasons," they could sign their own contracts.

"So," Arnold shouted, "knowing these little girls not capable of handling their financial affairs, you went into court and had the protection the law gives them set aside, so they could sign a contract with you?"

Myers was cornered. "Well," he said, backpedaling, "I do not mean to say these girls are crazy. They are far more intelligent than most girls of their age, but they do not understand business." Myers had the audacity to claim that Violet and Daisy cared nothing for money—they didn't want it. "Every time I would mention business matters to them they would fly into a rage and tell me they did not want to know anything about it."

"Were you under the impression that these little girls gave you the money?" Arnold asked.

"No, I wasn't under that impression," Myers said. "They always told me they did not need money, that they wanted for nothing and knew of nothing for which to spend it," he further testified. "There was no use in giving it to them just to let them throw it around."

"So you just took it yourself."

"Well, I was not going to throw it into the gutter."

"So you then considered it your money," Arnold said. "It did not occur to you to save it for the use of your wards. You used it to buy bonds in your own name."

"I considered it my money," Myers finally conceded. He "had no reason to consider it anything else" and had never opened a separate bank account to distinguish Violet and Daisy's funds from his own. "It all went into one lump, into the family treasury."

"So it was just a family affair," Arnold remarked.

"Yes, and a happy family, too," Myers snapped back, "until you corrupted it."

Arnold leapt to his feet. "If this man makes another remark like that," he proclaimed to Judge McCrory, "I am going to ask the court to protect me, or I will protect myself." Arnold's indignant outburst was likely in part for show, for provoking Myers into exhibiting the ugliest facets of his personality could only help Violet and Daisy's case. Martin Arnold excelled at preying on Myers's bad behavior. In response to the lawyer's "sneering remarks" and "ceaseless hammering," Myers became ever more irate and sarcastic.

As Arnold read off a list of the stocks Myers owned, Myers interrupted. Eager to downplay his wealth and project an air of generosity, he told Arnold dismissively, "You can have those."

"Yes, they are worthless and you would like to give them to these little girls," Arnold shot back.

"No, not to them," Myers bellowed, "but to you."

The barrage of shouting and snide retorts compelled Arnold to caution the witness, "I do not wish to make this a personal matter, but will do so if I have to."

Warned by both his lawyer and Judge McCrory, Myers calmed himself. Arnold then returned to 1927 and the question of the $36,142 Myers himself had said belonged to Violet and Daisy after the termination of his guardianship. "Did these little girls ever get that money?" Arnold asked.

Myers clammed up entirely for a moment, then admitted that they had not.

"Where is that money?" Martin Arnold shouted.

Probably deposited in the Trade Bank of New York or the City Central Bank of San Antonio, Myers said. He did not know for certain; his bookkeeper handled all the deposits.

"You mean to tell this court that you took this money belonging to your wards and used it?"

That was a question for his bookkeeper, Myers insisted.

Next Arnold scrutinized a contract with the Orpheum Theatrical Corporation. According to its terms, Myers had been paid $114,000 during the time he'd served as the Hiltons' guardian. Yet when his final report as guardian was submitted, it showed that only $79,380.80 had been received.

"Well, tell us what became of this thirty-six thousand dollars that was left," Martin Arnold pressed.

"I can't answer that question," Myers said. "I do not know."

"Do you claim to be a businessman?" The crowd guffawed openly at that. Myers's attempts to feign total ignorance of his finances, after asserting that Violet and Daisy weren't smart enough to handle their own business matters, were a wonder to behold.

. . .

If Myer Myers had done one honest thing with the Hilton sisters' earnings, it was not revealed in court that day. Even the diamond bracelets Violet and Daisy had begged for had been turned into an opportunity to pocket their cash. After withdrawing some $7,000, he spent just $4,525 on the jewelry (including Edith's pendant) and then proceeded to tell the sisters that only $700 remained. For this, he signed an IOU, which he never bothered to repay. In all, Myers admitted to spending $213,000 of Violet and Daisy's money—the current equivalent of just over $3.5 million.

Myers's account of his personal day-to-day treatment of his wards did not win him much favor, either. After watching him engage with Martin Arnold in a ceaseless "word war" throughout the morning and afternoon, it was especially difficult to take his claims of genteel conduct on good faith. According to the *San Antonio Light,* "Myers assured the court he had always treated the girls in a gentlemanly manner and had never cursed them outside the ordinary 'hells' and 'damns.'"

"Once in Nebraska I raised my hand as if to hit Daisy," he admitted. The sisters had flown at him, he testified, striking him and ripping his shirt from his back before Edith managed to disentangle them from him. The cause of their alleged fit of temper, however, Myers did not reveal—an odd omission from a man who wished to be viewed as a victim of their rage. That incident aside, Myers's efforts to paint Violet and Daisy as instigators were so petty as to sound ludicrous: they were backseat drivers, he said, who cursed him when he glanced at them in the rearview mirror. His claim that the ungrateful young women had been endowed with a lavish $100,000 education ($1.6 million now) was just as flimsy; Myers could recall the name of just one music teacher, who had earned no more than $2,000 for tutoring the Hiltons in violin and piano.

If Saunders's cross-examination of Myer Myers repaired any of the damage Martin Arnold had done, the papers did not see fit to print it. Once Myers had taken the stand and the facts and figures had started pouring out, there was not a speck of sympathy to be found for him in the press.

At the end of the day's testimony, Edith Myers again approached the plaintiff's table with both hands extended. All through the proceedings, this "quiet subdued little woman" had "stared wistfully" at Violet and Daisy. The two young women did not reach out to shake her hands in farewell. It took Edith a moment to realize that her foster sisters had no intention of returning her gesture. Slowly, her arms dropped to her sides and she made her way through the throng of spectators who had witnessed the silent rebuff.

Being on display for two decades had not fully prepared Violet and Daisy for the scrutiny they faced in the courtroom during such highly charged moments. The intense attention of the press and the public, though still overwhelmingly supportive, had begun to make the Hilton sisters a trifle uneasy. What if people came away with the wrong impression of their motives for bringing the Myerses to court?

Tears rimmed Daisy's eyes as she revealed her misgivings to a reporter that day. "Are we making a 'show' for publicity? No, we are merely humans making a fight for life—that something we have not yet known. Please," she begged the *San Antonio Light*, "don't let these dear people think we are seeking notoriety."

"Show people—that's what we are," Violet acknowledged. She could understand how their trial might look like a bid for publicity. It was a natural assumption, even. "But we are not in costume now and we have no grease paint on our faces," she said earnestly.

CHAPTER 18

BY THE TIME THE DOORS FINALLY OPENED AT NINE-THIRTY
Tuesday morning, the crowd outside the courtroom had already
been waiting for an hour and a half. Word had circulated that the
Hilton sisters themselves would be taking the stand. A throng of
women "rushed pellmell" for seats, pushing and shoving all the way.
As the room reached capacity, officers swung the double doors shut,
but the people kept surging forward. Glass shattered against the force
of the crush, and one woman's arm broke through a glass panel. Only
the sleeve of her heavy coat saved her from injury.

The day began with testimony from Erna Wynns, the Myerses'
former housekeeper. She related a disturbing incident she'd witnessed one night upon opening the kitchen door after hearing "loud
talking" in the dining room. The words were curses, coming from
Myer Myers. As Mrs. Wynns watched from the doorway, her em-
ployer stood up and lunged across the table as if to strike Violet and
Daisy. The sisters dodged the blow but said little and ate less for the
rest of the evening.

Next on the stand was a neighbor, Mrs. G. F. Harwick, who testified that she had tried to "make neighborly calls" on Violet and Daisy.
On her second attempt, the *San Antonio Light* reported, "she was met
at the gate by the yard-man, who told her to go away."

Then came the moment the spectators had been waiting for. Violet and Daisy rose. A burst of applause broke out. "This is no show," Judge McCrory admonished, "and spectators must respect the decorum of the court or they will be removed." No one in the packed courtroom even coughed as the Hilton sisters approached the witness stand.

Violet and Daisy sat down in an extra-wide chair. Never before had two people sat simultaneously on the witness stand. At just under five feet tall, they were so petite, their feet did not touch the floor. The court clerk fetched two big criminal case dockets to place under them so their legs would not dangle uncomfortably while they testified.

All eyes were upon them. The crowded courtroom was nothing like a theater. No footlights, no costumes, no music to buoy them. No script of carefully crafted banter.

Violet had been selected to testify first, since she sat nearer to Judge McCrory than Daisy. Both sisters were more nervous, perhaps, than they had been since the day they had stood on the vast stage of the empty Hippodrome at their disastrous first vaudeville audition. "Would the judge believe the story which would contradict the years of glittering ballyhoo about our lives?" they wondered. "On his belief hung our freedom and even more than that." It was one thing to reveal their mistreatment to Martin Arnold, or even to a newspaper reporter in the privacy of their little apartment; quite another to declare it in open court, with Myer and Edith Myers sitting just a few feet away.

Mr. Arnold knew exactly how to put his clients at ease. "Just think of being in my drawing room, girls," he instructed, "and tell the judge your story in your own way."

"Then I began to talk," Violet remembered. "At times I forgot my twin was linked to my body—perhaps because she was so closely in agreement with everything I said. Except for the beating of her heart vibrating through me, she was as quiet as any other person listening in that crowded room."

As Violet spoke, Daisy silently bolstered her. When she sensed that Violet might be about to falter, Daisy prompted her with a subtle nudge of her arm or shrug of her shoulder. "There are, you see, many times when being a Siamese twin has its peculiar advantages," Violet would say afterward. During her entire time on the witness stand, Violet could feel the intensity of her sister's concentration, which "stimulated and strengthened" her.

In spite of the sisters' high emotions, Violet's testimony was not nearly so exciting as Myer Myers's had been. Over and over again, her response was an unadorned *No, sir.* Yet the impact of those two words mounted slowly and steadily as Violet's answers accumulated into a catalog of Myers's financial misdeeds.

Once again, Martin Arnold brought out the final report of the guardianship that Myers had made in 1927, revealing to the court that Myers's records included a signed receipt for $36,142.67 that had allegedly been turned over to the Hilton sisters.

"Is that your signature?" Arnold asked Violet, showing her the document.

"Yes, sir."

"Did you ever get one dollar of that money?"

"No, sir."

"Did Myers ever tell you you had that money?"

"No, sir."

"Did you know you had it until you heard it here in court?"

"No, sir."

"Did you ever hear about the procedure in which your [status as a minor was] removed until you heard it in this court?"

"No, sir."

"Did you ever make Mr. Myers any presents of money?"

"No, sir."

"Did he ever tell you he was putting the money away for you or offer any explanation of what was done with the earnings of you and your sister?"

"No, sir."

Judge McCrory shook his head as he listened. Edith cried. Myer Myers glared, his hands latched tightly to the arms of his chair. But as long as Mr. Arnold stood between Myers and the witness stand, Violet and Daisy felt protected.

With Martin Arnold acting as her shield, Violet mustered the courage to tell the court that she and Daisy had signed that $36,000 receipt without receiving the money because Myers always covered any papers they were given to sign. Protesting was no use, she added. "He would roar and curse at us when we did not wish to do as he wished and ask us if we did not trust him and if we thought he was a thief. He would rage until we became frightened and did what he wished. We were always frightened of him." In addition to his anger, Myers's constant threats kept them under his thumb. "He told us we were born in England and had no right in this country," Violet said.

Fear of deportation proved stronger than shackles or chains, she told the court. Violet acknowledged that "there were no locks on the windows or doors" and that they could have used the telephone to call someone to take them away—if there had ever been a moment, aside from their singing lessons, when they were left alone without the Myerses or someone from the household staff, that is. Strictly speaking, Violet had to admit, nothing physically barred them from escaping. There was only the ever-present specter of Myers's threats. "But he always told us he would send officers after us and have us placed in an asylum," Violet testified, "so what was the use?"

Despite the brevity and simplicity of her answers, Violet's testimony riveted the court. Not only her story, but also the way she told it held the spectators in thrall. "The witness had difficulty in separating her own experiences from those of her sister and usually used the pronoun 'we' when replying to questions," the *San Antonio Express* noticed.

That was perhaps a simplistic view of what was happening on the witness stand. Violet was perfectly adept at mentally separating herself from Daisy, and had been since childhood. What the newspaper did not understand was that in many circumstances, *I* and *we* were interchangeable terms for the Hilton sisters. They did not simply go through life side by side. Each one's individual emotions and reactions, though not directly linked, affected the other, tinting their memories with additional hues. For Violet, speaking solely in the first person would have effectively erased Daisy from experiences that both sisters had contributed to.

On that witness stand, they were very much united in their purpose and their emotions, the very embodiment of the first person plural. Watching them, it was easy to see how accustomed they were to functioning as a unit. Daisy had to be warned not to whisper surreptitiously to Violet. Asked the names of their tutors, Violet listed several before habit compelled her to turn to her sister.

"Can you think of any more, dear?" she asked.

"Please confine your testimony to what you yourself remember, Miss Violet," Arnold gently reminded her.

Both sisters smiled at that. "I will do my best," Violet promised.

The newspapers failed to recognize the double standard their coverage was imposing on the Hilton sisters. The very same reporters who remarked on what they perceived to be Violet's inability to separate herself from Daisy nevertheless persisted in regarding the two women as interchangeable. Although Daisy testified, too, immediately after Violet, her voice is almost completely absent from the proceedings. She was even called as a witness by the defense, but the papers did not bother to print the questions posed to her by either side. As the *San Antonio Express* reported, her testimony "did not vary from that of her sister who had preceded her."

. . .

"You loved Mrs. Myers, did you not?" the Myerses' attorney, Thomas Saunders, asked Violet on cross-examination.

"Yes, we did."

"You love her now, don't you?"

"No."

"When did you cease to love her?"

"In about 1929, when we discovered we were not being treated right." Yes, Edith had always been kind, buying them nice clothes and looking after them as a mother would look after her own daughters, Violet admitted. "But she was just as anxious to hold us as he was." They had not even been allowed to attend church, she said, lest people see them without paying for the privilege. Instead she and Daisy made do with reciting the prayers Edith taught them at home.

Arnold rested his case by asking both Violet and Daisy if they had ever sworn or cursed at Myer Myers. Daisy said that she had not. Violet had to admit otherwise. "I never swore at him but once when he had used every foul word he could think of to me I called him a beast. That was the worst I ever called him."

. . .

Thomas Saunders opened the case for the defense with his star witness: Edith Myers. Once sworn in, she captivated the court with her recounting of Violet and Daisy's birth and early childhood. Tears streamed down Edith's cheeks as she "sobbed out" the dramatic story of how Kate Skinner had renounced her newborn daughters from the very moment of their birth, and Kate's relief at turning them over to Mary Hilton. A minute-long silence blanketed the courtroom at the end of these revelations, interrupted only by the sobs and hiccups of the female spectators in the crowd.

Edith's tears did not stop as she professed her lifelong devotion to her two wards. "In the twenty-three years I have been away from them three weeks and one day," she said. Daisy, Edith testified, was born with a twisted leg. "The doctor told us they could not possibly live, and if they lived could never walk," Edith told the court. "My mother and I massaged the deformed limb daily and it gradually straightened when she was about seven years old."

According to the *San Antonio Express,* Edith "said that she permitted them to have company and often left them alone." She denied ever hearing her husband threaten Violet and Daisy with deportation or an insane asylum.

"We gave them the best teachers we could find," she said, buttressing her husband's claim about their costly schooling. "I wanted them to be the smartest freaks that ever lived."

Violet and Daisy both hung their heads at that. Daisy's cheeks colored, and she bit her lip. Whether it was a reaction to the knowledge that Edith truly had cared about their education or a reaction to the shame of being referred to as freaks in open court is impossible to say. Either way, it was the sisters' only display of emotion during the entire courtroom ordeal.

"I always have and always will love them," Edith testified. Her voice shook with the words.

Although it is true that Edith was largely responsible for whatever semblance of affection Violet and Daisy had known as children, there is reason to question at least some of her testimony. For instance, Dr. James Rooth, who was present at the Hiltons' birth, made no mention of any anomalies to their limbs in his 1911 report to the *British Medical Journal.* Photos of Daisy in infancy and early childhood also contradict Edith's claim about the twisted leg she had so lovingly coaxed into straightness.

Martin Arnold seemed to begin his cross-examination gently, asking Edith "if she had always been willing to give the girls what they wanted." Edith replied that this was so.

Arnold sprang his trap. "Are you willing to give them that thirty-six thousand dollars for which they signed a receipt and did not get?" he demanded.

"I have nothing to do with the money," Edith said.

"Since these girls have been in your care they have earned about five hundred thousand dollars, have they not?" Arnold challenged. "How much of that do you want to take?"

Edith's seldom-witnessed temper blazed up as suddenly as her mother's so often had. "How much do you expect to take?" she shouted, pointing an accusing finger at Arnold in startling contrast with her earlier display of tearful maternal devotion.

Saunders appears to have called just one other witness on Myer Myers's behalf, a traffic manager for the Al G. Barnes Circus. He considered Violet and Daisy's $500-a-week salary under Myers's contract "very liberal," considering that Myers had lifted them from the sawdust-filled pits of the carnival to vaudeville's "big time" theaters. After that, the defense either rested or produced no more witnesses that the papers considered worthy of reporting on.

"I knew that my client, Myers, was at a disadvantage when he took the stand, due to the mob rule of the audience," Saunders said in his closing, adding the grandiose comparison of Christ being crucified by the whim of a crowd. "Though scoffed at by the rabble, Myers sat there and told truth after truth. I knew he'd make a bad impression." The only thing Myer and Edith Myers were guilty of, Saunders professed, was granting "too many luxuries" to Violet and Daisy Hilton.

Few of Martin Arnold's closing remarks survive. The *San Antonio Light* quoted a single sentence: "The whole thing smacks of fraud." Arnold also read aloud a one-line note handed to him by an unidentified spectator. "A farmer feeds and provides harness for his mules," it said, casting Myers as the stingy farmer and Violet and Daisy as his stock.

"Which one of your press agents gave you that?" Saunders demanded in a heat of irritation.

There was no jury; the entire decision rested with Judge McCrory. The judge did not hold the court in suspense while he deliberated. His mind had already been made up before the lawyers offered their closing arguments.

Judge McCrory nullified the 1927 contract, ordered an investigation of the Myerses' financial records, and appointed a receiver to manage the Hiltons' income while the investigation was pending. In short, Violet and Daisy were free.

McCrory offered Myer Myers a few words of sincere praise as consolation. "Jack Dempsey was nothing but a ham-and-egger until Jack Kearns took hold of him and developed him into a world champion," the judge declared. "The Hilton twins would not be where they are today had Myers not managed their affairs and proved a good promoter." Nevertheless, Myers was ordered to turn over all the books, bonds, contracts, cash, and property that had been mentioned during the hearing. All of his financial records would be thoroughly scrutinized by the receiver, and based on those findings, the court would reconvene to decide how the money and property should be split between Myer and Edith Myers and Violet and Daisy Hilton.

How did Violet and Daisy and the Myerses and the hundreds of spectators packed into the courtroom behind them react? Remarkably, not one of the reporters present that day described the scene. Nor are there any direct quotes from the sisters or their former guardians. The curtain abruptly fell the moment Judge McCrory issued his ruling.

• • •

"For the first time in their lives, they say, they see ahead of them a vista of freedom, of mingling with throngs and of being their own bosses," reported the *San Antonio Express* about Violet and Daisy the next day. At home in their little apartment, "where they reign as queens for the first time in their lives," Violet and Daisy had not tired of luxuriating in the everyday duties of sending out laundry and ordering groceries. They couldn't wait to plunge fully into the world they had seen so much and so little of, to make friends and ride streetcars.

Larger celebrations brightened the Hiltons' first days of freedom, too. "Attorney and Mrs. Arnold threw open their beautiful home in our honor," they remembered over a decade later. They smoked, drank wine, and danced. Don Galvan played his guitar and sang, winning over the whole party.

"The 'don'ts' of our childhood were all 'dos' now, and we reveled in it," Violet and Daisy confessed of their indulgences. "It seemed as though we had been transported into another world."

Exactly one week after Judge McCrory's ruling, "glowing with the thrill of their first solo business venture," Violet and Daisy signed a contract for a week's engagement at the San Antonio Theater. "Although we have been in vaudeville work for eight years, this is the first contract that is really ours," they said. "And we are glad to make our new start here, where people have been so kind to us." In their excitement, they had already gone out shopping—alone—and picked out new evening gowns for their act.

Independence would prove to be a prize Violet and Daisy never ceased to cherish. But it was not to be their only reward. Three months after the accounting of Myer Myers's finances began, a compromise was reached. The two legal teams agreed that Myer and Edith Myers, for their successful promotion of the San Antonio Siamese Twins, were entitled to keep the mansion on Vance-Jackson Road, as well as their horticulture farm in the neighboring county. Violet and Daisy received cash and bonds totaling $80,000, in addition to their costumes and stage sets, worth an additional $20,000.

The news reached Violet and Daisy in a Fort Worth café, where they were lunching before their next show.

"You don't mean it!" Daisy exclaimed.

"Is it really true?" Violet asked.

They had every right to be astonished. In all, the settlement granted the Hilton sisters a fortune worth nearly $1.7 million today.

PART TWO

CHAPTER 19

LIFE AS VIOLET AND DAISY KNEW IT WOULD NEVER BE THE same—though not for the reasons they supposed.

The heyday of vaudeville had passed. Sound motion pictures, initially known as talkies, had taken moviegoers by storm in 1927. Not only were sound films wildly popular, but they were also much cheaper for theaters to book than a full bill of singers, dancers, magicians, and trained animals. Movies and vaudeville formed an uneasy truce at first, sharing the bill in many venues. By the early 1930s, though, talkies were elbowing live performers out of theaters entirely. The year after Violet and Daisy's victory over the Myerses, the most famous vaudeville stage of them all, New York City's Palace Theatre, would convert to a movie theater. Home radio sets were becoming commonplace, too, making it possible for millions of Americans to enjoy music, comedy, and drama without setting foot outside their living rooms. To top it off, the stock market had crashed in 1929, and the Great Depression loomed on the horizon.

Violet and Daisy were too busy basking in their newfound independence to appreciate what these changes meant for their future. Even the fact that they were now making $1,000 to $2,000 a week instead of their former $3,850 doesn't seem to have set off any alarm bells. After all, in 1931, $1,000 had the same purchasing power that

$16,000 does today, and the sisters no longer had to support Myer, Edith, and Theresa Myers. With tens of thousands of dollars in the bank and a whole world waiting to be explored, perhaps a smaller salary didn't matter.

Money had certainly never mattered before. It had always come easily, and more quickly than even the Myerses could spend it. That in itself was a problem. Violet and Daisy had no experience in managing finances. They had no understanding of how quickly everyday expenses could eat away at a bank account. They'd never paid rent or utility bills, balanced a checkbook, or written out paychecks for their musical staff. Myer and Edith's extravagances had also accustomed the Hiltons to fine food and hotels, to private sleeper cars on trains and trunks filled with satins and velvets, sequins and furs.

To these expensive tastes, they added a whirlwind of new pleasures: nightclubs, dinner parties and stage shows, cigarettes and cocktails. Theirs was "a hummingbird's life," one newspaper later said, "of glamour and wealth, color and glitter." Violet's and Daisy's glee had a fierce quality to it. They seemed determined to enjoy everything that had ever been denied them, both as adults and as children. Simply exploring downtown San Antonio unchaperoned ignited their old youthful enthusiasm, transforming them almost into little girls again. "They loved to go to picture shows and they loved to go shopping, which they had never been allowed to do by their manager," Lucille Stotzer, Martin Arnold's secretary, said. They chose their own clothes now, scorning the "frilly" dresses they'd been forced into since childhood, in favor of "sophisticated" styles. Yet childish pleasures, particularly ice cream sodas, were among their favorite indulgences, Miss Stotzer added. "I remember that very well."

"We love to go walking," Violet and Daisy themselves told a Houston reporter. "We are always amused, never annoyed, when people stop to look at us."

Maybe it was true. They had been starved for human company

Kate Skinner, Violet and Daisy's mother. She died in 1912, following the birth of her fourth child.

Courtesy of Shelagh Childs

The only known image of Mary Hilton, a studio portrait taken in Kent before her first marriage, likely around age twenty.

Courtesy of the family

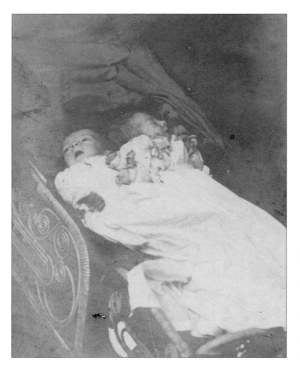

A picture postcard of three-week-old Violet and Daisy in their pram, marking the occasion of their christening in March of 1908.

D. B. Denholtz Collection/ showhistory.com

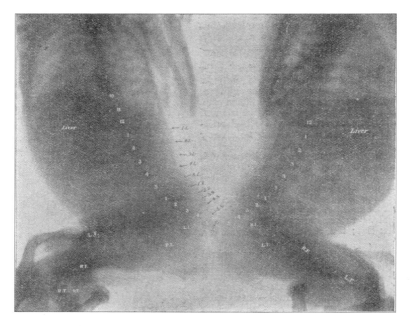

An X-ray showing that the Hilton sisters shared a single tailbone, marked "c" for coccyx.

Collection of the author

Violet and Daisy at three months old. The woman holding them is almost certainly Edith Hilton.

CSU Archives/Everett Collection

This photo of Violet and Daisy around age five featured prominently in Luna Park's advertising.

CSU Archives/ Everett Collection

Fashionable clothing, an abundance of toys, and a pair of camera-ready smiles masked Mary Hilton's mistreatment and created an impression of perfect happiness.

D. B. Denholtz Collection/showhistory.com

By early 1915, newspapers began remarking on the girls' musical skills. Violet played piano, and Daisy played violin. This photo remained in use until they were ten years old.

The Wellcome Collection

The captions of most photos and postcards, like this one from about 1918, inexplicably reverse the Hiltons' names. Violet is always on the left when she and Daisy face the camera.

Courtesy of Michael Wilde

At age fourteen, Violet and Daisy still dressed much like little girls half their age. This photo was featured in advertisements until they were at least sixteen years old.

Collection of the author

An exceptionally rare snapshot of the Hilton sisters posing outdoors with other youngsters.

The Hertzberg Circus Collection, Witte Museum, San Antonio

At birth, Violet and Daisy were oriented almost completely back-to-back, but as they grew, their ligature became flexible enough to form a V-shape. With an extra twist of the waist, they could even face forward simultaneously.

The Wellcome Collection

Demonstrating their signature expressions: Violet's grin, and Daisy's demure smile. Despite these characteristic differences, it once took Edith two weeks to realize that the girls had convinced a photographer to print one of their portraits in reverse as a joke.

The Wellcome Collection

Music was a true joy for Violet and Daisy. Over the course of their lifetime, they mastered violin, piano, two types of saxophone, clarinet, and ukulele.

The Wellcome Collection

Myer and Edith Myers pose for a formal "family" portrait with Violet and Daisy. Edith holds the girls' beloved Pekingese, Boy.

The Wellcome Collection

Violet types while Daisy sews. The public's fascination with seeing the girls do two different things at once was endless.

The Wellcome Collection

The girls bought their clothes—including their bathing suits—off the rack, and altered them at home with Edith's help.

The Wellcome Collection

Though this photo was posed in a studio, Violet and Daisy did enjoy tennis and other active sports like golf, boxing, handball, swimming, and archery throughout their lives.

The Wellcome Collection

Demonstrating their footwork in 1925. The sisters' grace and agility never failed to astonish theatergoers.

The Wellcome Collection

Violet and Daisy with Ruth Roland, an early producer and star of silent films. The Myerses kept the girls so isolated that their only chances for friendships came in these brief encounters with fellow performers.

Collection of Amanda Clay

For the grand finale of their act, Violet and Daisy danced a double fox-trot with a pair of twin boys, bringing down the house every time.

The Wellcome Collection

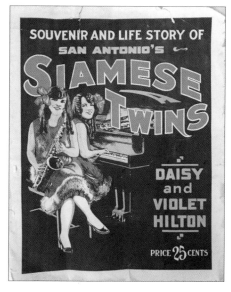

The twenty-five-cent souvenir booklet commissioned by Myer Myers for the San Antonio Twins' smash hit vaudeville tour.

Collection of the author

Edith and Myer Myers outside the mammoth estate on Vance-Jackson Road that they built with the Hiltons' earnings in 1927.

0395-F, San Antonio Light, UTSA Special Collections

By the late 1920s, Violet and Daisy (pictured here with prizefighter Jack Dempsey's mother) had grown visibly too mature for sausage curls and hair bows, yet the Myerses refused to let the sisters shed the little-girl image that had proved so lucrative.

Collection of the author

The Hiltons' hero, attorney Martin Arnold, in the courtroom with his famous clients.

Courtesy of the Everett Collection

REIGNING
SENSATION OF VAUDEVILLE
SAN ANTONIO'S
SIAMESE TWINS
DAISY AND VIOLET HILTON
BORN JOINED TOGETHER

RIALTO THEATRE JUNE 20
BOONE
MATINEE & NIGHT THURSDAY
NOT A MOVING PICTURE

A lavishly illustrated theater program, produced at the height of the Hiltons' popularity.

The Hertzberg Circus Collection, Witte Museum, San Antonio

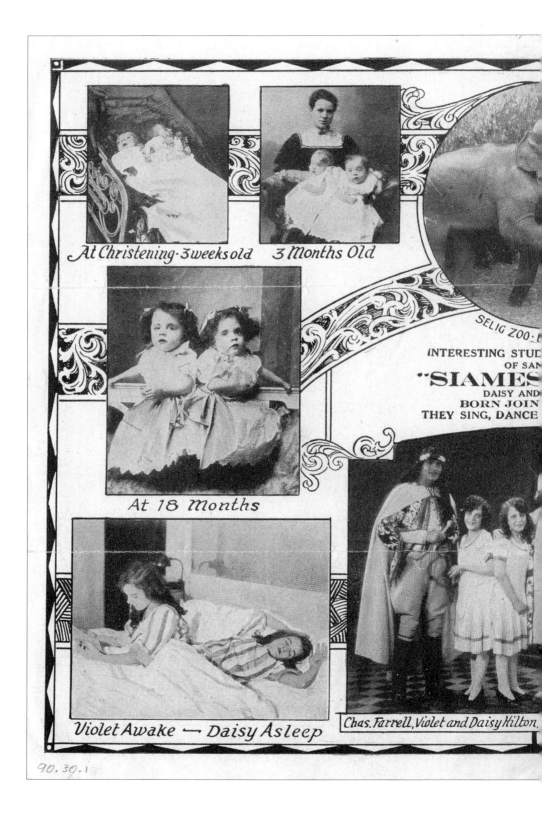

At Christening · 3 weeks old   3 Months Old

At 18 Months

Violet Awake — Daisy Asleep

SELIG ZOO · L

INTERESTING STUD
OF SAN
"SIAMES
DAISY AND
BORN JOIN
THEY SING, DANCE

Chas. Farrell, Violet and Daisy Hilton,

90.30.1

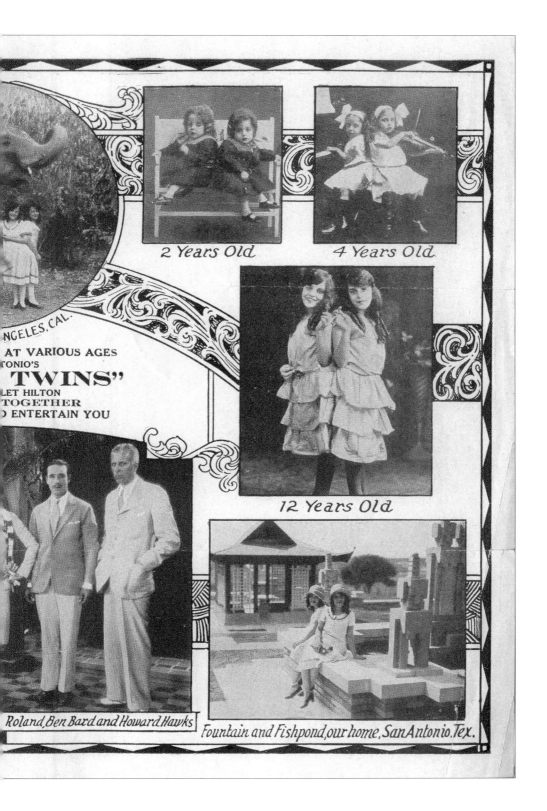

NGELES, CAL.

AT VARIOUS AGES
TONIO'S

"TWINS"

LET HILTON
TOGETHER
ENTERTAIN YOU

2 Years Old

4 Years Old.

12 Years Old

Roland, Ben Bard and Howard Hawks

Fountain and Fishpond, our home, San Antonio, Tex.

Good Night   Page Ted Lewis   Good Morning

Violet   and   Daisy

At Luncheon   Accomplished Musicians

Edith and Myer Myers pose alongside Violet and Daisy during the jam-packed emancipation hearing in January 1931.

Bettman via Getty Images

Violet and Daisy wasted no time in casting aside their long hair and short dresses upon winning their independence.

Collection of the author

On the set of *Freaks* with actor Wallace Ford in 1931.

Collection of the author

Strolling the streets of London during their 1933 tour of the British isles.

akg-images/ullstein bild-Martin Munkacsi

Having their
hair coiffed in the
latest style, 1933.

*akg-images/ullstein bild-
Martin Munkacsi*

Violet and Daisy with Maurice
Lambert, in a pose that
certainly did nothing to ease
worries of bigamy, after being
refused a marriage license
in both New York City and
Newark in July 1934.

Courtesy of the Everett Collection

Primping on the boardwalk in Atlantic City.

CSU Archives/Everett Collection

Jim Moore and Violet proclaim their marriage vows at the Dallas Cotton Bowl on July 18, 1936, while Daisy stands aside.

Collection of the author

A glamorous
1940s pose, signed
by Daisy.

Collection of the author

Daisy married Harold
Estep (aka Buddy Sawyer)
before the justice of the
peace in Buffalo, New York,
on September 17, 1941.

Bettman via Getty Images

The Hilton Sister's [*sic*] Snack Bar opened to considerable fanfare in June of 1955. The Hiltons were forty-seven years old when they launched their first business venture.

CSU Archives/Everett Collection

Violet and Daisy's tell-all autobiography, *Intimate Loves and Lives of the Hilton Sisters,* autographed by Violet.

Collection of the author

Daisy and Violet (in profile) working their scales in the produce department of Park-N-Shop in the mid-1960s.

Courtesy of Linda Reid Beatty

Grocery store owner Charles Reid (left) and Blue Cross Blue Shield rep Sam Bell look on as Violet and Daisy review a brochure for Park-N-Shop's employee health insurance plan. The Reids' compassion and generosity ensured that the Hiltons were secure and comfortable in their final years.

Courtesy of Linda Reid Beatty

A rare candid snapshot, taken at a North Carolina service station in the late 1960s. The man is Leo Wingate, who often drove the Hiltons home from work in a Merita bread truck and bought toys for their dogs.

Collection of the author

for so long that they could well have gloried in even the most casual interactions with strangers on the street. How long, though, before they began to see that people were far more interested in snapshots and autographs from San Antonio's Siamese Twins than in forging a sincere friendship with Violet or Daisy Hilton?

"Only by a hard inner struggle, apparently, have they succeeded in making the cheerful aspect of life dominate its darker side," one observer mused, "and they have had to be jolly in a very noisy way to drown the low voice of their inner doubts, shyness, and uncertainty." Camille Rosengren, who had gotten to know Violet and Daisy as a child thanks to her mother's friendship with Edith Myers, found that tenacity endearing. "There was a kind of desperate 'I'm OK-ness' about them that was admirable," she said.

"More than anything else," Lucille Stotzer recalled, "they wanted to live normally—to be able to do like other people." That was not as simple as it sounded. "Normal" life was more than nightclubs and ice cream sodas. Because they were conjoined, Violet and Daisy hardly knew what an ordinary existence was like—though not for the reasons most people assumed at first glance.

Physically, the Hiltons were very much able to "do like other people," as Lucille Stotzer had put it. Their intelligence, health, and mobility were as good as or better than anyone else's. Yet there is no way around the fact that being conjoined had permanently altered the trajectory of their lives from the very moment they were born. The era and the circumstances of their birth conspired against them, confining Violet and Daisy to a paltry range of possibilities from the start.

Regardless of how smart, agile, attractive, or capable they were, people like the Hiltons were universally considered unemployable. No one would so much as entertain the possibility of hiring conjoined twins to work in a school, a hospital, a restaurant, or a factory. And so for those branded as freaks in the eyes of society, just three paths were open: live in an asylum, depend on the charity of family (or strangers), or make a living through exhibition. Mary Hilton had yanked Violet and Daisy onto the third path, and as a result, at age twenty-three they knew next to nothing about how the world outside a theater worked.

The greed of Mary Hilton and the Myerses had narrowed the sisters' opportunities further yet. They'd been deliberately deprived of the chance to form meaningful relationships with anyone but each other. They'd been deceived, used, and abused by the people they'd thought were family. They had no close friends to offset the damage inflicted by the Myerses, and though they had developed an affinity and loyalty toward San Antonio, they had no true sense of home.

After a lifetime of mistreatment, it was remarkable that Violet and Daisy emerged as pleasant and outgoing as they were. "They were just simply delightful girls," Lucille Stotzer said. She, like nearly all who came to know the Hilton sisters personally, quickly lost her fascination with the fact that they were conjoined. "You were not conscious of it after you were with them—they were just average little girls, giggling and talking to themselves."

Between their small stature and a lingering air of immaturity left over from two decades of isolation, nearly everyone referred to them as girls, even after they had become adults. Stunted in some ways and mature in others, they seemed simultaneously older and younger than their years. It remained a winning quality on the stage, but the way it played out in day-to-day life was another story.

Isolation had permanently handicapped Violet and Daisy in ways their physical bond never would, leaving them ill equipped to navigate the world beyond theater doors. "Under the Myerses they were taken care of, but they had absolutely no chance of any kind of freedom that would have enabled them to handle fame on their own," said Camille Rosengren. "They were malleable and passive in a way— Daisy more than Violet. They couldn't tell a real scam or conman from a good person. They had no ability to judge anybody or anything."

Violet and Daisy were oblivious to their ignorance. In their own eyes, they were seasoned professionals. Their lack of business sense or ability to measure integrity made it impossible for them to know whether they were being treated unfairly. "They were just so generous with their money," another friend said. "Money meant nothing in the world to them." For a while, Joe Freeman, their court-appointed receiver, handled their business affairs. Soon, though, Violet and Daisy were on their own—just as they'd always wanted to be. None of it boded well for the future.

. . .

Now that they were in charge of their own lives, the Hiltons had to learn to harmonize in new ways. There were more opportunities than ever for their wishes and desires to differ. As they had done for so many years already, Violet and Daisy managed to unite two opposing qualities into a surprisingly cohesive whole: compromise and independence.

"In almost all human relationships," they said, "friendship, love, marriage, even business, one person rules. In our relations, neither dominates." That was true in the sense that neither bullied the other. Compromise remained a solemn point of honor between them. From the outside, though, it was apparent that Violet had the more forceful personality. She was the one who was apt to take charge. Daisy, despite her impulsiveness, had always been the more docile, the more naturally inclined to comply with another's wishes for the sake of smooth sailing. Yet Violet did not have free rein to pull Daisy along any way she pleased. "When we were eight years old," Daisy said, "we shook hands and decided that neither one would make any decisions that the other was against." Though she did not exercise it as often, Daisy always had the right to object, as did Violet. Rarely did one flat-out refuse to accommodate the other. "We just saw that tolerance would be absolutely necessary if we were to have any happiness at all in life," Daisy explained. If she wanted to go shopping, for instance, and Violet had a headache, Violet made a promise to go the next day. "Having once given her my word, nothing will stop me—at least, nothing has," Violet said.

They had always thought of themselves as distinct individuals. "All this talk about 'identical' twins is just bosh," they insisted in spite of their undeniable physical resemblance, "because we've never liked the same things—food, clothes, or people." Now they could indulge in new ways of proving that point. They began experimenting frequently with different hair colors, dousing their "horrible brown" with shades of red and auburn. Platinum blond became Daisy's habitual favorite, while Violet grew partial to black. Offstage, they quickly abandoned the habit of dressing identically, as outward evidence that "each of us has an individual personality." Their reading habits were just as polarized. Violet leaned toward "sweet romantic stories"; her books were nothing but "trash," according to Daisy, who favored "sophisticated literature." Both of them continued to relish a steady diet of detective and crime stories, though their tastes in plots and authors diverged predictably—old-fashioned stories for Violet and modern ones for Daisy. The one thing that required mutual agreement was going to the movies. If there wasn't a picture both sisters were interested in, they didn't go at all. "It's a big bore to sit through a movie you don't want to see," Violet said.

With freedom came the opportunity to exert deeper, more substantial independence from each other. "So we decided early on that each would make her private life her own," Daisy said. "What Violet does is her business, and what I do is mine."

They maintained their individual autonomy along strict lines, including separate bank accounts in separate banks. "If Daisy wants to give her money away she can," Violet said. "But she can't give away mine." Likewise, when Daisy misplaced an envelope full of cash, Violet had nothing to do with her sister's hunt to track it down. "She did not help me, although she heard all this about the lost money, she never interfered. I was not in the least angry with her on account of this, as I can settle my own affairs alone," Daisy said. "If one of us is in trouble, the other does not as a rule take any notice of it. We sympathize with each other, but we don't want to settle one another's troubles."

More surprisingly, the sisters developed distinct circles of friends that did not always overlap. That was tricky in the beginning, Daisy acknowledged, especially when it came to visiting those who lived in different towns. "One of us just goes along and doesn't pay any attention. We thought it couldn't be done at first, but you learn to act as if you didn't even know the others." The same mind-your-own-business policy applied to romance; she and Violet trained themselves "not to act the mother-in-law." When Violet had a date, Daisy said, "I just read, did crossword puzzles, and ate the candy her boyfriend brought."

They needed a rule to govern their pair of "healthy tempers," too. Violet had always been the more irritable, but Daisy had to admit that she, too, was prone to momentary outbursts of anger and frustration. Their mutual policy was to stand aside and wait for the storm to pass without attempting to calm it. "When I get mad I just blow off steam and say anything I want about anything," Daisy said. "She doesn't say a word until I'm finished."

"That's right," Violet said. "I let her get it all out of her system." When the smoke cleared, that was the end of it. Long ago, Henry Hilton had shown them that clinging to words spoken in anger only allowed them to fester into something more poisonous.

"It's lucky that neither of us holds a grudge," Daisy said. "We have our little flareups, occasionally, to be sure. I get jealous of men," she admitted, though she didn't say under what circumstances. Was her temper more apt to spark when her boyfriends paid attention to Violet, or when Violet had a date and she didn't? "But we never get jealous of each other, thank goodness."

"And we do not magnify or minimize our weaknesses and strengths," the two of them agreed. "No facets of our characters are hidden, or can be, from each other." While Daisy characterized herself as "high-strung, quick-tempered, and jealous," she admired Violet's "quiet and broad-minded" temperament. Though Daisy did not rely on her sister to bail her out of her own personal dilemmas, Violet's opposing personality steadied her, providing an emotional ballast that Daisy found invaluable. Violet was also the more patient, which had its advantages in business. Being "the diplomat," she was better equipped to handle "irate and hard to please theater managers." That didn't mean Violet always held sway professionally, though. The Hilton sisters had different opinions about their career, a problem they managed with the most straightforward solution. "We settled that by deciding that we would take turns being the boss." Every six months, they switched. They also divvied up their mundane business duties, with Violet handling the bookkeeping and Daisy managing secretarial tasks like buying railway tickets.

People who could not manage to live as harmoniously as they did baffled the Hiltons. "When we see married couples having their scraps and spats over little trifles, Violet and I have to smile," Daisy said. "If we could settle things without hard feelings, why can't they?" It was all so simple to them. "We try to extend the same courtesies to one another roommates would do," Daisy explained. "We have to give in to one another, like any two intelligent people would do."

"If we can get along, anyone can do it," Violet declared.

Within their own private sphere, the Hiltons' system worked nearly flawlessly. "They were very congenial between themselves," Lucille Stotzer confirmed. "I never heard a cross word between them."

. . .

Well over a decade after gaining their freedom, the Hiltons would convince their fans that they had faced another monumental decision in 1931—one they'd never spoken of at the time. Soon after the court victory over Myer Myers, Daisy confessed to *American Weekly* in 1944, Don Galvan had proposed to her.

If it was true, it must have been an invisible whirlwind of a romance. One moment Don and Daisy were gazing shyly at each other from theater wings, sending "thought messages" across the stage, and the next, he was imploring, "Marry me, Daisy, and forget about show business. Come to Mexico and live with my family." Daisy herself offered no explanation of how their relationship had leapfrogged from one phase to the other. To hear Daisy tell it, the dream-come-true moment of Don's proposal had taken her by surprise as well, though for altogether different reasons.

"Actually confronted with this odd situation," she said, "it was very different from what I had imagined." She felt Violet's jolt of surprise, too, and did not know what to say to Don. How could she answer only for herself in a situation like this? It was not possible to factor Violet out of the equation. "I thought that he couldn't very well ask her consent to marry me," Daisy pondered. The decision whether or not to marry the man she loved belonged to Daisy and no one else. Violet would have been the last person to dispute that fact. "Yet—I wondered if she should not be consulted," Daisy said, "since she would share every moment of my life with my husband."

It wasn't the thought of exposing her most intimate moments with Don to Violet that troubled Daisy. Both sisters were immune to that kind of shyness. "It gave us grave moments and much wonderment when our suitors were embarrassed by the inevitable presence of a third person," they said. The Hiltons had long ago accepted the impossibility of physical privacy. In response, they'd learned to drop an invisible curtain between themselves at will for the sake of mental and emotional solitude. The thought of a set of prying eyes and ears might have intimidated Don, but Daisy knew that the last thing Violet would be doing was looking or listening during the couple's intimacies. The real problem with marrying Don was the more difficult matter of forcing Violet to abandon the career she loved and move to another country.

"Don, have you thought this out?" Daisy asked.

Don assured her that he had. "I'm sure I can make allowances for Violet," he said confidently.

"How?" both sisters asked together.

"This way: You will be my wife for six months of the year. Then, for the other six months you may go wherever Violet wants to go. And if she should get married then, naturally, you must spend six months with her and her husband."

Don's solution stunned both Daisy and Violet into silence. It was completely fair in one sense, completely in accord with the way she and Violet managed their daily lives, yet completely unsatisfying in another. The thought of being parted from Don for half the year was as unpleasant to Daisy as the prospect of asking Violet to relinquish her freedom for six months at a time.

Solving the riddle of how to be fair to Violet was not the only thing behind Daisy's hesitation. Don's manner as he'd proposed had robbed a portion of the joy from the moment. "Even as he asked me he took the cigarette from my hand, pushed my wine glass aside," Daisy recalled. "Even he would suppress me!" After so recently winning the simple freedoms that had eluded them for so long, Daisy had no patience for any kind of patronizing behavior.

"Give up my little pet habits!" she lamented to herself. And Violet, too—if Don disapproved of things Violet enjoyed, would his distaste compel her to give up her own decadences and indulgences for Daisy's sake? "Should she be subjected to such restraint?" Daisy wondered.

Perhaps worst of all was Don's request that Daisy give up show business. She and Violet had been adamant about remaining on the stage once they were emancipated from the Myerses. "It is the only life we know," Violet had recently told a reporter, "and we could not be happy anywhere else." Vaudeville was more than a career—the stage was the nearest thing to home, and the audience the nearest thing to community, that Violet and Daisy had known.

Love, Daisy concluded, could not be expected to conquer all of those barriers to happiness. "Why should I submit both of us to another life of censorship in which we couldn't be ourselves?" she decided. Daisy turned Don down. The parting with Don left her—and everyone who read the article—with a tantalizing question: "Could either of us marry? Could any man adjust himself to our lives?"

· · ·

Only one person disputed the authenticity of Daisy's tear-jerking tale: Don Galvan. "Those stories were entirely wrong," he told *American Weekly* in 1945. According to Don, his relationship with Violet and Daisy was "confined to a few chance meetings" in Newark and Kansas City. "They dropped in to catch my act and, of course, we had a chat." A few years later, he ran into them at a San Antonio party, where, he claimed, the Hiltons told him they wanted to hire him as their manager once they were free of Myer Myers. There was no more to their acquaintance than that. As for the singing and the adoring gazes across the stage? That was a constant problem for Don Galvan, *American Weekly* explained. To his chagrin, Don had discovered that "women who disbelieve anything a man tells them will, however, become very earnest about anything he sings to them, even if he doesn't mean a word of it."

When Violet and Daisy called him after winning their freedom, Don agreed to meet in New York to discuss the possibility of becoming their theatrical manager. He arrived at their hotel to find another roaring party in progress. Don was not impressed. "I told them they should stop having parties if they wanted to keep their public," he recalled. "They said they had just freed themselves of one domineering man and didn't want another. I said 'Okay girls, if that's how you feel about it, get someone else to manage you!' And that's the last I saw of the Siamese twins."

· · ·

Was Daisy's love story just another extravagant piece of ballyhoo, like the Hiltons' account of dazzling the city of Berlin with their musical debut at the tender age of four? It is certainly possible. Nevertheless, there may have been more than a grain of truth to the Hiltons' version. The fundamental elements matched, after all. Daisy had been impressed by Don Galvan's talent and wanted him to be part of her life. But the way he turned up his nose at the sisters' self-indulgences gave her pause, and ultimately their lives proved to be incompatible. Consciously or otherwise, the Hiltons may have exaggerated the core of that basic story to dramatize a deeper truth about their own reality: the sanctity of their sisterly bond would always be prized above all others. Never in their lives would Daisy or Violet jeopardize the other's happiness for her own sake.

CHAPTER 20

BEFORE THAT FIRST GIDDY YEAR OF FREEDOM WAS OUT, AN opportunity to steer their career in a brand-new direction fell smack into Violet's and Daisy's laps—the chance to appear in a movie unlike anything that had been filmed before, or has ever been filmed since.

Spearheaded by Tod Browning, the unofficially crowned king of horror who had directed *Dracula*, the project was conceived as "a horror story more horrible than all the rest." It would be called, simply, *Freaks*.

The plot centers around Hans, a three-foot-tall sideshow performer in a European circus who becomes smitten with a trapeze artist named Cleopatra. The affection of a child-sized man is nothing more than a joke to Cleopatra; only the promise of enjoying Hans's immense fortune persuades her to marry him. She attempts to hasten her inheritance by poisoning him, but when Hans's sideshow comrades discover Cleopatra's treachery, the "so-called code of the freaks" compels them to unite and avenge one of their own in a grotesque and terrifying conclusion.

The story line toyed cleverly with the idea of monsters, asking who was worthier of revulsion, a beauty savage enough to commit murder for profit, or the so-called physical monstrosities who upend her foul plan?

Browning did not task the makeup and costume departments with creating his cast of freak show characters. Instead, he sent casting agents to comb the amusement world for the real-life stars of carnivals and sideshows. Their efforts resulted in a roster as impressive as it was unrealistic. Browning's fictional one-ring circus had "three times as many freaks as a Ringling show," *Variety* wryly remarked.

The cast of human curios starred three-foot-three-inch-tall Harry Earles, who would eventually play a member of the Munchkin Lollipop Guild in *The Wizard of Oz,* as Hans. Harry and three of his six siblings had been born with dwarfism; one of his diminutive sisters, Daisy, was cast to play the woman Hans jilts to marry Cleopatra. Two other supporting actors also had forms of dwarfism: Angelo Rossitto stood two feet, eleven inches tall, and Jerry Austin three feet, six inches tall.

All of them towered over Johnny Eck, the twenty-year-old "Half Boy" whose body appeared, as he put it, "snapped off" at the waist. In fact, Johnny Eck did have a complete body, but because of a condition called sacral agenesis, his legs and feet were too drastically underdeveloped to support him. Johnny made his living by concealing his lower limbs under his clothing and pretending they did not exist at all. Instead, he entertained his audiences by walking, running, and climbing ladders with his hands. He stood eighteen inches tall.

Tod Browning hired three performers who would have been known as limbless wonders in sideshow vernacular. Frances O'Connor and Martha Morris both had been born without arms and used their toes as deftly as fingers for tasks such as eating, writing, and sewing. Prince Randion was the grandfather of the cast—quite literally. Born in Guyana without any limbs at all, he was sixty years old and had eight grandchildren. Randion had astounded Coney Island audiences for forty-five years by shaving himself with a straight razor by manipulating his shoulders, and rolling and lighting cigarettes with his lips.

People with microcephaly had also been popular sideshow attractions for decades. The condition prevents the brain from developing to average size, which in turn results in a small skull and sloping forehead. In sideshows, such people were dubbed with a particularly cruel moniker: pinheads. To accentuate the distinctive shape of their heads, all of their hair except for a tiny ponytail at the crown was usually shaved. Browning signed three so-called pinheads to appear in *Freaks:* Elvira and Jenny Lee Snow (known as Pip and Flip, the twins from the Yucatán, though they were neither twins nor Mexican) and a much-beloved performer who went by the stage name Schlitzie and effortlessly stole every scene he appeared in.

Jane Barnell, who called herself Lady Olga on the stage, had hirsutism, which had caused her to sprout the beginnings of a beard at age two. By the time she'd reached adulthood, her beard could grow as long as thirteen and a half inches when left unshaven. Peter Robinson, the Human Skeleton, claimed to weigh "fifty-eight pounds soaking wet." He was cast as Lady Olga's husband.

The features on the left side of Josephine Waas's body were feminine, while the right half appeared masculine. She went by the stage name Josephine-Joseph, billing herself as "Half man, half woman. Brother and sister in one body." Though she claimed to be a true hermaphrodite (a term abandoned in favor of *intersex* today), Miss Waas had also pled guilty to a charge of fraud in England the year before *Freaks* began filming, and therefore may have been gaffed, or fake.

Then there was Elizabeth Green, the Stork-woman; and Minnie Woolsey, who called herself Koo Koo the Bird Girl. Both women had genetic conditions that affected their skeletal growth, resulting in narrow limbs, bulbous heads, and long beaklike noses. They dressed in feathered suits and wore shoes shaped like bird feet.

And, of course, the biggest stars of the entire cast—Violet and Daisy Hilton.

It was an odd move for the Hilton sisters. All their lives, Violet and Daisy had shunned the notion that they were run-of-the-mill freaks. They had not appeared under a freak show canvas since they were three or four years old, considered so rare and beautiful that they deserved their own exclusive venue. Never before had they deigned to rank themselves alongside bearded ladies and human skeletons. Perhaps they were asserting their independence. Perhaps they hoped that signing with Metro-Goldwyn-Mayer studio would launch a film career. They never publicly explained their decision to participate in Browning's project.

Their roles were small. Violet spoke around twenty lines, Daisy ten. Not one word was critical to the plot. Instead, they were part of a series of diversions from the main story, too small even to be called subplots. These scenes functioned as a kind of on-screen sideshow, each constructed to highlight some aspect of a carnival performer's skills or circumstances as the characters interacted. While on-screen husband and wife Martha Morris and Angelo Rossitto discuss their misgivings about Cleopatra, for instance, Martha sews with her toes.

By contrast, the sole purpose of the Hiltons' scenes was to tickle the audience's imagination with sly innuendos about conjoined twins' romances. Violet bickers endlessly with Daisy's fictional husband, who chides her for keeping his wife in bed all day with a secondhand hangover; later, Daisy thrills in tandem with her sister when Violet seals a marriage proposal from her own suitor with a passionate embrace.

No scene embedded itself more firmly in the popular consciousness than the wedding feast, when the entire sideshow cast assembles to celebrate the marriage of Hans and Cleopatra, complete with entertainment by the sword-swallower and fire-eater. In a gesture of generosity, the freaks spontaneously decide to induct Cleopatra into their fellowship. Angelo Rossitto and Johnny Eck climb to the tabletop and fill a loving cup with wine, which then passes from one person to another in a mimicry of Holy Communion as the guests drum the handles of their knives on the table and chant, "Gooble-gobble, gooble-gobble, one of us, one of us!"

Violet and Daisy, curiously, are not seated at the table during any of this spectacle. As had always been the case back in their carnival days, they are set apart from the rest, sharing a chair placed a few feet away from the corner of the table, blithely playing their saxophones as the rest of the guests drum and chant in unison. The distance between the Hiltons and that table eerily mirrored their uneasy relationship with the carnival freak shows of their past. In their own minds, they were something more than just a sideshow attraction—they were entertainers in their own right, accomplished singers, dancers, and musicians. Yet to the public, their physical bond would always be the primary attention-grabber.

Even within the studio itself, Violet and Daisy occupied a blurry area between freak and movie star. One producer led a protest to set up a separate outdoor cafeteria for Browning's sideshow performers, so that everyone else on the MGM lot "could get to eat in the commissary without throwing up." The ban did not apply to Violet and Daisy, however. Once again, their attractiveness granted them special status, allowing them to rub elbows with the studio's biggest stars. (Harry and Daisy Earles were also permitted into the commissary. Thanks to their relatively ordinary proportions, people considered their miniaturized features cute. Angelo Rossitto and Jerry Austin, whose forms of dwarfism had altered the proportions of their bodies, were relegated to the outdoor freak table.) Even so, author F. Scott Fitzgerald, who was screenwriting for MGM, would claim that the sight of the two sisters contemplating a single menu had once triggered a wave of nausea that made him bolt from the table. He conveniently left out the fact that he'd been suffering from a walloping hangover that day.

• • •

Freaks debuted in early 1932 to what *Variety* called "astonishingly variable results." In Los Angeles, "some horrified spectators got up from their seats and ran—did not walk—to the nearest exit," while in San Diego, the film "smashed all house records" in a week.

Panicked at the reactions of preview audiences, the studio frantically tried to tone down the more grotesque aspects of the picture. A third of the film ended up on the cutting room floor, never to be recovered. The remaining sixty minutes lurched from scene to scene, sometimes without apparent logic, snipping jokes in half and leaving threads of story dangling. The studio also tacked on an attempt at a happy ending, reuniting Hans with the woman he'd abandoned for Cleopatra. It did no good. Browning's vision had been butchered. "His theme is never permitted to bloom," lamented the *Pittsburgh Post-Gazette*.

Critics' reactions were as polarized as the public's. While one thought Browning had succeeded in presenting the cast "as human beings rather than curiosities," another was declaring that the film was doomed to fail because "it is impossible for the normal man or woman to sympathize with the aspiring midget."

A perceptive reviewer from the *Los Angeles Times* reflected that an individual's response to *Freaks* depended "upon your own reaction to the immemorial side show of the circus."

The public responded not so much with horror as with revulsion. Looking at people like Violet and Daisy, Schlitzie, and Johnny Eck made audiences squirm, and rather than ask themselves why they felt uncomfortable, they blamed Tod Browning for daring to film people they did not like to look at. Many of them had undoubtedly enjoyed watching superstar Lon Chaney play a criminal who disguises himself as an armless circus performer in Browning's 1927 hit, *The Unknown*. Watching actual armless people on film, however, proved to be more than most moviegoers could stomach. The hypocrisy of this situation seems to have been lost on audiences and critics alike in 1932. "To put such creatures in a picture and before the public is unthinkable," one woman wrote to Browning. "You must have the mental equipment of a freak yourself to devise such a picture," pronounced another. The controversy threw the motion picture industry into "an uproar."

MGM tried to double down and turn the intensity of audiences' reactions to its advantage, concocting advertisements that dared apprehensive moviegoers to brave the horrors of the film. "Are you afraid to see *Freaks?*" one openly taunted. "You will laugh at them, shudder at them, but you will never forget them," it promised. "Slimy . . . Gibbering Creatures of Nature," another read. "Not Recommended for Children or Adults in Delicate Health."

It was no use. *Freaks* was banned in Atlanta. It did not debut in New York City for six months, presumably out of fear that the industry's most influential reviewers would eat it alive. Petitions circulated in Washington, DC, and other major cities to have the movie thrown out of the theaters.

Fortunately for Violet and Daisy, few critics singled out their performance for comment. Those who did varied just as widely in their opinions as they did on the film as a whole. *Variety* declared that the attempt at comedy in Violet and Daisy's scenes "reaches the very pinnacle of bad taste in a picture overboard with offensiveness," while the *San Antonio Express* was pleased to note that the Hilton sisters "happily are not in the repugnant sequences of the film."

Remarks on *Freaks* from Violet and Daisy themselves are scarce. In a May 1932 interview, Violet said simply of the venture, "We thought it was wonderful." Whether *it* was supposed to refer to the film itself or to the sisters' entire Hollywood experience was left unclear—perhaps deliberately so. Though the Hiltons did not speak out against *Freaks* publicly, the very idea that they could be lumped together with carnivals and sideshows never failed to incense them afterward. "We most certainly do not consider ourselves freaks and you would be amazed at what normal lives we lead," Daisy said many years later. Violet was just as adamant. "We, however, are not in carnivals and never have been," she boldly insisted as though the first sixteen years of her life had been surgically extracted from her memory. "We are of the theaters and night clubs. It is a different life altogether—much more dignity, if you follow me."

They swept the whole experience under the rug, never mentioning *Freaks* again.

. . .

Calculating the impact of *Freaks* on the Hilton sisters' popularity—or lack thereof—is tricky. After all, their salary had already been steadily sinking for a year by the time *Freaks* debuted. Coincidence or not, 1932 marked an unmistakable turning point in Violet and Daisy's career.

Their act had remained more or less unchanged since 1925, with the recent exception of one amusing tweak: instead of relying on their accompanist or emcee to ask questions, their dancing partners now posed as felt-hatted reporters to act out a spoof press interview. With their playful answers, the Hiltons gently mocked the hundreds of silly questions they'd fielded from audiences over the years. "For instance," one newspaper recorded, "when Violet goes to play tennis, Daisy says she plays a round of golf." The sisters' own amusement at turning the tables on the imaginary interviewers gave the audience as much pleasure as the jokes themselves.

Nevertheless, business was not what it used to be. Although some critics considered them "still good vaudeville," the days when people would line up around the block for tickets were behind them now. "Applause was mild, audience lethargic," another review read. "Siamese Twins have been pretty common in recent seasons."

Copycat acts had sprung up almost immediately in the wake of their phenomenal success. Terry Turner, who had so painstakingly restored the Hiltons' confidence after their disastrous audition with Keith-Albee, had signed the Gibb sisters, Mary and Margaret of Holyoke, Massachusetts, the first known set of American-born conjoined twins, to a vaudeville contract in 1926. Conjoined Filipino brothers Lucio and Simplicio Godino were touring the globe with their identical twin wives under the management of none other than Myer Myers and William Oliver in 1931. Violet and Daisy had been so popular that they'd even inspired a pair of impersonators who buttoned themselves together and called themselves the Milton Sisters.

None of them were as entertaining, profitable, or popular as the Hilton sisters; nevertheless, their acts made conjoined twins seem commonplace, robbing Violet and Daisy of their aura of rarity. That said, the Hiltons had been touring America's theaters for most of a decade. Hundreds of thousands of people had already seen them onstage. Even without copycats siphoning away business, their popularity would inevitably have waned.

The drop was so steep, it must have felt like falling off a precipice. Gone were the days when audiences desperate for tickets demanded that the Hilton sisters be held over for a second week. Violet and Daisy were doing split-week engagements now, performing for just three days before moving on. In Boston, where they'd crushed the box office record with a single $30,000 week in March 1925, they grossed just $8,300 during their 1932 booking. *Variety*'s assessment was brief and brutal: "Hilton Sisters not a good draw."

Their salary plummeted accordingly, from its all-time high of $3,850 a week to $750. At a time when unemployment was skyrocketing and the average manufacturing worker was lucky to take home more than fifty cents an hour, the very thought of $750 a week (over $13,000 today) would have been enough to make most Americans nauseous with envy. If Violet and Daisy mourned the drop in pay, they had sense enough not to lament to the press.

The Hiltons' solution echoed the wisdom of Ike Rose and Myer Myers: Seek out fresh territory. That fall they applied for American citizenship, obtained passports, and booked an eight-week engagement on the other side of the Atlantic.

CHAPTER 21

ON DECEMBER 21, 1932, VIOLET AND DAISY ARRIVED IN SOUTH–
ampton, England, for what they had every reason to believe would
be a triumphal return to the country of their birth. For over twenty
years, they had charmed audiences on three continents. Yet the success of their United Kingdom tour is not a simple thing to gauge.

From the beginning, the trip was fraught with uncertainty. The
theater circuit that had booked them, Moss-Empire, cabled with a cancellation notice just before the Hiltons were to set sail from New York.
Violet and Daisy dug in their heels. The theater, they were informed,
had not procured the necessary labor permit for their performance.
The Hiltons would not be deterred. They hired an English law firm
and defiantly boarded their ship. By the time they arrived, all the paperwork had been sorted out, and the bookings proceeded as planned.

Had it been an honest case of a crucial detail slipping through
the cracks, or had Moss-Empire gotten cold feet at the last moment
and scrambled for a loophole? Despite Violet and Daisy's American
success, Moss-Empire found itself contemplating the same question
Loew's had wrestled with almost ten years before: Would audiences
pay to see conjoined twins on the vaudeville stage? Moss-Empire had
no choice but to find out. Violet and Daisy had promised to sue if the
bookings were canceled.

As Moss-Empire had likely anticipated, the British seemed taken aback by the prospect of watching conjoined twins sing and dance. Violet and Daisy's first performance, in Leeds, became "the subject of a great deal of controversial talk," despite the *Yorkshire Post and Leeds Intelligencer*'s assurance that "there is nothing distasteful about their act."

The Hiltons soldiered on to London, where publicity was scanty and a flu epidemic was raging. In London's Finsbury Park Empire theater, almost half the seats were empty, a phenomenon *Variety* would later explain as "primarily due to the British being antagonistic towards freak attractions." Still, there was a glimmer of hope. "Act sustains interest throughout," noted a London critic, "and, given good publicity, is a cinch here."

At the very least it's safe to say that those who ventured in to see the Hiltons' show enjoyed themselves. The difficulty lay in filling the seats in the first place. British publicity was comically, stereotypically, subdued. Where American newspapers printed illustrated articles and advertisements two or three columns wide and several inches deep for days before each booking, British notices for the Hiltons' appearances were just a fraction of an inch tall.

English audiences may have been reluctant to pay to see conjoined twins perform in a theater, but they had no qualms about gaping at Violet and Daisy in public. Boxing matches turned out to be a reliable place to spot the famous sisters, who'd enjoyed practicing the sport themselves since their teens. They were "crazy on attending boxing matches," Violet and Daisy told the *Derby Daily Telegraph*. Their fellow boxing fans were just as keen on seeing them. "Hilton sisters create a sensation at the Ring, when spectators more concerned in watching the girls than the fights," ran one report.

The British public, Violet and Daisy themselves noticed, tended to be "more warm-hearted" outside the theater than in. Thousands of people jammed train stations to witness their arrival as they crisscrossed the country, requiring constables to manage the crowds. Even with police in attendance, at least one "mild scuffle" broke out as the Hiltons made their way from train to taxi. It seemed that Mary Hilton just might have been correct all those years ago—people would rather glimpse Violet and Daisy on a train platform for free than ante up for the cost of a seat at their show. If those thousands of spectators could only be convinced to crave more than a fleeting glance, surely money would start pouring into the Moss-Empire box offices the way it once had in the States.

Was it only a coincidence, then, when two weeks after their lackluster London show, Daisy startled the press with a thrilling announcement? She was engaged, she declared, to a twenty-one-year-old Chicago orchestra leader named Jack Lewis.

Even the most ardent of Hilton fans had to wonder who this Jack Lewis was. His name had never been associated with the sisters before. The only Jack Lewis to be found in the pages of *Billboard* or *Variety* was an older, married vaudeville producer by the same name who worked in New York. Likewise, the Jack Lewis who appeared regularly in the *Chicago Tribune* that year was a boxer, not a musician. In short, the man Daisy described as her fiancé did not seem to exist.

Skepticism did not tinge the reaction to Daisy's glad news, however. British interest immediately perked up. Newspaper articles swelled from sentences to paragraphs, and some reporters began seeking out Violet and Daisy for comments and even interviews. Daisy happily informed them all that a civil ceremony at Gretna Green, a village just over the Scottish border, renowned as a refuge for "runaway" weddings since the 1750s, would follow in six weeks' time.

Reporters were even more curious about Violet's reaction. "Do I mind?" she replied to one. "Not at all. I am quite keen on her being happy and we are not the slightest bit jealous of each other." She quipped to another reporter, "He's a charming boy, and anyhow, I shan't miss my sister, shall I?"

Oddly, the news of Daisy and Jack's engagement took longer than an ocean liner to travel from England to the United States. February, March, and most of April passed before the story broke, in a single article that never once quoted Daisy or Violet. Stranger still, although the story occupied an entire page of *American Weekly*, the prospective groom spoke just six lines, in response to the question why he found Daisy more appealing than Violet. ("Both of the girls are swell, but Daisy is so smart and cute at the same time.") His picture—the only image of him that would ever appear in connection with the Hiltons—looked suspiciously like something halfway between a photograph and a drawing.

The clearest hint that the story had little basis in reality was the comical claim that the sisters had had a special lovers' phone booth installed in their apartment, with a partition that could be lowered between the two women for privacy. A photo showed Daisy leaning over a telephone mounted on the right half of the booth, while Violet stood waiting outside. Both wore hats and fur coats, and Violet held her purse, *inside* their apartment. That was because the picture had actually been taken on the street in front of their hotel in London in January and doctored for the newspaper. If such a phone booth had actually existed, it would have been useless to Violet for the same reason that she couldn't drive a car, at least in the United States—the phone was on the wrong side of the booth. The whole thing had a fanciful quality to it, almost reminiscent of the souvenir booklet Myer Myers had dreamed up years before.

Six weeks passed with nary a sign of Mr. Lewis, or the promised wedding. "Now I don't think he'll be able to get here, and I shall see him when we get back to America," Daisy said. No one seemed to mind. Reviews of the Hilton sisters' act had become perceptibly more favorable, though none would ever match the fervent tones of their American counterparts. "Enjoyable and meeting with approval," a Scottish critic said. In Aberdeen, they were declared "a hit" and received the unusually forthright praise of "an enthusiastic reception."

Moss-Empire must have found their box office returns satisfactory, for they extended the Hiltons' initial eight-week contract into March and beyond.

Brighton in particular greeted the sisters with open arms, offering "a warm welcome to their natal town." There, at least, they packed the house. At a local department store, Violet and Daisy signed hundreds of autographs while a constable devoted his "whole-time attention" to managing the great press of well-wishers. Absent from the throng was any member of Violet and Daisy's biological family, including two younger siblings they did not know existed. Kate Skinner had died of complications after the birth of her fourth child in 1912, crushing any slim hopes of a reunion with the mother who had given them up. If any other relatives made an attempt to connect with them, the meeting has been lost to history. The Skinners, recalled a cousin, seemed embarrassed at the thought of allowing anyone to discover "that Siamese twins were in our family tree." Only Edith Myers's sister Alice, who had attended Violet and Daisy's birth, welcomed them into her home.

For the rest of the spring and summer of 1933, Violet and Daisy traversed the British Isles, drawing great crowds in the streets and apparently unremarkable attendance in theaters. In the end, a tour that should have been "a cinch" ended up being remembered as a "brodie," as *Variety* would put it in vaudeville slang—a colossal, almost suicidal flop, at least by American standards.

There was likely nothing the Hiltons could have done about it. From an American point of view, the sorry state of British publicity had hampered Violet and Daisy's chances at making a runaway hit from the start. "Many a good attraction out of town has lost good money through managements keeping the show a secret," *Variety* complained. Exhortations like *remarkable, amazing,* and *sensational* didn't have the same impact when they appeared in modest little articles, wedged at the bottom of a page beneath columns of horse racing statistics and hemmed in by illustrated quarter-page advertisements for bakery bread and camera film. At a glance, the notice of the Hiltons' appearance in Lancashire was no more eye-catching than a neighboring article extolling a cure for hemorrhoids. Even a story headlined "The Best of This Week's Shows" devoted exactly two sentences to Violet and Daisy, describing their act in the most matter-of-fact terms. Word of mouth helped but tended to reach its height just as the show was closing anyway.

In spite of the disappointing turnout, the Hiltons may have been a bit better off financially when they departed for home that fall than they had been the year before. At £300 a week, or around $975, their British salary was more generous than what they'd been forced to become accustomed to in the United States.

. . .

No sign of discouragement dimmed the Hiltons' return home. Violet and Daisy stepped ashore in New York that October brimming with news. "Dancing Siamese Twins to Double in Matrimony," the *Brooklyn Daily Eagle* announced. Violet had fallen for a man she would identify only as "a prominent English boxer"—"the dearest boy in the world." Daisy still planned to marry the enigmatic Mr. Lewis. For a week straight the story rocketed across the nation, putting the Hiltons' picture in all the papers from coast to coast. A Christmas double wedding was in the works, the stories promised.

Christmas came and went, and no wedding bells chimed. News of the Hiltons had once again slowed to the thinnest of trickles. The dearth of news articles could easily have led anyone reading the paper in the winter of 1933 to conclude that Violet and Daisy Hilton had retired.

Now and then the engagement announcement popped up in an obscure pocket of the country that had somehow neglected to print the news earlier. The story always carried the same photo: Violet and Daisy waving from the deck as their ship arrived in New York on the sixth of October. The prospective grooms' faces never appeared. The name of Violet's fiancé remained a mystery.

After the initial flurry of publicity, both relationships seemed to evaporate without anyone's notice. When next the Hiltons emerged in the limelight, the only talk of "engagements" concerned theatrical bookings. Had the sisters truly been in love? Or had they only capitalized on the public's titillation over their romantic prospects? Violet's and Daisy's own accounts of these relationships are so thoroughly muddled, it's easy to wonder if anything the Hiltons said about their love life had been true in the first place.

The initial version of Daisy and Jack's love story, printed in the United States in April 1933, had the two meeting for the first time outside the New York City office of the booking agent that Lewis and the Hiltons all shared, presumably sometime in 1931 or 1932. That was plausible enough. But as she stood on the deck of the *Aquitania* in New York Harbor in October 1933, Daisy told a reporter for the *New York Daily News* that she'd known Lewis for five years, and had refused to accept his proposals until Violet was also engaged so they could be married simultaneously. If that was true, it put Daisy's first meeting with Jack in 1928, when she was still under the Myerses' strict supervision. More dubious yet, Jack Lewis would have been a mere sixteen years old.

A decade later, the Hiltons would change the story yet again, telling *American Weekly* in 1944 that while Violet was dating her prizefighter in England, Daisy had been the lonely third wheel until Jack Lewis entered the picture. This scenario shifted Daisy and Jack's meeting across the Atlantic Ocean and into early 1933. After Jack swept Daisy off her feet, the sisters claimed, the two couples became "a gay foursome," enjoying a year of convivial double-dating.

That was impossible. Daisy herself had told the British press in May 1933 that her wedding was delayed because Jack hadn't been able to make the trip to England. When the Hiltons returned to the

United States in October, Violet's fiancé did not accompany them. The two men had never been on the same continent at the same time, let alone met each other.

The *American Weekly* version stretched credulity further yet with the claim that Jack did not propose to Daisy until mid-1934. "After a while," Daisy said, "I realized that too many of my conversations with Jack took place over the phone. And when he asked me over the wire to marry him, I knew that his shyness made him unsuitable for the husband of a Siamese twin." Every bit of that story was at odds with the actual events of 1933. If Jack had indeed proposed over the phone, it was almost certainly because Daisy had been in England, leaving him no other option. And if Daisy had known then and there that Jack was not the man for her, why had she promptly announced their engagement?

The details of Violet's boxing-ring romance were even sketchier. Initially, she stoutly refused to divulge the identity of her British sweetheart. Almost a year passed before the name of Britain's welterweight champion, Harry Mason, became associated with the Hilton sisters, when suddenly Daisy began telling the press *she* was engaged to the boxer. In 1944, Violet would reverse the story once again, claiming that Harry Mason had been her intended groom all along. By all accounts, the relationship ended by mid-1934, as abruptly as it had begun.

The stories tangle, intersect, and contradict each other at every turn, as though Violet and Daisy could not be bothered to recall what they'd said from one telling to the next, or, for that matter, as if they never imagined anyone else would take the trouble to remember the most basic details, either.

What did it matter, so long as no one protested? A lifetime of carnival ballyhoo and publicity stunts had shown Violet and Daisy again and again that the truth had only the smallest of roles to play in their success.

CHAPTER 22

IN FEBRUARY 1934, THE HILTON SISTERS SUDDENLY RESUR-
faced. They'd written an autobiography, the papers said, entitled *Double Life*. The book, due out in May, never materialized. Instead, Violet and Daisy began touring with a show of their own devising, called the Double Rhythm Revue. The "colorful, melodious, fast-moving" variety program featured a twelve-piece orchestra, a pair of comedians, three dancers, two acrobats, and "a large chorus of well-trained Broadway beauties."

The Double Rhythm Revue lasted almost four months. At the end of May, *Variety* printed a tiny notice that the Hiltons' show had "folded." The show's failure made no sense. In April, *Billboard* had reported that the revue had been doing "good business" all along the upper Ohio Valley. Another story in *Variety* soon followed, revealing that Violet and Daisy had left the thirty-seven members of their show stranded in Philadelphia without pay, where the sheriff had seized $300 worth of the sisters' property to compensate the orchestra. An Albany restaurant was on the verge of suing them for an unpaid tab of $83 (over $1,500 today). Adding to the chaos, two different agents were embroiled in an argument over who represented the act.

How could the venture have nose-dived so quickly? Financial ineptitude? An unscrupulous manager? Costumes, sets, and equipment beyond their means? For a pair as trusting and inexperienced as Violet and Daisy, any combination of these ingredients—and more—could have come together to create a foolproof recipe for quick and easy financial disaster.

"Financial security never seemed to be the least bit of concern to Daisy and Violet," vaudeville performer Rose Fernandez recalled. "When they came into a new town with their show, you half got the impression that the Ringling Brothers and Barnum & Bailey Circus had arrived. The twins had a reputation for being very kind to their help. They were always surrounded by hangers-on who had their hands out."

"That's where their hundred thousand dollars went," said one of their dancers. Everything they'd won from the Myerses had been invested in that show.

"They were making the best of their world after they got free," Camille Rosengren said, "but they could not cope."

. . .

Two weeks after *Variety* had aired their financial woes, a brand-new Hilton story burst like a shower of fireworks into newspapers across the nation.

"Siamese Twins Denied Right to Get Married"
"Double Trouble for Siamese Twins Seeking Wedding
    License"

Violet Hilton, the papers said, was engaged to be married to one Maurice Lambert, a tall, shy member of their orchestra—a man unheard of before that day. The abruptness of Maurice's appearance in Violet's life went unremarked upon, however. The quandary their engagement had spawned was so sensational, it commanded every speck of both reporters' and readers' attention.

When the happy couple presented themselves at the Manhattan

Municipal Building for a marriage license, the deputy city clerk, ruffled by the sight of Daisy in her matching black velvet dress, refused the application. Clerk Hines's reasoning was "rather vague," the *New York Times* reported, citing "moral grounds."

That was not good enough for Violet. Hadn't Eng and Chang Bunker married, she demanded, and Josefa and Rosa Blažek? (She was right about the Bunkers and wrong about the Blažeks.) Daisy piped up with the news that she was engaged, too—to Harry Mason, the English welterweight boxer—though she wasn't applying for a marriage license just yet. Clerk Hines didn't have an answer to any of that. He referred the matter to his boss. "The whole thing shattered the aplomb of Chief City Clerk Julius Brosen, usually iron nerved about marriage matters," the *Charlotte News* reported, "and he threw up his hands in despair after listening to plural answers to singular questions."

Violet protested again, "not in the least dismayed" by the stares she and Daisy were drawing. Clerk Brosen turned to Mr. Tarbox at the Corporation Counsel's office, who wrote across the form, *"Application is denied on the ground that bride is a Siamese twin."* When Violet's attorney started making a stink, Tarbox turned to *his* boss, William C. Chanler.

Mr. Chanler stood firm. The city clerk "was vested with discretionary powers," which allowed him to turn down applicants he deemed unfit to marry due to insanity or illness. Though Chanler had to admit that no specific regulation denied conjoined twins the right to marry, he proclaimed, "The very idea of such a marriage is immoral and indecent." Wouldn't a man who married a Siamese twin have two wives? Wouldn't that be bigamy?

With Daisy in tow, Violet and Maurice marched out of the Manhattan city hall and caught a train to Newark to try again there. "Nothing doing," said the New Jersey clerk. "Moral reasons."

Violet and Maurice's predicament leapt into headlines literally overnight—the very next day, the trio filmed a newsreel for Fox Movietone News. "I don't see any reason in the world why we should be denied the privilege of being happy," Violet asserted while Maurice sat on her right, his face stock-still and his eyes darting self-consciously to and from the camera. "My sister Daisy feels the same way. Her only wish is that I will be always happy." Then in a careful, measured tone, Maurice recited their plan to petition the courts of New York for the right to marry. "I think my sister's marriage will be a very wonderful thing," Daisy chimed in as Violet grinned her broadest grin, "because I am very sure they love each other."

Newspapers erupted in lively controversy. "Are Twins People, or a Person?" the *Jersey Journal* asked. If the Hiltons could travel on trains and planes for a single fare but required two steamship tickets, how many marriage licenses did they need? And how many grooms? One city hall official was allegedly willing to grant a pair of licenses to Violet and Daisy for a dual wedding but refused to allow them to marry singly.

"It's a shame, unjust, cruel," Violet lamented. "I am a normal human woman with a woman's feelings and a woman's desire of fulfillment. I am in love with my fiancé and the natural culmination is marriage."

"Won't it be a little embarrassing?" a reporter from the *New York Daily Mirror* asked. Violet and Daisy both gaped at her.

"Why should it?" they asked in unison.

Maurice sounded downright jolly when asked the same question. "Good Lord, why! I've known them always like this. I'd not feel the same any other way." As a matter of fact, he said, "I wish I were twins so I could marry both of them."

In less than ten days' time, the story mushroomed to outlandish proportions. The *New York Times* reported a dubious claim that Violet and Maurice had applied for marriage licenses in "more than twenty states," and suddenly, it became as good as fact—no matter that the other nineteen states were never named. *Time* magazine ran an article on the conundrum, referring to "Violet-&-Daisy Hilton" as "a double-monster joined at the buttocks."

Ten years before, the Hiltons had introduced themselves to the cities on their itinerary by presenting themselves at police stations for fingerprinting. Now they visited city halls instead, trailed by a phalanx of reporters and photographers, their conversation muffled by the "recurrent booms of a dozen flashlight cameras."

The avalanche of publicity revived Violet and Daisy's career like a magical elixir. By the end of July, an audience of one thousand attended the newly rechristened Hilton Sisters Revue in Owensboro, Kentucky. "Owensboro is the only city in Kentucky which has been booked for an appearance of the Hilton Sisters," the *Messenger-Inquirer* bragged. By October the band was bigger, the show longer. In addition to comedy and acrobatics, there was a trick piano duo, a "goofus dance," and a man who billed himself as "Chief Eagle Feather, full blooded Cherokee." One of the new cast members was none other than Jim Moore, the Texas boy who'd gazed so wonderingly at Violet and Daisy during the San Jacinto Fiesta in 1917. He'd persevered and become a dancer, just as he'd always dreamed. When the Hiltons ran into him at a San Antonio dancing school owned by old vaudeville acquaintances, they hired him and his partner, Anita. For Jim, it was a stroke of luck worthy of a fairy tale.

All too soon, the story of Violet and Maurice's quest for a marriage license began to smell of a hoax. If the couple were truly in love, truly desperate to be married, their actions did not prove it. A photograph of the Hiltons and Maurice with a marriage license clerk in Chicago, captured mid-chuckle, flatly contradicted the previous stories' tone of disappointment and unfairness. Crown Point, Indiana, a city renowned as "one of the nation's most sensational marriage marts" for its willingness to marry couples denied licenses in Chicago, issued Violet and Maurice a public invitation, which they evaded. Similar invitations from North Carolina, South Carolina, Maryland, and Arkansas also went unheeded. Violet's lawyer had allegedly "vetoed" the other states, demanding that a precedent had to be set in New York. "We're going to have a showdown on the matter," he proclaimed. "Our pride makes us insist on being married here," Violet agreed in the *New York Daily Mirror.* "We resent the suggestion of immorality. The marriage is natural and normal and we are going through with it."

The newspapers were not convinced. In Indiana, the *Hammond Times* was confident that the Hiltons' press agent would send them everywhere *but* Crown Point. And was it possibly a coincidence that a full-page advertisement for the Hilton sisters' act had appeared on page two of *Billboard* within days of Violet and Maurice's being turned away by city clerks in both Manhattan and Newark? "Write! Wire! Phone! For Open Dates," the ad urged.

To entertainment insiders, Violet and Maurice's dilemma had all the appearances of one of the most brilliant publicity stunts in recent memory. "Weep for These Poor Girls!" implored a tongue-in-cheek headline in the very same issue of *Billboard* as their full-page ad. "Tears are dropping from Midway Bill's eyes as he pens these words— not on account of the wrecking of their love life, but because of the publicity the Associated Press has given to three broken hearts." The writer could barely contain his envy and admiration. "Shades of Myer-Myer . . . who made the twins a worthwhile theater attraction, come before me, and when I read of the terrible love catastrophe (?) that has befallen these petted and pampered beauties of the carnival side show I am inclined to shed more tears!"

William Rice, the Great Wortham Shows press agent who had discovered the Hiltons in San Francisco in 1916, sent Violet a telegram urging her to let him arrange a public wedding for her and Maurice in Hawaii, "if you are really getting married." Putting on such a spectacle could earn them upwards of $3,000, Rice promised. According to Rice, Violet and Daisy promptly wired back: "This is a real marriage. We are booked solid for two years. Mind your own business."

"I doubt both statements," Rice wrote in a *Billboard* gossip column the following week, "and I will mind my own business from now on."

Perhaps Violet and Maurice's predicament had been authentic to start with. If so, the problem had become much too lucrative to solve. It didn't matter whether the papers believed they were in love, so long as people kept buying tickets to the show. "With the reams of newspaper publicity reaped by the pair, it should be an easy sell," *Variety* concluded. It was. The Hilton Sisters Revue coasted on Violet's notoriety until it ran down to fumes.

· · ·

By early 1936, enthusiasm had cooled. "The 40-minute show built around them is sad," said the very same *Variety* critic who had praised the revue in 1934.

They were taking in $135 a day—close to $2,500 in today's currency—while the rest of the nation was only beginning to scrabble its way up out of the Great Depression. And yet once again Violet and Daisy could not make ends meet. The Hilton Sisters Revue employed a full orchestra, a manager, an advance man, dancers, comedians, acrobats, an emcee, and a so-called Indian chief. All of them had to be paid, all of them needed hotel rooms, and all of them had to eat. The band's bus needed gasoline, and newspapers would not print the show's advertisements for free. With a Dallas woman on the verge of suing them for $65.08 in unpaid rent and telegram charges, the situation was looking as dire as it had been two summers earlier. When the band's bus rolled into a ditch outside Platteville, Wisconsin, in June, injuring several musicians, the Hiltons found themselves at an all-new low.

The act needed a fresh tonic. Reinventing the performance itself or cutting down on expenses would have been the sensible thing to do. Instead, the Hiltons hit back with the biggest publicity stunt of all.

CHAPTER 23

THE SCHEME WAS TERRY TURNER'S IDEA—THE VERY SAME Terry Turner who had turned Violet and Daisy Hilton into the sensation of vaudeville in 1925. How exactly the Hilton sisters' path happened to cross with their onetime vaudeville coach remains unknown, however.

Only one story could top Violet's being refused a marriage license in twenty-one states—a wedding. And not just any wedding. Turner cooked up a public ceremony on the fifty-yard line of the Dallas Cotton Bowl stadium, right in the middle of the Texas Centennial celebration— at twenty-five cents a head. Afterward, the Hilton sisters would present "a complete stage show" for the crowd, backed by the Dale Stevens Orchestra and topped off with music and dancing for one and all.

"If I can get a license, will you go through with the ceremony?" Turner asked.

"I'll be the goat, if you can manage," Violet volunteered. All they needed was a groom. Maurice Lambert was out of the picture. That romance, like others before it, had silently extinguished itself. Dancer Jim Moore was just the man for the job, Turner decided. Tall and debonair with a trim mustache, he'd suit the part perfectly in photographs. "He'll mean more publicity for the act," Turner said. "Are you game, Jim?"

According to Violet, "Jim smiled good-naturedly and shrugged his willingness."

That was not how Jim Moore remembered things at all. He "bucked" at the idea at first, but eventually agreed to participate under a fictitious name—after Turner had threatened him with the cancellation of a contract, which would have left him $850 in debt. When he arrived in Dallas and saw *Jim Moore* plastered all over the billboards, he was almost sick with a mortification so intense, he struggled to adequately describe it forty years later. "Well, my family, of course, were absolutely . . . my daddy disowned me; he just told momma, you see: 'just . . . don't even write to the boy.' They still called me a boy. I was twenty-six." It could have been an opportunity to advance his career, to have his face recognized in every state in the union. That wasn't who Jim Moore was, though. "If I was smart, I would capitalize on it," he said, "but I was too embarrassed."

Meanwhile, Violet feigned dismay at all the publicity, playing the role of the blushing bride. "No, we didn't want public attention drawn to this," she would say afterward, "but how could we get out of it? If we had been secretly married, pretty soon there would have been unpleasant stories of too much intimacy, and we would have had to tell. We thought we might as well have it over in one big explosion."

It was nothing short of an explosion. Daisy wrote a series of four articles that appeared in papers across the country in the week leading up to the July 18 wedding date, and another full-page illustrated feature in *American Weekly* soon followed. A few weeks earlier, the public had been too apathetic about the Hilton Sisters Revue to buy tickets to their show. Now Violet and Daisy had millions of readers eating out of the palms of their hands as Daisy described the ins and outs of her sister's unique romance.

"I think every girl has to get married to be really happy, anyhow," Daisy wrote. "It makes her life complete."

Were these her true feelings about marriage? Given that the article was written as publicity for a sham wedding, it's risky to take these words at face value. Years earlier, Violet and Daisy had solemnly professed that marriage was not for them, but that had been in an equally dubious source—Myer Myers's propaganda-filled souvenir booklet. Judging by their actions rather than their words, it's tempting to conclude that to the Hilton sisters, marriage was simply a tool to increase their celebrity.

. . .

Daisy's articles toyed with the public's fascination, heading off every salacious dilemma the newlyweds were likely to face, and providing a prim and proper answer. At the root of it all was a single question: How could anyone enjoy romance without privacy?

For the Hiltons, it was second nature. Though the engagement between Violet and Jim was a fraud, the sisters' ability to create individual bubbles of privacy around themselves was perfectly authentic.

Since childhood they had honed the knack of dismissing each other by retreating to the private spaces within their own minds. "We had learned how not to know what the other was doing unless it was our business to know it," Violet said. It worked both ways. When Daisy wanted to share an intimate moment with a beau, she could trust Violet to simply tune herself out. And they did have beaus— boyfriends the press never heard about—whom they were perfectly comfortable canoodling with.

Their friend Lucille Stotzer recalled, "Daisy would have a date, for example, and Violet would sit there and read a book. She never knew what was going on. They had trained themselves that way."

Violet and Daisy were so adept at it, the two of them told reporters, that Daisy had not even realized when Jim proposed to her twin. "I was right in the middle of a good short story when Vi nudged me a couple of times and asked me to put the magazine down because she and Jimmy wanted to tell me something," Daisy said. "I had not heard a word they were saying."

Everyday married life would be no different. During "private discussion of matters of interest only to husband and wife," Daisy went on, she would be as uninvolved "as if I had gone out and shut the door." Daisy even dared to hint at how a three-person honeymoon would work. "When Jimmy kisses me goodnight . . . it will be good-bye, too, until time to get up, unless the hotel catches fire or for some reason they want my spiritual as well as my physical presence."

"That's the real truth," Violet chimed in, "although I know most people won't believe it. She won't bother us any more than a nice kitty sleeping on the other pillow."

"I have known the girls two years," Jim added, "long enough to know that what they say about presence of body and absence of mind is absolutely true. Daisy doesn't embarrass me at all, and what's more, I hope she finds the right man soon to make her as happy as Vi and I are."

The notion left the public's imagination reeling. Could anyone be so fully oblivious to what was going on right beside them—neither notice it nor remember it? Perhaps for Violet and Daisy it was more a matter of schooling themselves not to react in the moment, and never to remark afterward on what they'd witnessed, an unorthodox type of privacy forged out of necessity and mutual agreement. Or perhaps we underestimate how much the human mind is capable of.

Regardless of how they achieved their unique type of solitude, Violet and Daisy knew the public would never understand or believe it. The thought of so much as cuddling with a beau while a third person sat inches away was enough to make anyone else squirm. And so the Hiltons began telling newspaper reporters that they'd learned their mental escape trick from none other than Harry Houdini.

It was a brilliant concoction. Houdini could escape any lock, could even make an elephant disappear. If anyone could teach two young woman how to mentally vanish from each other's consciousness, it was Houdini. Though Violet and Daisy never actually claimed that their ability to absent themselves at will was magic, invoking the name of the greatest magician the world had ever known certainly implied that it was. And paradoxically, the idea that magic was involved made the whole thing sound plausible.

The way Daisy told the story in her newspaper columns leading up to Violet's wedding, it sounded as if she and Violet had been the darlings of the American stage since earliest childhood—a childhood in which Houdini became a surrogate father, whispering advice and encouragement from theater wings on everything from reading to spiritualism. "Houdini wanted to make us self-reliant," Daisy said, "to save us from the people who were exploiting us."

In fact, their vaudeville careers coincided for just nineteen months, between the Hiltons' stage debut in March 1925 and Houdini's death on Halloween the following year. If Violet and Daisy ever appeared in the same theater as the great magician, the evidence has yet to be uncovered. The possibility is a long shot at best. Houdini was traveling the Keith-Albee circuit in 1925, while the Hiltons had signed with Loew's. They did, however, perform in neighboring theaters in Cleveland for a week in March 1925.

Perhaps Houdini managed to attend one of their performances, or presented himself at their dressing room door. (The odds that Myer Myers permitted Violet and Daisy to attend Houdini's show, where they would have been seen by thousands of other spectators, are infinitesimal.) If such a meeting took place, it occurred under utmost secrecy, for there are no newspaper photos or articles to document it. The utter silence of the newspapers strongly suggests that the three never met, for how could Myer Myers have resisted the chance to print a photograph of Violet and Daisy with the greatest magician of all time in every newspaper in the nation?

Could Houdini possibly have snuck in to meet the Hiltons without the Myerses' notice? He was the master of escape, after all. But even a magician as formidable as Harry Houdini would have been hard-pressed to teach Violet and Daisy a mental vanishing trick within the space of the fleeting encounters that happen at stage doors and in dressing rooms. The Hiltons' ability was far more likely the result of a lifetime of practice, rather than any kind of backstage hocus-pocus.

. . .

Long after it was over, Violet would boast that 100,000 people had attended her wedding, but in fact the crowd in the Cotton Bowl on July 18, 1936, was underwhelming—between 4,200 and 5,000 people paid a quarter apiece to watch the spectacle, in a stadium that seated over 45,000.

Violet wore a white satin gown without a train and carried a bouquet of white rosebuds. Daisy flanked her in a dark dress of flowered chiffon and a wide-brimmed black hat that partially obscured her face from the cameras. It was the first time anyone could remember seeing the Hilton sisters dressed differently from each other in public. Violet mounted the rostrum on the arm of Mrs. Henry May, the minister's wife, while Jim waited beside Reverend May with his best man, an administrator for the Centennial Exposition who'd been recruited by Terry Turner to fill the role.

Jim could not entirely hide his qualms over the whole thing. His pinched expression betrayed a perceptible sense of unease, "but that does not mean anything," the San Francisco Examiner assured its readers, "because most bridegrooms manage to look as unhappy as a dog being washed."

The kiss was tinged with comedy, for Jim towered more than twelve inches above his petite bride. Daisy "convulsed with mirth" beside them.

As the kiss ended, the band launched into a swing number and the announcer's voice boomed, "Come on down and congratulate the bride!" Spectators swarmed the newlyweds. Jim and Violet shook hundreds of hands, then joined the throng of dancing. Daisy "glided along behind" without a partner, the *Des Moines Register* marveled.

"It's swell," a relieved Jim told the *San Antonio Light* after he'd pronounced his vows. "All this excitement about getting married has me a little bewildered though. I'm glad we only had to go through with it once."

"I've been in love with Jimmy since I met him two years ago at San Antonio," Violet gushed to another reporter. "You know we tried in several Eastern states to arrange a wedding but strict state laws calling for the establishment of a residence stopped us." It was an audacious thing to say. Either the newspapers botched the story badly, or Violet had the gumption to believe she could fool the public into forgetting that her marriage license woes had occurred with an entirely different fiancé, for entirely different reasons.

Even with the details blurring beyond recognition, everyone in the nation seemed willing to play along. "Because the twins endured so much tragedy, I don't think there was anybody in America who didn't want them to find great happiness," said their friend Camille Rosengren. Violet and Jim's over-the-top show-biz marriage, she reflected, "was one of those loopy, feel-good stories in which an entire nation could take a little giddy joy."

"A crowd pursued us to the very door of our wedding suite," the Hiltons remembered. Terry Turner; Jim's dance partner, Anita; and other members of the revue waited there to toast the grand hoax over supper and laughs.

The three of them—Violet, Daisy, and Jim—continued to play their parts to the hilt. They even posed for a rather suggestive photo for *American Weekly*, showing Violet and Daisy in slinky flowered bathrobes and disheveled hair, seated on a couch next to Jim, who wears a jacket and tie. Daisy blithely reads a newspaper, held to block her view of her sister as Violet and Jim sit cheek to cheek, sharing cold drinks and a cigarette.

Years afterward, the Hiltons declared that the stunt had paid off just the way Terry Turner had promised. "We went to Hollywood and made several films," they bragged of the aftermath.

Nothing of the sort happened.

. . .

Less than two months passed before word leaked that Violet and Jim's marriage was on shaky ground. An "unimpeachable source" had told the *San Antonio Express* that the bride and groom were maintaining separate residences during their nightclub bookings in New Orleans. On September 9, Mr. and Mrs. Jim Moore petitioned the court in New Orleans for an annulment, declaring that they had never lived together as husband and wife. The wedding, the two confessed, had been "forced on them by booking agents."

"Jimmy and I are the very, very best of friends," Violet assured newsreel cameras. "He sure is a swell guy."

"I think the world of the girls, and they still think the same of me," Jim agreed in a separate film interview. Though the three would indeed remain close, their days of performing and traveling together were already at an end.

The judge, however, seemed skeptical and requested further testimony from additional witnesses. The case was put off until October, and the papers reported no further on the matter. Perhaps the media had begun to weary of the Hiltons' matrimonial antics. It is also possible that the annulment was never granted. Violet later claimed she and Jim had "never gone through the formalities of a divorce," and she would continue to refer to herself as a married woman for several years. It certainly made for enticing advertisements: "Two Lovely

Girls! One Husband! Yet it's Not Bigamy!" read a 1940 theater ad. And after all, when had Violet and Daisy let the truth get in the way of good publicity?

But the fraud, and the coolly casual way the Hiltons admitted to it, had finally tarnished beyond repair the pristine image Mary Hilton had cultivated since Violet and Daisy were three weeks old. "Maybe the poor little Siamese twins weren't so sweet and pure after all," Camille Rosengren said of the public's reaction. "What everybody thought was a real life fairytale turned out to be a sick joke. People felt disappointed by them, if not betrayed." There came no public outcry, no huffy denunciations in the press. People simply quit caring.

The disillusionment affected more than just audiences. "Vi and Daisy put their careers at risk by agreeing to that phony-baloney wedding in the Cotton Bowl," fellow nightclub performer Rose Fernandez agreed. "Even the twins' most loyal supporters felt deceived by them. And just like that, a lot of the powers in the entertainment field—the agents, the bookers, the managers of theaters and clubs— saw them as damaged goods."

For the first time in their lives, the Hiltons found themselves confronted with the lies they'd been telling for years. In Minneapolis that October, a *Tribune* reporter cornered them at the depot, demanding to know if they were the same twins who'd just gotten married in Texas "after all that fuss and fume" over not getting a license in twenty-some states.

Violet and Daisy were visibly tired from an uncomfortable train trip and irked to find no one waiting at the depot to see them to their hotel. No one had even booked them a room, in fact, or informed them which club had scheduled them to perform.

"Don't reporters ever read their own newspapers?" an irate Violet barked back at him.

"And I wouldn't blame them if they didn't," Daisy retorted.

Unwilling to leave well enough alone, the *Tribune* man asked how the marriage had worked out. "It didn't," Violet said. "It was a publicity gag."

The reporter boldly prodded further yet, wondering if they'd ever lived with Violet's husband.

"No," Violet snapped.

"And it's nobody's business but our own if we had," Daisy said, cutting off the conversation as "they turned their joint backs."

Hostility of this sort was so alien and bewildering to them, the Hilton sisters even tried hiding behind dark glasses when they went out, to avoid similar encounters. "They were joined together physically, for Betsy's sake," Rose Fernandez scoffed. "Did they really think that dark glasses were going to hide who they were?"

CHAPTER 24

THE HILTON SISTERS OUGHT TO HAVE THANKED THEIR LUCKY
stars that the press and the public had turned its back on them, for in
the midst of the Cotton Bowl hoopla, a much bigger crisis had been
secretly brewing.

Daisy was pregnant.

Millions of people had gaped at the newspaper photos of Violet's
wedding without realizing that a more explosive story was staring
right back at them—the maid of honor was due to become a mother
within four or five months.

The identity of her baby's father, once known to a select few, has
by now been lost to history. According to Jim Moore, both of the
sisters had boyfriends in their orchestra, and the father of Daisy's
child was one of those fourteen musicians. Neither Jim nor Daisy
ever divulged the man's name. Only once did Daisy give a clue as to
his identity. "Well, maybe there is someone in our band I do like,"
she'd said in 1934, ". . . yes, a lot . . . but there will be no question of
marriage, for anyway, a very long time."

That old show business adage "There's no such thing as bad
publicity" would not apply in this situation. Twenty-eight years had
passed since Kate Skinner had faced the same dilemma, but attitudes
had scarcely budged. Unwed mothers were still the stuff of scandal,

and after the furor over Violet's sham marriage, an illegitimate birth could very well cost the Hiltons their career.

Daisy's solution was to seek an abortion. "They wanted to have it done right . . . and have it done clinically and in a sanitary place," Jim Moore remembered. That meant doing the thing they hated most in the world. For the first time in their lives, Violet and Daisy voluntarily walked into a doctor's office. "That's the only time that the girls ever consented to go and see a doctor all the time I knew them," Jim Moore said.

The doctor examined and measured. "This young lady is perfectly capable of having normal child birth," he concluded, and refused to perform the procedure. Giving birth was not a risk to Daisy's health, but undergoing an abortion without medical supervision most certainly would have been. Her only remaining option was to deliver the baby and give it up for adoption.

Whether Daisy would have chosen to keep her baby under different circumstances is impossible to say. Five years before, in the midst of their emancipation trial, the Hiltons had confided to the *San Antonio Express* their dream of creating a little family for themselves. But what they had wanted then was a child old enough to attend a fine boarding school while the sisters traveled the vaudeville circuit. Only during the periods between tours would they be together as a family. Nowhere could this cozy fantasy accommodate a newborn baby. By 1934, Daisy had changed her tune completely. "I don't want children," she told the *New York Daily Mirror* point-blank. Many years later, Daisy elaborated for a Canadian reporter, "We could have children, too, the doctors told us, but frankly we do not care for that. Wouldn't fit in with our way of life; wouldn't be fair to the children, either."

Violet and Daisy continued touring and performing throughout Daisy's pregnancy. How they managed to hide her condition from their audiences is a mystery. By September, Jim Moore recalled, it was "quite noticeable, almost." Perhaps the Hiltons' audiences simply refused to believe their eyes. It was hard enough to fathom a conjoined twin's marriage; motherhood stretched the limits of credulity further than most people's minds could follow. "As Daisy got bigger and bigger, she just had to buy bigger size dresses," Jim said.

The Hilton sisters' schedule did not waver that autumn. From early October to the second week of November, Minneapolis newspapers advertised Violet and Daisy's appearances in theaters and nightclubs. And then, after November 9, the headlines and ads dried up. Sixteen days later, the Hiltons reappeared in Winnipeg, Canada.

Sometime during that two-week gap, Daisy Hilton's son may have been born. This apparent lapse in their performance schedule aligns with Jim Moore's suspicion that Daisy gave birth in Minnesota near the end of 1936.

By coincidence, Jim had been booked to perform in Minneapolis in late autumn as well. When he called Violet and Daisy's booking agent to try to get in touch, he found himself stonewalled. "She treated me as if I were the big bad wolf," he said. "And she would give me no information. She would not tell me where the girls were. They may have been there in Minneapolis at that time. I don't know."

There is also a chance that Jim Moore's recollections muddled the year, and that Daisy's child was actually born in Wisconsin in late November or early December 1940. That Thanksgiving week, the Hiltons were performing a series of one-night stands in and around Minneapolis. On November 29, the *La Crosse Tribune* announced that Daisy had been taken ill in Tomah, Wisconsin, 170 miles southwest of Minneapolis, and was confined to her hotel. All of the Hilton sisters' bookings for the next two weeks were canceled. "Her illness was at first believed to be appendicitis, but later her physician said it was definitely not that," the *Tribune* reported. The actual cause of Daisy's malady was never revealed, but the Associated Press ran a photograph of the two sisters in bed with their lapdog while Daisy recovered.

Whenever and wherever he was born, the baby boy's adoption,

like the majority of closed adoptions at that time, remains shrouded in secrecy. Daisy never saw her son again.

. . .

With the Cotton Bowl fiasco and the ordeal of Daisy's pregnancy behind them, Violet and Daisy fixed their gaze firmly ahead. "We had to turn our thoughts again from emotion and think of the only thing we ever really were masters of—work," they wrote. "We had lived a variety of lives, virtually as prisoners and as rich playgirls. . . . We had known freedom, had celebrated it, and then had failed to enjoy it. Work alone had never failed us. And it isn't strange that we again longed to return to it."

But the stage, which had always been the central axis in their lives, could no longer provide the stability it once had. Their act was down to seven minutes now—one song, followed by a series of "impertinent questions about Violet's marriage" that shifted the tenor of their performance away from the dewy-faced innocence that had delighted fans from one hemisphere to the other for almost three decades. "The Hilton Sisters grow older, it is apparent," *Billboard* had noted in a 1937 review, "and when they are not smiling at the audience their faces reveal a look of unhappiness, which isn't exactly entertaining." Their expressions were of little consequence. People were growing impatient with the singing and dancing anyway, *Variety* noticed. They were "dying to know" the juicy details of Violet's and Daisy's personal lives, and rather than listen to the Hiltons harmonize with their accordion-playing emcee, the audience would have preferred to pelt the sisters with the "intimate questions" the advertisements promised they'd answer from the stage.

Just as it had in the winter of 1933–1934, publicity quietly dwindled as the 1930s faded into the 1940s. A six-month tour of Canada in 1937 had brought steady work, yet removed them further and further from Americans' consciousness. Returning to the United States, they had skirted the West Coast with two more sets of twins in a show called the Seeing Double Revue until the end of that year. No one east of the Cellar lounge in Los Angeles's Ambassador Hotel had heard a peep about the Hilton sisters for most of 1938.

Two years of near silence followed. It seemed the Hiltons had drifted entirely from the spotlight. "Freak Acts," according to *Billboard*, were "Not So Hot" anymore. The chief booker for Loew's, the same vaudeville chain that had hired the San Antonio Siamese Twins in 1925, now complained that freaks "usually get the theater publicity, but they don't draw crowds."

Consequently, Violet's and Daisy's names were more likely to pop up in "Ten Years Ago Today . . ." columns than in the news itself. One account has them entertaining aboard the Cunard liner RMS *Berengaria* for several months during the lull, reveling in luxury as the ship ferried its wealthy passengers back and forth across the Atlantic. The *Berengaria*, however, caught fire in New York Harbor in March 1938 and was scrapped that autumn. Another version explained away their obscurity with a three-month tour of South America, though they had not been south of Mexico since 1935.

The less-than-glamorous truth was that Violet and Daisy's theater engagements from 1939 to 1941 were hardly worthy of notice. The Hiltons were trouping from town to town, performing one, two, or three nights at a time before moving on. A cocktail lounge in Reno, a circus in Massachusetts, a theater in British Columbia, a nightclub in South Carolina. Sometimes they performed in two towns in one night—a far cry from shipboard caviar breakfasts and tropical sojourns. Unbeknownst to most civilians, they spent July and August 1941 traveling with the United Service Organizations (USO) Mobile Unit F, entertaining servicemen at forts and training camps across the Great Lakes region.

And then, in September 1941, the Hilton sisters suddenly bubbled up from obscurity once again. There they were in the papers, in the embrace of a blond, baby-faced young man whose smile beamed out from between Violet's and Daisy's. In his hand, he clutched a sheaf of congratulatory telegrams.

Daisy had gotten married.

. . .

Her groom was the tap-dancing emcee of their act, Harold Estep, who called himself Buddy Sawyer on the stage. This would be the fifth time a marriage announcement had followed a career lull. Perhaps it was a coincidence, but by now it was looking much more like a predictable pattern. Though unnamed "friends who attended the wedding" said the marriage was the culmination of a six-year romance, Buddy's mother, Mrs. Florence Estep, told her local newspaper that "she had not been aware of her son's plans."

Violet had had immediate reservations. "I felt then that her marriage with Buddy would not be right," she wrote somewhat cryptically afterward. "I thought she had not weighed the idea well." Violet did not elaborate on her ambivalence toward the marriage, leaving the impression that the couple was somehow unsuited for each other. More likely Violet, always the more sensitive and cautious of the sisters, still felt the sting of the fallout from the 1936 Cotton Bowl debacle more acutely than Daisy and dreaded the public's reaction to yet another Hilton wedding.

Nevertheless, Violet had not tried to persuade her sister to change her mind. She said nothing. It was one of their cardinal rules: "We never consult or advise. We simply tell each other our wishes."

Daisy and Buddy were married at the city clerk's office in Buffalo on September 17, 1941. (The couple apparently had no trouble procuring a marriage license from the State of New York, as Violet and Maurice Lambert had half a dozen years earlier.) Newspaper coverage was halfhearted—a photo and a few sentences at most. Violet and Daisy, however, insisted they were relentlessly hounded by newspapermen for ten solid days. "Then," the sisters recalled, "one morning when we looked across at the twin bed where Buddy had been when we drowsed between the incessant phone calls from reporters, Buddy had disappeared."

He never returned.

"Daisy is a lovely girl," Buddy eventually told the press when he resurfaced. "But I guess I am not the type of fellow that should marry a Siamese twin. As a matter of fact, I am not even what you would call really gregarious. In the show business, there are times when you get tired of seeing anybody—let alone twin brides. As far as being a bridegroom under such conditions is concerned, I suppose I am what you might call a hermit."

But if the attention during their honeymoon had been so constant and unbearable, how is it possible that the news of Buddy's desertion did not break until over two years later, when Daisy formally sought a divorce in Pittsburgh in December 1943?

"The marriage was just totally and simply a publicity stunt," their agent Philip Morris admitted in 2014. It had always been the most reliable way to commandeer attention from the media. Morris also recalled the Hiltons asking a fellow performer if he was interested in becoming the most famous magician in the world. When the man asked how, the Hiltons replied, "Marry one of us."

Buddy, however, would insist half a century later that his affection for Daisy had been genuine. "Some people thought we got married only for the publicity," he said in a 1997 interview. "They were wrong. I loved Daisy very much. She loved me. Even when we parted, I thought that when the hysteria of the press died down, maybe we could get together again and have a life together after all. It just never happened. She went her way, I went mine. People get badly hurt by love sometimes."

CHAPTER 25

FOR BETTER OR WORSE, DAISY AND BUDDY'S MARRIAGE HAD no effect on the Hiltons' career prospects. Violet and Daisy were dumbfounded by the fact that theater owners weren't beating down their door for bookings. "They really could not understand why it was that they could no longer draw *thousands* of people into the theaters," agent Philip Morris later said.

By December 1941 the situation was dismal enough that they'd turned to performing in burlesque theaters, wearing scanty costumes as they danced and waved ostrich-feather fans and filmy scarves. Burlesque in the 1940s was not entirely unlike vaudeville. There were comedy acts, singing, and dancing, but the jokes were bawdier, the costumes far more risqué. What truly set burlesque apart was the apex of the show—the striptease. That was what sold tickets and filled seats.

Violet and Daisy were not the main attraction of the burlesque shows they performed in but one of the minor acts leading up to it. "I worked with them at a theater in Steubenville, Ohio," remembered dancer Carole Licata, who went by the stage name of Val Valentine. "Their dressing room was right next to mine. They did a nice little act. They played ukuleles and they did harmony, and they had perfect little Barbie Doll bodies." Burlesque required Violet and Daisy to expose those bodies in a way they had not done since the days when Mary Hilton would take them on her knee and pull up their skirts so the audience could gawk.

Since gaining their freedom, Violet and Daisy had made the choice to continue capitalizing on their identity, their unique status as conjoined twins. Never before had they exploited their bodies, however. Their ploy had always been to draw an audience's attention *away* from their physical connection, priding themselves on their ability to earn genuine applause for their music and dancing. Burlesque demanded precisely the opposite, and the contrast was stark.

Bud and CeCe Robinson, who'd performed in variety shows with the Hiltons years before and still exchanged occasional Christmas cards and letters with the sisters, decided on a whim to take in Violet and Daisy's burlesque performance during a visit to Louisville, Kentucky. "When we saw them onstage, it just broke our hearts," Bud recalled. "As they danced, they peeled off parts of their costumes. They did some bumping and grinding. As strip-tease performances go, their exhibition was pretty tame. Still, it tore us up watching them. They were lovely, vivacious girls. They had genuine talent as entertainers. Now they were reduced to this." Bud and CeCe had planned to knock on Violet and Daisy's dressing room door and surprise them with an invitation to dinner, but after seeing the show, they couldn't bring themselves to face their old friends. "We were embarrassed for them," Bud said, "and we knew that they, too, would have been terribly shamed at knowing we had been in the audience."

Yet it wasn't the baring of their flesh that embarrassed the Hiltons. "Actually, we hate doing something which demands no talent," Daisy told a reporter in Cincinnati. What really galled them was working alongside women who'd previously waited tables and served ice cream sodas.

Violet added, "We've made the big switch to this sort of dancing for two reasons—money and fun. Mostly for money."

And what did the audience think of their big switch from "the legitimate stage"?

"They still love us," Violet said. "Of course now that we're in clubs we run into drunks and hecklers, but we just ignore them. Our motto is always to be gracious under any circumstances."

. . .

The 1940s saw Violet and Daisy performing under a vast array of circumstances, from theaters and movie houses, to nightclubs and cocktail lounges, to VFW posts and fairgrounds. Some of their performances were advertised for "Adults only"; others welcomed children at a quarter apiece.

"It didn't matter to them if they were playing to an audience in a ritzy nightclub or to some farmers sitting in bleachers downwind from a fairground pig barn," said a trampoline performer who toured on a grandstand show with the Hiltons one summer. "They just seemed to genuinely enjoy putting on their show."

As World War II progressed, the sisters continued to donate their time to USO variety canteens, even allowing themselves to be simultaneously hypnotized for the amusement of a crowd of servicemen in Pittsburgh. "The Hilton Sisters, Siamese twins, blinked drowsily until their false eyelashes fell on their cheeks like unrolled awnings," the *Pittsburgh Post-Gazette* reported. Under the hypnotist's instructions, they ate lemons without puckering and didn't flinch when he held a lit match under their hands. It was perhaps the first time in history that conjoined twins had ever been hypnotized.

When they weren't thrilling soldiers with such antics, they were selling war bonds and donating blood to the Red Cross. Both Jim Moore and Buddy Sawyer had enlisted, lending the Hiltons additional motivation to contribute to the war effort on behalf of the men they had married. However dubious the marriages might have been, Violet's and Daisy's friendships with Moore and Sawyer were authentic.

For a time the Hiltons played repeated engagements at Club Casino in Pittsburgh, setting up residence in the Kirkwood Hotel. The next year, their act at Club Bali and other nightspots did "turnaway business" in Miami, thanks in large part to an illustrated six-part series of tell-all articles in *American Weekly* entitled "Private Life of the Siamese Twins."

The series resurrected every one of the stories that had garnered them the biggest headlines in the past: the emancipation trial, the Hiltons' dual engagements to Jack Lewis and Harry Mason, Violet and Maurice Lambert's thwarted pursuit of a marriage license, and the Cotton Bowl wedding. To this, they added the never-before-told tale of Don Galvan's proposal to Daisy. Readers devoured these juicy stories of the sisters' glamorous love lives, then came flocking to see them in Florida—so many that some had to be turned away at the door.

In spite of all evidence to the contrary, Violet and Daisy persisted in believing that the spike in nightclub attendance was due solely to their talent. Critics disagreed. "The famous Hilton Sisters have been around as headliners since before most of you could vote," noted the *Miami Herald*'s stage critic, "indicating that they must be worth seeing, at least once. As one who has seen them several times, I find them more pathetic than entertaining." Terry Turner, who had so painstakingly groomed them for the stage in the 1920s, later offered an equally blunt assessment. "People didn't care what the Hiltons did, they just wanted to see two people joined together."

But as far as Violet and Daisy could tell, their fame was back on the rise. Buoyed by their apparent popularity, they rented a little place of their own in Miami. There, the Hilton sisters posed by the kitchen sink and in the living room with two vacuum cleaners to show off their domestic skills for *Pix* magazine. Mostly, though, the road was their home. They played the Hirst circuit and toured with Trudy Russell's "Swing It Girls" Revue, filling in the gaps between tours with nightclub engagements that bounced them like pinballs from the southernmost tip of Florida to the southwest corner of Canada and back again.

It was as if they were everywhere and nowhere all at the same time. The sight of the sisters at a train station, hotel, or gas station could make local news in cities as big as Atlanta or as small as Melvin, Illinois, yet overall they remained curiously invisible to the public at large. "In case you care, Violet and Daisy Hilton, the 'original' Siamese Twins, have launched a theatrical comeback at a spot called Jimmy's in Miami," the *New York Daily News* reported in November 1945, apparently ignorant of the fact that "those old standbys of show business" had been working steadily, if not conspicuously, for years.

Glowing reviews had become a thing of the past. The Hilton sisters "try hard with their harmonies but fall flat vocally and with audience," *Variety* noted that December.

Burlesque kept Violet and Daisy afloat for another six months. Then, in 1946, they took a notion to try their hands at retirement. After more than thirty-five years in the public eye, they'd more than earned it. In fact, they'd been idly toying with the thought of what to do when they left the stage since at least 1940. The idea of running their own cocktail lounge held particular allure. They'd finally be able to put down roots, yet still keep a finger on the pulse of show business. Violet had her eye on a little spot in Ely, Nevada.

Their attempt to forsake the stage lasted a year at most. "Like monkeys in the zoo," they said in June 1947, "we got lonesome for people." That summer found them touring Midwestern state and county fairs. "That is what we call our vacation," the sisters told a reporter in Illinois, casually brushing aside any implication that such bookings were a significant step down. The newspaper noted that they were "middle-aged." In fact, Violet and Daisy were thirty-nine years old.

"I don't know why some people think we are feminine Methuselahs," Daisy griped when reporters persisted in overestimating their age. "Perhaps it's because we've been on the stage so long."

By the late 1940s, Violet and Daisy's stage was expanding and contracting with confounding irregularity. One summer, they returned to the Johnny J. Jones Exposition as the leading attraction in a "girl show," a type of all-female variety act that very likely featured a striptease, though whether the Hiltons did the stripping is unknown. Two years later, they appeared on the bill at New York's Palace Theatre, once the most coveted booking in all of vaudeville. In between, they took up residence for five months at Bob's Tourist Court in Highland, Indiana, a motorists' lodge thirty-five miles south of Chicago—"vacationing," they told a local reporter, because of the area's "diversified weather." It was a far cry from a tourist hot spot, nestled as it was between the steel mills of Hammond and Gary. Granted, the area's anonymity could have appealed to the Hiltons if they were craving some peace and quiet. Peace and quiet had never been Violet's and Daisy's style, though. Vacations rarely if ever crossed Daisy's mind, and Violet's idea of a thorough rest was two weeks at a mountain lodge with a big fireplace and plenty of people to talk to. And no more than two weeks. Violet was adamant about that. "I wouldn't like to go unless I knew it was only for so long," she said. All their lives, they'd felt more at ease on the stage than anywhere else. A five-month lapse in performances hints that bookings were becoming fewer and farther between than ever—a reality the Hiltons refused to admit, perhaps even to themselves.

CHAPTER 26

WHAT CAME NEXT WAS THE UNLIKELIEST OF LEAPS—FROM dwindling burlesque and nightclub gigs to the big screen. Violet and Daisy's latest agent, Ross Frisco, had concocted a story just for them, a story he was convinced could be turned into a Hollywood feature film.

At the outset, the premise looked like a rubber-stamped version of one of the most familiar episodes in Violet's and Daisy's lives. They were to play Vivian and Dorothy Hamilton, a pair of sisters with a vaudeville singing act. For the sake of publicity, Dorothy/Daisy agrees to stage a marriage ceremony with a vaudeville sharp-shooter named Andre. Here, Frisco's plot veered from reality. Seeing an opportunity to use Dorothy for her money during their feigned courtship, Andre woos her until she falls desperately in love—so desperately that the sisters consult a surgeon in hopes of separation for the sake of a "normal" marriage. When Andre deserts Dorothy the day after their wedding, Vivian/Violet shoots him during his act with one of his own revolvers. Vivian ends up on trial for murder, which leaves the court with the dilemma of how to punish the guilty twin without simultaneously violating the rights of her innocent sister.

It had to have been a tough sell to Violet and Daisy. For starters, the Hilton sisters were more than a little snobbish when it came to the film industry. "The stage had real talent, in their opinion," the *Lansing State Journal* had reported in 1942, "while the movies in a whole lot of instances depend on glamour boys and girls to get a picture over." Not only that, but this picture promised to be an exploitation film in every sense of the word—meant to shock and unsettle with its tawdry plot, while also capitalizing on the fascination with Violet and Daisy themselves.

Maybe flattery did the trick. A plot custom-made for them, based (however loosely) on their own lives, must have been at least a little enticing. Or maybe it was the prospect of artistic control, something the Hiltons found woefully lacking at their nightclub venues. That control came with a hefty price tag, however. In order to be in charge, Violet and Daisy would have to fund the entire production themselves.

That ought to have been a red flag. Throughout their vaudeville career, Camille Rosengren said, "they were used by guys who took their money." This must have seemed different. Ross Frisco wasn't exactly pocketing their money—not the way Myer Myers had. The choice to participate was entirely theirs.

Violet and Daisy took the bait. At age forty-two, they returned to Hollywood to film a picture with the dubious title *Chained for Life*.

. . .

Filming took place on a closed set, in hopes of building up intrigue. "I'm fascinated by *Chained for Life*," wrote Hedda Hopper, Hollywood's premier gossip columnist. "The title fits the story, for it features the Hilton Sisters, famous Siamese Twins. The set is chained, too. No visitors are allowed."

That was a blessing, for progress was anything but smooth initially. What had begun as a courtroom melodrama was morphing into a variety show as Violet and Daisy pushed to have musical

211

numbers and other acts included. Director Harry Fraser recalled, "I was assigned the picture after one or two directors had been fired, or had quit in disgust." The Hiltons found it impossible (or made it impossible, depending on who tells the story) to work with anyone who didn't understand vaudeville. Fraser was different. He'd been a headliner in Orpheum theaters the very same year Violet and Daisy had toured the Orpheum circuit, traveling just two weeks ahead of them. Fraser knew exactly how to handle a pair of former stars. "Once we got together for the film, I took the girls under my wing, and escorted them to a supper club for a night on the town. As a result, when we started shooting, the scenes rolled along smoothly, like water off a duck's back."

Fraser remembered the Hiltons as "cheery and happy" on the set, as pleased with their own work as they were with Fraser's. "We were able to be the puppets of the director, emoting exactly as he wished us to," they proudly told the *Lowell Sun*. Unbeknownst to the would-be stars, that was not a tall order. "It was not a production in which I took much pride," Fraser admitted in his memoirs.

The Hiltons, by contrast, were in raptures over the way the film was developing. "Their hopes for how the movie was going to turn out were higher than the moon," cast member Whitey Roberts recalled. It was a peculiar reaction on their part, considering how completely the script contradicted their own feelings about living as conjoined twins.

Chained for Life could have been an opportunity to show the public the reality of being conjoined. Instead, it fell back on the same old clichés and assumptions. Despite Dorothy/Daisy's proclamation that "we decided that our physical bond would never be our cross," the plot insisted on treating that bond as though it were a burden, an obstacle that left any sense of fulfillment dangling forever out of the sisters' combined reach.

The visual stunner of the film, a cleverly shot dream sequence with a body double enacting Dorothy/Daisy's fantasies of cavorting through a garden alongside her fiancé, had no basis in the Hiltons' reality. Regardless of whether they did entertain momentary fantasies of how it would feel to walk and dance alone, the very idea that Violet and Daisy would have contemplated surgical separation for the sake of marriage was ludicrous. Never in their lives had the Hilton sisters hinted at a desire to be separated for any reason. It was all a facade, telling movie audiences what they wanted and expected to hear—things like "The only way I can be happy is to be alone with a man I love" and "I'd rather be dead than go on like this."

Scattered among the melodrama were tiny glimmers of sentiments closer to the truth. "All our lives we've had to bury every normal emotion," Dorothy/Daisy says. "I'm not a machine; I'm a woman. I should have the right to live like one." The context of the scripted lines was vastly different, but the underlying reality remained true to life. Violet and Daisy had known since earliest childhood how it felt to hide their darkest feelings, as well as how it felt to be treated as living wind-up toys whose only purpose was to amuse others.

Other fragments of the script might have had nothing or everything to do with the way the Hiltons had come to view the world by the 1950s. "We've reached the top in show business," Vivian/Violet wistfully observes, "and there isn't a thing we can't have."

"Except happiness," Dorothy/Daisy returns. "We've fooled ourselves that by entertaining others, we were making ourselves happy." After forty years in show business, it could have been the tiredest of clichés, or the bitterest of realizations.

Be that as it may, filming galloped ahead at breakneck speed; within two weeks, *Chained for Life* was complete. Then an inexplicable nine months passed before its release. Director Harry Fraser remembered the movie getting "tied up in litigation shortly after its completion" but kept quiet about the reason why. Financial troubles? Difficulty with the censors? Given Violet and Daisy's history of financial instability, as well as the movie's lurid premise, it's purely a gamble to guess which possibility is the stronger.

There was also the matter of figuring out how and where to release *Chained for Life*. It was not the sort of movie that was going to get a red-carpet premiere on Hollywood Boulevard with searchlights and limousines. Not by a long shot. What prestigious theater would choose *Chained for Life* when it could have the latest offerings from box office magnets like John Wayne, Marilyn Monroe, Frank Sinatra, or Bette Davis? Besides, Fraser suspected that if the picture was widely released, "the exploitation would have capitalized on the twins' physical handicap in a way which might appear cruel and embarrassing."

The solution was to offer the movie to drive-in theaters, with the added bonus of a personal appearance by the Hilton sisters. Ross Frisco advertised *Chained for Life* in *Variety* as "a full length feature musical"—a laughable claim for a B-movie being released in the same year as one of Hollywood's all-time greatest musicals, *Singin' in the Rain*. Though Violet and Daisy did sing on-screen, the three romantic ditties they performed hardly transformed a dramatic potboiler into a musical extravaganza. In essence, Frisco was duping theater owners—who knew what would or would not appeal to their audiences—into booking the movie.

Consequently, box office returns were as unimpressive as the film itself. False advertising and lack of authenticity were not the movie's only flaws. *Chained for Life* was also hobbled by a no-name cast; a stilted script; and a preposterous, tissue-thin plot. "'Chained for Life' Chained to Dullness," complained the *Miami Herald*. "The story . . . is told ponderously, awkwardly and downright badly." Everyone but Violet and Daisy, the *Boston Traveler* said, "is being dreadfully pompous in trying to make a quite monstrous story acceptable to the censors." The director had done "probably the worst job on record," and the plot was "terrible," continued the paper's film critic, "matched in horror only by the vaudeville acts which the audience is forced to sit through."

Mercifully, *Chained for Life* lasts barely more than an hour. If not for the Hiltons' three musical numbers, as well as the juggler, the accordion player, the sharpshooter, and a bike-riding clown, it would have been shorter yet.

Violet and Daisy's in-person appearances did little to boost the movie's popularity. Outlandish advertising often set them up to disappoint their audience. "Never-before-told stories of their loves, romances, heartbreaks and yearnings, physical and spiritual, will be revealed by the girls in this dynamic stage interview," promised the *Cincinnati Enquirer*.

They sang, and they did answer questions. Only certain questions, though. The topic of their marriages, once the centerpiece of the act, was now firmly off-limits. "We don't discuss that," Daisy told a reporter in Ohio. "That's our private lives—something the nosey public isn't going to find out." It may well have been a matter of privacy, or it may have been a ploy to lure moviegoers into dishing out fifty cents for a signed copy of an autobiographical booklet entitled *Intimate Loves and Lives of the Hilton Sisters*.

"The Hilton sisters were well aware that their chained for life condition was the one merchandisable asset which they possessed," Harry Fraser claimed. "And like the good troupers they were, they made the most of it, with poise, dignity, and unfailing good humor."

Reporters never failed to come away with the impression that Violet and Daisy loved commanding center stage for the entire show, even if the "stage" was the roof of a concession stand. They "simply gushed" about the luxury of having these makeshift platforms all to themselves, the *Akron Beacon Journal* said.

Along with their enthusiasm, an unmistakable air of haughtiness had begun to color their conversations, the first perceptible sign, perhaps, that the Hiltons were beginning to weary of a life on the road, being perpetually in the public eye.

. . .

After three more years of trouping from one drive-in to another, Violet and Daisy began to realize they'd had their fill. Of everything. Show business just wasn't what it used to be—at least according to the Hiltons. Few had seen the view from a pinnacle as high as they had achieved, and from where they stood in 1955, the contrast was bleak.

"There's no courtesy, no art in the business today, it's just another job," Daisy said.

The venues were no better. Violet complained, "We can't have perfection in these gin mills. Nobody knows how to put shows on."

The time had come, Daisy said, "to get out of this crazy business."

For years, they had mused with reporters about opening a cocktail lounge in Nevada when they retired from the stage. That dream had metamorphosed during the intervening decade. The Hiltons would take one "last fling" at entertaining, the *Miami Herald* reported, and then in two years they'd retire to Florida and buy a motel. Both sisters looked forward to devoting time to their hobbies—Violet had a passion for collecting autographs and pocketbooks, and Daisy sought out rare perfumes.

Instead, just two months passed before the Hilton sisters made their break with the stage. They'd suddenly become joint proprietors not of a motel or a cocktail lounge but of a tiny restaurant on First Street in downtown Miami, just two blocks west of Bayfront Park. Called the Hilton Sister's [*sic*] Snack Bar, the "open-air snackery" featured a counter with half a dozen stools arrayed under an awning. Tourists strolling along the sidewalk could step right up to the counter and order hot dogs, hamburgers, and orange juice from Violet and Daisy Hilton themselves. The venture cost them a reported $4,500.

Publicity photos from the grand opening that summer of 1955 show Violet and Daisy decked out in full-length gowns with spaghetti straps tied halter-style behind their necks. Large earrings dangled from Violet's ears, and fancy combs glittered in Daisy's blond curls. "I don't think that I've ever had as bad a case of nerves onstage opening a production or doing pictures as I did serving a hamburger," Daisy confessed to a reporter as Violet smothered giggles beside her. "I actually had stage fright serving hamburgers! I was so scared I didn't know what to do."

"We intend to make Miami our home and hope eventually to buy a house here," Daisy added. For the first six months, business went well. The novelty of being served by conjoined twins no doubt compelled tourists to choose the Hiltons' hot dogs and hamburgers over the hundreds of similar meals Miami had to offer. In December, Violet and Daisy felt confident enough about the restaurant's prospects to send word to have their furniture removed from storage and shipped to Florida.

But by May 1956, the snack bar was permanently shuttered. The Hiltons, it turned out, had no better luck running a restaurant than keeping their show business act out of debt.

CHAPTER 27

IT WAS BACK TO THE "GIRLIE SHOW" CIRCUIT, THE DRIVE-IN theaters, and the state fairs. Violet and Daisy were almost fifty years old, competing for space onstage with women half their age, who had twice their stamina. As fiercely as they clung to their conviction that their talent set them apart from other performers, it simply wasn't true anymore. To the public, the Hilton sisters would always be Siamese twins first and foremost. The fact that they could sing and dance was only a convenient bonus—something that allowed the spectators to stare a little longer without feeling awkward. Though Violet and Daisy refused to acknowledge it, their act had become a freak show in disguise.

That same ferocious pride forced Violet and Daisy to make a razor-thin distinction between their state fair bookings and carnivals. At the fairs, they'd been up on the grandstand, where they'd fancied themselves so far above the sawdust of the midway that the indignities of carnival life could not reach them. By 1959, even that illusion had evaporated, with *Billboard*'s announcement in August that the Hilton Sisters Siamese Twin Revue would play the midway at the Wisconsin State Fair, "the first time on a fun zone in years." They needed the publicity, but how it must have burned to see *Billboard* pointing out their decline. Still, they insisted they were somehow different—better. "We don't talk to carnie people and they don't talk to us," Daisy informed a reporter.

Their snobbery was nothing but pretention. It wasn't as though *any* kind of people were knocking each other over for the chance to speak to Violet and Daisy Hilton anymore. In fact, the Hiltons' lives had to be on the line in order for the sisters to make headlines the way they used to.

. . .

"Siamese Twin Has an Operation—While Sister Sweats," the *Detroit Free Press* informed the nation on September 8, 1959. Daisy had fallen ill at the Michigan State Fair and landed in Detroit's Mt. Carmel Mercy Hospital.

Actually, she'd started to feel ill at the state fair in Milwaukee, ten days earlier. The exact nature of her symptoms is unknown, but Daisy's discomfort had been severe enough for Violet to break one of their lifelong rules and interfere with her sister's business. Violet had pressed Daisy to see a doctor. Daisy had refused.

"People in show business don't run to a doctor," Daisy told incredulous reporters afterward.

Daisy had held out for a week and a half, insisting on finishing their song-and-dance routine at the Michigan State Fair, before consenting to consult with Dr. James Fryfogle, a heart surgeon who'd been exhibiting his research at the fair. Dr. Fryfogle had diagnosed a hernia and ordered Daisy straight to the hospital.

A hernia occurs when an organ gets pushed or squeezed into an area where it doesn't belong—usually through a weak spot in the surrounding muscle. Most often it happens when some portion of the stomach or intestines bulges up into the chest cavity or down around the groin or navel. When shoved out of place through a small opening, the dislodged segment's blood supply can be strangled. If that tissue dies, or blocks the flow of digestion, a hernia can be fatal within a matter of hours.

Daisy needed surgery.

Violet and Daisy were fifty-one years old and had never been inside a hospital in their lives. They did their best not to show it, but they were terrified. For as long as they could remember, they had dreaded surgeons and their scalpels, and now Daisy's life depended upon them.

"I'm not the patient," Violet wisecracked as she and Daisy walked into the operating room. "My sister is the one who is ill. I don't know what I'm doing here."

They lay down on adjoining operating tables and Daisy received local anesthesia. Violet remained entirely unsedated during the two-hour operation. "We don't feel a thing," she managed to joke.

"It was a tense situation," assisting doctor Charles Polentz told the press afterward. "Violet didn't say it in so many words, but you could tell she was fearful for her sister and apprehensive at the same time about what would happen to herself." If anything went wrong, consequences could be just as dire for Violet as for Daisy.

"Naturally, I was worried," Violet said. "Whatever happens to Daisy happens to me." But everything went off without a hitch. The head surgeon, Dr. Paul Connolly, pronounced the surgery "successful in every way."

Violet and Daisy were just as satisfied with the treatment they received from the staff at Mt. Carmel. "They didn't act like we were a clinical experiment," Daisy told the *Detroit Free Press*. Coming from a woman who had not a single pleasant memory of a doctor's care and attention, that curt sentence was an unparalleled compliment.

The Hiltons would accept no sympathy from the press or anyone else over their unexpected setback. "This is not a sob story. We don't want anyone feeling sorry for us," Daisy commanded from a room at Detroit's Royal Palm Hotel, where she'd been confined for a two-week recovery period. The only thing the sisters were worried about, now that Daisy was on the mend, were the two pet dogs they'd had to leave behind when they'd been rushed from the fairgrounds to the operating room. Everything else was business as usual. "We've got our agent looking for a night club date for us, something we could do standing on our heads," Daisy said as she smoked and sipped coffee.

· · ·

But the Hiltons did not bounce back into the nightclub circuit as they'd expected. Frustrated and baffled by what they could only comprehend as their booking agent's ineptitude, Violet and Daisy switched to a new agency—Kemp-Morris and Associates of Charlotte, North Carolina.

Philip Morris recalled the day Violet Hilton rang his office. "Do you know who I am?" the voice on the other end of the line asked.

"Absolutely," Morris replied, no doubt instantly endearing himself to Violet. "You were the highest-paid act in vaudeville. You were the sensation of the show business world for many, many years."

"Well, my sister and I have decided to go back on the road, and we wondered if you would be kind enough to book our act." Morris agreed, promising to be in touch when he'd arranged some engagements.

A day or two later, a taxi driver knocked on Morris's door. At the driver's request, Morris accompanied the man down to the curb. "And there in the backseat of the cab," Morris remembered, "were the two Hilton sisters." Once out of the cab, they headed straight toward the office, as resolutely as if they'd scheduled an appointment with Morris weeks ago. "They were coming up the steps, like spiders—you know, four legs coming up the steps, but they were lovely girls."

"Well, we're ready to work," Violet and Daisy said.

Morris was flabbergasted. He'd told Violet on the phone it would take at least a couple of weeks to set up some performance dates. The task had proven more difficult than he'd anticipated. Morris had immediately sensed reluctance on the other end of the line when he'd spoken to theaters, prompting him to request trial dates rather than solid commitments. "We can put them in as an engagement and let's see how they do," he'd told the skeptical bookers. So far, no one had taken the bait. Audiences in the early 1960s were attuned to rock 'n' roll, the bookers insisted, not the sweet-voiced harmonies of the World War II era that had been the Hiltons' specialty for the last twenty years.

And now here were Violet and Daisy themselves, standing expectantly on his doorstep. Not only that—they needed Morris to pay their cab fare from the train station.

"It'd be better for you to go back home—"

"We do not have a home to go to," one of the sisters interrupted.

"Is there a theatrical hotel in town?" asked the other. "Do you think they would check us in on the cuff?" That phrase—*on the cuff*—confirmed Morris's suspicions that they were broke. The Hiltons were depending on a hotel to trust them to pay their bill when they began collecting salary from the performances he had not yet booked. Once, they'd raked in $3,850 a week, a salary that would add up to the present-day equivalent of $2.2 million in a single season. Now they had nothing. Their $100,000 court settlement was long gone, eaten up by the failures of the Double Rhythm Revue, the Hilton Sisters Revue, *Chained for Life,* and the Hilton Sister's [*sic*] Snack Bar. Whatever money Violet and Daisy had made from nightclub and state fair bookings had evidently never lasted long enough to save or invest.

"They were like a couple of scared, shaking and hungry little puppies," Morris remembered later.

The Hiltons were also a curious combination of jaded and naïve. They'd begun to sound like the hardened, fast-talking dames in the detective stories they still loved to read, yet dressed for their act in frothy lace dresses that Mary Hilton might have approved of—Violet in white and Daisy in orchid, with coordinating gloves and handbags.

It was as if, Morris said, they were trapped in a "time warp." When he asked how they intended to travel from town to town, the Hiltons replied that they'd take the train. Violet and Daisy had no idea that trains had ceased to be the primary means of travel in America; it would be almost impossible for Morris to book a route that did not rely at least in part on automobile.

Nevertheless, by the summer of 1960, Morris had managed to get the Hilton sisters back on the road again, touring drive-in theaters with *Chained for Life*. From Boston's Twin Drive In they hopscotched along the eastern seaboard to Lowell, Massachusetts; Saco, Maine; Washington, DC; Richmond and Newport News, Virginia; and Wilmington, Delaware. November saw them swing inland for bookings in the Carolinas at Greensboro, Greenville, and Charlotte.

In December, the newspaper advertisements for in-person appearances abruptly stopped at the Fox Drive-In in Charlotte, North Carolina.

The story of what happened next in the neighboring town of Monroe is always told in the vaguest of terms. "They said an agent brought them here and promised to come back for them," an acquaintance later recalled. Violet and Daisy had parted ways with the Kemp-Morris agency when the trickle of engagements Philip Morris had managed to book had run dry a few weeks before Christmas. "We tried to suggest that they start exploring ways to survive outside the entertainment world," Morris said. But the sisters could not imagine separating themselves from show business any more than they could imagine separation from each other. After all, they'd just been held over for an extra day at the Fox Drive-In. Didn't that mean people were as eager to see them as ever? "They still imagined themselves to be stars," Morris would say later. "I think they thought that somewhere out there, they still had a big adoring public, but that somehow this audience just happened to have gotten misplaced."

Unable to conceive of any other future for themselves, Violet and

Daisy took matters into their own hands and hired someone new to help handle their drive-in engagements. Agent, manager, chauffeur—whoever he was, this unnamed scoundrel checked the Hiltons into the Mary-Lynn Motel in Monroe before making off with their earnings, never to return. Violet and Daisy found themselves stranded and destitute, thirty miles southeast of Charlotte.

It was apparently not the first time. Letters found among their possessions after their death would indicate that "the sisters were constantly being duped by managers who claimed they couldn't find jobs for them. . . . They were always ending up in hotels without any money in a strange town, with the hotel manager growing more and more impatient."

Clegg Keziah, owner of the Mary-Lynn, leapt to the rescue, offering the Hiltons free lodging in the back corner room for as long as they needed it. Keziah also invited them to eat, free of charge, at his restaurant next door. It was a godsend. Keziah's son remembered Violet and Daisy as "very delightful" people, overwhelmed with gratitude for the safety net his father had so spontaneously unfurled beneath them.

Remarkably, Clegg Keziah's patience and hospitality extended not for days but for months. It is difficult to fathom how Violet and Daisy could have been left in the lurch for so long. Were there no friends they could turn to for a helping hand? Nowhere else they could go? Surely a man as generous as Clegg Keziah would have loaned them the cost of a telephone call, cab ride, or train ticket. If they were too proud to appeal to the Kemp-Morris agency once again, shouldn't someone, somewhere have noticed when they fell out of touch altogether? If any of these scenarios played out in Monroe, those facts have never come to light.

Just like that, the life they had known for over fifty years ended. Violet and Daisy Hilton never set foot on a stage again. "We laid their career to rest right here," Fox Drive-In manager W. F. Lemmonds recalled.

CHAPTER 28

DAY AFTER DAY, MORNING, NOON, AND NIGHT, VIOLET AND
Daisy walked from their room at the Mary-Lynn Motel to the Orange
Bowl restaurant. Every time, the customers at Marlene's Beauty Parlor plastered themselves to the window to watch the thrice-daily pro-
cession. "They looked so sad and lonely and bedraggled," said owner
Marlene McCauley, who was just sixteen at the time. "To this day, it
bothers me that I didn't do more to extend myself to those ladies. I
could have at least invited them into my shop for some hair styling.
I don't know why I didn't."

Eventually, a church in the area heard of the sisters' plight and
arranged for them to move to an unoccupied unit in Tanzy's Trailer
Park on Wilkinson Boulevard.

No matter how strongly Clegg Keziah and his wife, Helen, insisted that the Hiltons need not worry about settling their motel and
restaurant bills, Violet and Daisy wanted to pay their own way.

The Hiltons needed work.

Being conjoined did not make finding a job simple. The mere
sight of two identical women standing shoulder to shoulder and
hip to hip had the power to discombobulate prospective employers.
People looked at their joined bodies and assumed they wouldn't be
able to do all kinds of things. Contrary to first impressions, there

wasn't much the Hiltons couldn't do. The only task they were unable to share equally, Violet had once pointed out, was driving a car. The true obstacle was that, with the exception of their short foray into the restaurant business, Violet and Daisy had never held down a conventional job in their lives. All their training, all their skills, were oriented toward the stage.

An opportunity was closer than they realized. Only a mile or so down Wilkinson Boulevard from Tanzy's Trailer Park stood the flagship store of the local Park-N-Shop grocery chain. Its owner, Charles Reid, had made a name for his independent supermarkets by providing his customers with a combination of excellent service and playful sales gimmicks. Watermelons at half price—if you showed up in pajamas. Free breakfasts featuring North Carolina food products. Clowns and other entertainment for kids. Special appearances by TV characters, like Timmy from *Lassie.* Giving away a deed to a square foot of Alaskan territory with every $10 purchase. Violet and Daisy had done a gig there once, as a promotion for twin-pack potato chips. They'd stood with the display at the front of the store, gamely autographing joined-together boxes of chips for Reid's customers. "Now, that's a good sport," one of Park-N-Shop's customers marveled years afterward.

Something about Charles Reid and his store must have struck a chord with Violet and Daisy. With no money and nowhere else to turn, they showed up at Park-N-Shop and knocked on the office door.

"We want to see Mr. Reid," the Hiltons announced. "We want a job."

Oh my gosh, the receptionist thought. *These people can't work here.* Nevertheless, she showed the two women into her boss's office.

Reid's daughter, Linda Reid Beatty, remembered, "They sat down on one chair—kind of cuddled—and they said, 'Mr. Reid, we need a job. And you only have to pay one.'" Any job would do.

"They told me they could mop my floors and stock my shelves

and do just about anything I needed around the store, and I'd only have to pay for one of them," Mr. Reid himself recalled.

It's hard to say what aspect of Violet and Daisy's appearance troubled Charles Reid more. The fact that they were joined was one thing; their style was something else altogether. "They caused quite a stir," Linda Reid Beatty said.

Anyone could see that their hair was dyed, and not particularly skillfully. For years, Violet had favored an intense black, while Daisy prided herself on her bleached-blond curls. Now Daisy was fond of red, which had faded to brassy shades of orange. Bright red polish shone on their long finger- and toenails. Their makeup, ideal for combating the harsh lights of the stage, looked garish and overdone in ordinary daylight. Their fashion sense, too, was better suited for nightclubs and theaters than grocery shopping. Long accustomed to lush costumes adorned with ostrich feathers and sequins, Violet and Daisy seemed oblivious to the fact that their clothes not only were bolder and flashier but were also cut higher up the back and lower down the front than just about anyone else's in town. On top of all that, their outfits that day looked like they'd been slept in.

"Well, I gotta think about it," Mr. Reid answered. "Let me get back to you."

"And he prayed and prayed," remembered Reid's daughter. "He was a quiet man, a quiet Christian."

"Lord, I know you want me to do something with these people," Mr. Reid implored. *"What in the world would I do with them?"*

"I wanted to help them, but I wasn't quite sure what kind of job I could offer them," Mr. Reid said later. What kind of work could two people do simultaneously, all day long? He could hardly bring himself to imagine the two of them down on their hands and knees with buckets and scrub brushes. What would his customers think of such a sight?

Before long, an answer came to him: produce. In the 1960s,

checkout lanes did not have scales for weighing fruit and vegetables. That was done by an employee in the produce department, the way deli counters weigh, package, and price freshly sliced meats and cheeses today. Mr. Reid realized that if he positioned two counters in a V shape and equipped each side with a produce scale, Violet and Daisy could each work one scale, serving two lines of customers at the same time.

Charles Reid did for Violet and Daisy Hilton what everyone before him ought to have done—he made a simple adjustment to accommodate their unique needs. Everyone benefitted. Violet and Daisy landed the job they so desperately needed, and the Park-N-Shop customers received speedier service in the bargain.

There was one domain in which he insisted on conformity, however. "I told them their hair had to be the same color and that they would need to get rid of the long nails and their stage clothes—they couldn't wear them to work."

Shepherded by Mr. Reid's wife, LaRue, Violet and Daisy submitted to haircuts and allowed their hair to be dyed a matching shade of brown. They toned down their makeup and clipped back their nails. Mr. Reid bought them each three Park-N Shop-uniforms, which they altered by hand to accommodate the bridge between them. Every morning they arrived at eight-thirty, dressed in those matching red-and-white-checked blouses and long denim skirts. Every afternoon, they went home at four. Mr. Reid paid them both.

Violet and Daisy kept busy every minute they were on the clock, readily accepting additional tasks like shucking corn and bagging apples or potatoes. "I don't know if they had ever done any manual labor before," their supervisor, Guy Rodgers, said, "but they turned out to be excellent employees." He got a kick out of watching them work together, "a-fussin' and a-gabbin' every minute." Customers and coworkers alike recalled the sisters as pleasant and talkative. "They are perfectly charming people," one of Park-N-Shop's employees informed the *San Antonio Light* when the paper called to inquire about the Hiltons. "They stay out of the limelight and are working for a living like all the rest of us."

The way their work space was arranged halfway disguised the fact that Violet and Daisy were conjoined. Even someone standing right behind them would not necessarily have realized they were anything but two women in a cramped area, working "fanny-to-fanny," as Linda Reid Beatty put it.

Months passed. A year and more went by, and the pair of identical women working the produce scales became as familiar a fixture to Park-N-Shop's customers as the bunches of bananas and towers of oranges. Even so, a certain level of curiosity proved impossible to fully dispel. Charles Reid himself couldn't help being a little fascinated by the way they moved together. "They never said, 'Let's go over yonder' or anything like that. They just got up and started walking."

Children sometimes snuck around behind their scales, eager to see how they were connected. "Some even tried to look under their dresses," Mr. Reid remembered. After a lifetime of stares, Violet and Daisy had no patience for that kind of nonsense anymore. Nor were the sisters subtle about letting children know when they were out of line. "I'd be in another part of the store," Reid said, "but I could still hear it—that slapping noise as Daisy or Violet would pop some little boy on the head because he got too close. You'd just hear that pop and some kid would take off running."

Violet, who had always been "the diplomat," developed a slow-burning fuse when it came to youngsters. As far as she was concerned, "they all became meanies by the time they were eight or nine years old." She had no patience for unruly children who monkeyed with her scale or upended her displays of fruits and vegetables. As these perpetual irritations slowly but surely accumulated, abiding by the store's policy of tolerating such misbehavior became the toughest part of Violet's job. Despite LaRue Reid's periodic warnings, one day Violet let loose with a tirade about "irresponsible parents" within earshot of a customer who'd just allowed his son to run rampant through the produce department. The boy's father took it personally.

According to the Hiltons' supervisor, the man "stormed into the store's office and told someone there that he was not going to take insults from a lowly store clerk. He left his cart filled with groceries right there and walked out, announcing that he would never set foot in our store again."

Kind and quiet though he was, Charles Reid could not have that kind of scene playing out in front of his customers. Personal boundaries were one thing. The Reids always permitted Violet and Daisy to protect their physical space, as well as their privacy. Park-N-Shop's management did its best to help fend off reporters, but now and then one slipped by. "We want no part of the press," Violet and Daisy said when a *Miami Herald* reporter approached them at work; they turned their backs as one and walked away. That was the one and only type of rudeness Charles and LaRue Reid would let the Hiltons get away with. In any other circumstance, the customer reigned supreme, whether they were nine years old or ninety-nine. Violet and Daisy knew that as well as anyone—perhaps even better, given the talking-tos they'd had from LaRue. This time, Mr. Reid could not look the other way. He instructed Guy Rodgers to fire the Hiltons.

True to their own lifelong code of conduct, Violet and Daisy held no grudges. They continued to buy their groceries at Park-N-Shop each week and always stopped to chat with Rodgers. When after some weeks it became apparent that the Hiltons were descending into dire straits all over again, Rodgers appealed to Mrs. Reid (who happened to be his sister) to give the sisters a second chance. She agreed.

The gamble paid off. "They were model employees—two of the hardest workers I ever had," Rodgers said.

. . .

As it turned out, the Reids' soft spot for Violet and Daisy extended well beyond making sure they had a steady paycheck. The Reids' church, Purcell United Methodist, owned a two-bedroom cottage on grounds that had been the site of a World War I camp. Somehow Charles and LaRue arranged for the Hiltons to rent the cottage from the church for less than they were paying for their trailer at Tanzy's. The Reids also made sure a couch, dinette, and bed were delivered.

The cottage at 2204 Weyland Avenue was the very image of the home twenty-three-year-old Violet and Daisy had imagined for themselves in the midst of their emancipation trial in 1931: "Nothing big and fancy, but just a little place that will be cozy and comfortable."

"We never had a home; we've always traveled," Violet said in 1960. After so many years of living out of suitcases and trunks, residing in carnival wagons, train cars, boardinghouses, and hotels, and collecting their forwarded mail from *Billboard* magazine's Cincinnati office, the Hilton sisters finally had a place all their own, with a permanent address fixed to the front of their little black mailbox.

. . .

Within the community, Violet and Daisy initially held themselves at a distance, creating a small bubble of privacy around themselves. "I would say they weren't *un*friendly, but they were a little more stand-offish," said Robert Tanzy, whose father owned Tanzy's Trailer Park.

Decades of fending off curious multitudes had taken their toll. "The twins are a little haughty—which may be only protective armor," one perceptive reporter had concluded in the early 1950s. He was absolutely correct. "We never allow people to get too close to us," Daisy said. "Some people tend to pry. And we have to keep our private lives our own." They were particularly wary of women. "We never get close to any woman," Violet had told a reporter a few years earlier. "It's hello and good-by and that's it." Female interviewers had always tended to presume an unwelcome level of intimacy, asking "all sorts of questions" that the Hiltons had no intention of answering. And women also had a maddening tendency to yank items right out of Violet's and Daisy's hands when they went shopping, eager to see if they were buying the same things.

Carving out a comfortable space for themselves in the everyday life of a close-knit neighborhood proved a gradual process. "I think the first reaction that everybody had was to feel sorry for them a little bit by the time they got here," reporter Tommy Tomlinson of the *Charlotte Observer* said, "because they were really down on their luck, they were basically broke, they were looking for work." Pity never drew the Hilton sisters closer to anyone. Stares must have been inevitable, too, though Violet and Daisy had long ago learned to disregard curious looks. "Being stared at doesn't hurt you," Violet had said as a teenager.

Most days the two sisters went to work and came home and that was that. Their neighbors could expect a pleasant *Good morning* and a wave hello, and little else. "Daisy's the one that did most of the talking," Leo Wingate, the man who delivered Merita bread to the supermarket, remembered. "The other one didn't have anything to say, except once in a while Daisy would be talking about somewhere she had been, and Violet would poke her in the ribs and say, *I was there too!*" Daisy's coworkers also recalled her as the one who'd perk up at an invitation to a barbecue or party, while Violet preferred not to socialize. Violet always prevailed.

They did occasionally attend services at Purcell United Methodist Church, though whether out of spiritual hunger or a sense of obligation for the church's role in finding them a home is anyone's guess.

They also participated in the men's Sunday school class, rather than mingle with the ladies.

"Housewives are the dullest people on earth," they'd said in no uncertain terms in 1952. "All they talk about is dirty clothes, dirty dishes, and dirty children." The years in between had done nothing to temper their distaste for conventional female roles. "We don't like homes, families, and kids," Daisy reiterated in 1960, "but we have two little mixed-breed dogs. We both love dogs."

Those dogs were perhaps the most direct route to Violet's and Daisy's hearts, as the bread man at Park-N-Shop learned. He endeared himself to the sisters by bringing toys for their beloved pets—rubber rats he bought in batches of two dozen—as well as saving them cab fare. "He lived close to them, and he'd take them home in the bread truck a lot of times," Linda Reid Beatty recalled.

Companionship, it seemed, was not something the Hiltons felt a need to seek out. Simple kindnesses and loyalty, though, were generously repaid, despite the sisters' modest hourly wage. "They were always giving things away," Reverend John Sills of Purcell United Methodist remembered. "Every Christmas they would buy expensive gifts for some of the regular customers of the store."

• • •

By the late 1960s the Hiltons had slipped almost completely from public view. Now and then their names might appear in newspaper columns when old fans wrote to inquire, "Whatever became of the Hilton Sisters . . . ?" Or sometimes fragments of their past turned up in the corner of a page, where papers like the *San Antonio Light* dredged up snippets of articles from decades past to fill empty space under the headline "10 and 20 Years Ago."

To Jim Moore, it seemed like a sad decline. But Jim had not been in touch with Violet and Daisy for years. He could only speculate on their feelings. "I guess they felt like they were doing an honest day's work," he said. "They had finally come to the place where they resented show business, I do believe."

In that, Jim was correct. A Charlotte television actor confirmed, "I asked them not long ago if they'd like some old pictures I had, made when they were young. 'No,' they said, 'we want to forget those days forever.'"

Violet and Daisy had been exposed—in every sense of the word— to the public since they were three weeks old. After half a century in the glare of the spotlight, the cool shade of obscurity seems to have provided a long-overdue haven.

"They were eager to appear, for once in their lives, as something other than freaks," the *Charlotte Observer* reported. That sense of normalcy and acceptance was a little easier to come by in North Carolina than it might have been anywhere else. Over a century earlier, Eng and Chang Bunker, the original Siamese twins, had settled on adjoining farms one hundred miles north of Charlotte, in Mount Airy, and alternated living at each one. Several of the Bunkers' dozens of grandchildren and hundreds of great-grandchildren still lived in the vicinity. Millie-Christine McCoy, too, had been born in North Carolina. The state had come to take a certain pride in its conjoined residents, which possibly played a role in the way Charlotte's citizens subtly but firmly made Violet and Daisy welcome.

Whatever the reason, the hospitality was unmistakable. Never before had the Hiltons had a home, or been surrounded by so many honest people who took a genuine interest in their welfare. "I think the sisters were happiest here in Charlotte," said Reverend Sills. Linda Reid Beatty agreed. "I remember them telling me once that in some ways they were happier than at any time in their lives."

To those who worked with them, the Hiltons seemed happiest of all in the Park-N-Shop break room. There, in a haze of smoke, Violet and Daisy found their final stage. With cigarettes dangling from their lips, the Hilton sisters laughed and talked, regaling their coworkers with glitzy tales of their former life in show business. Out on the sales floor they had to "be good," or LaRue Reid would fix them with a warning stare, but in the break room they were free to air memories of their sensational marriages and rattle off names of all the famous folks they had met. "I don't know how many were really true," Linda Reid Beatty confided. "I think they enjoyed startling people, to a degree." It didn't matter. No one who sat with Violet and Daisy in the break room needed the God's honest truth to have a good time. The Park-N-Shop staff enjoyed hearing the Hiltons' stories every bit as much as Violet and Daisy loved telling them. "They just liked to entertain," Linda Reid Beatty remembered fondly. "They were still entertaining."

CHAPTER 29

JUST BEFORE CHRISTMAS OF 1968, VIOLET FELL ILL WITH IN-fluenza. All their Christmas gifts for their coworkers and favorite customers had been wrapped and tagged. Too sick to work, the Hiltons arranged to have the presents sent to Park-N-Shop. As Violet began to get back on her feet, Daisy was laid low. Usually when the sisters passed an illness from one to the other, the second had a milder bout. Not this time.

The flu that year was "mean stuff," Linda Reid Beatty recalled. It must have been, for on December 28, Violet and Daisy put aside their lifelong hatred of doctors and consulted Dr. Thomas Leath. Then they returned home, possibly in disregard of the doctor's advice.

As the days stretched into a week, and then two, their absence troubled Mr. Reid more and more. "They were very rarely sick and hardly ever missed work," he said. "So we were worried when they were so sick they couldn't come to work." Aware that the sisters had no family and few close friends, the Reids took it upon themselves to telephone the house "just about every day to check on them." Someone also looked in on the Hiltons on New Year's Eve.

. . .

No one knows precisely when Daisy died. No one, perhaps, but Violet. Her own death was now assured—unless she called for help and consented to allow doctors to separate her from her sister's corpse.

It is possible that the thought did not so much as cross Violet's mind. In February 1967, Dr. George B. Callahan, then the nation's foremost expert on conjoined twins, traveled from Illinois to Charlotte and "tried to talk with them." Dr. Callahan had no luck. Violet and Daisy had sensed early in their lives that the surgeons who proposed separating them were interested most of all in something they prized above the sisters' health and well-being. "We are firmly convinced that . . . we could be used as propaganda for certain doctors, who desired to become famous by exploiting our curious condition," Violet explained in 1937. The two of them had never wanted any part of that. "We did not believe in sacrificing our young lives for any scientific purposes," Daisy agreed. At age fifty-nine, Violet and Daisy remained as disinclined to submit to medical examinations as they had ever been. Separation remained totally out of the question as far as the Hiltons themselves were concerned, despite the knowledge that advances in surgical medicine were slowly but surely making the prospect of dividing and reconstructing their shared tailbone and rectum less and less risky.

No matter how confident the doctors might be, an unavoidable element of risk remained. "There is no doubt that all the surgeons who wished to operate on us would have been very careful up to the end," Violet had acknowledged in her twenties. "But if the operation had been a failure, they would have said, 'It was not possible to foresee the unknown workings of Fate in the case of this unusual phenomenon!'" She was absolutely correct. Each and every set of conjoined twins is unique, and even today, separation surgeries occasionally end in heartbreak when an undetected anomaly thwarts a medical team's most meticulous preparations.

The intervening years had not weakened their resolve to remain physically united. Nor did the sudden reality of Daisy's death change that conviction for Violet. "Violet and I have always been together in life," Daisy had said in 1925. "We've shared our joys and triumphs and ambitions. We love each other so dearly that life for one without the other would be too sad to endure. No, we want to go both together." Their feelings were not at all unusual. Even some conjoined twins who have been surgically separated in infancy would rather die in tandem than go on alone. Better to die as one than endure the unfathomable emotional trauma of existing "half dead."

. . .

On Saturday, January 4, 1969, nobody picked up the phone at 2204 Weyland Avenue. That wasn't cause for immediate concern. Sometimes, Charles Reid knew, Violet and Daisy took the receiver off the hook so they could rest undisturbed. Usually they'd answer later. Not that day, though. "I knew they hadn't gone out of town or anything because they didn't know anybody to go visit."

Mr. Reid dialed their number every hour, his alarm mounting with each unanswered call. When he couldn't stand it any longer, he and his wife drove to the house. No one came to the door. The Reids phoned the police at 7:15 p.m. Officers arrived within fifteen minutes and broke down the door. There were Violet's and Daisy's bodies, collapsed over the heating grate in the central hall.

Both death certificates gave the date of death as "before January 4, 1969." Influenzal pneumonia was listed as the cause of death for both Violet and Daisy. It was true enough for Daisy, but Violet's case is not so clear. As their coworkers remembered it, Violet had recovered from her bout of Hong Kong flu before Daisy fell ill.

238

By the time they were found, the effects of rigor mortis had worn off—an indication that both sisters had been dead for thirty-six to forty-eight hours. Daisy's body was in visibly poorer condition, however, and that could only mean that Violet had survived her sister for several hours at the very least. It might have taken as long as two days for Violet to succumb.

How the death of one conjoined twin results in the death of the other is to some degree a matter of conjecture. As a consequence of their wholly unique anatomy, the mechanisms are somewhat different for each pair. In Violet and Daisy's case, the fact that all of their most vital organs were individual may have prolonged the process.

Violet's brain, heart, and lungs initially continued to function without Daisy. Her stomach, liver, and kidneys were also not directly affected. But tissue that is deprived of circulation dies. From the moment of her death, Daisy's body was unable to return any blood Violet pumped into her via their connecting bridge. If Violet's blood supply did gradually diminish in this way, so would her ability to absorb oxygen and nutrition. It is also possible that Violet's heart became overtaxed by the effort of trying to circulate blood between two people. Further, any blood that managed to make its way back into Violet's circulatory system from Daisy was doubly compromised by lack of oxygen and the presence of bacteria as the process of decomposition began taking hold of Daisy. Sepsis, most often caused by the spread of such toxic bacteria throughout the body's systems, could also have affected the Hiltons via their merged intestinal tracts; any unexpelled waste harbored in Daisy's body had a direct connection to Violet via their common rectum.

For most of us, it is far, far beyond imagining—the stuff of nightmares and horror stories. Yet for Violet, awaiting death was a lesser horror than the prospect of living without Daisy. "Other girls may be able to do things we cannot," the two had said in 1924, "but they haven't anybody they love as much as we love each other." Their bond was so deep, so fundamental to her being, that Violet could not bring herself to break it, even as the decomposition of Daisy's flesh inched its way into her own. *"We were born this way and we will stay this way,"* they had said time and again. *"This is the way we want to be."*

"When the time comes to die," one paper had reported when they were just seventeen, "they will die willingly with each other."

• • •

Whether or not Violet's and Daisy's bodies were autopsied is unclear. The *Greensboro Record* reported that Mecklenburg County medical examiner Dr. Hobart Wood had ordered an autopsy; six days later, the *Miami Herald* reported that specialists' requests to examine the women's remains had been denied. "No autopsy was performed," the *Herald* stated, quelling rumors that the sisters had been separated for burial.

To the medical world, the Hiltons' remains represented a rare and precious source of information that was otherwise impossible to obtain. Nevertheless, there can be no question that Violet and Daisy would have wanted their bodies to remain intact, and joined. Their abhorrence of doctors was so ingrained, it had been a struggle even to get them fitted for eyeglasses. If the Reids had any say in it—and they may well have, since Mr. Reid had applied and been approved as the administrator of Violet and Daisy's estate—the Hiltons were not permitted to become specimens. "They said to me, Mr. Reid, we've been together our whole life. We don't ever want to be apart."

• • •

"Perhaps the only normal thing, by commonplace, human standards, that ever happened to the Hilton sisters was their funeral," the *Charlotte Observer* wrote on January 9.

For almost ten years, Violet and Daisy had held their neighbors and coworkers at arm's length. Now that they were gone, those who knew them felt compelled to close that gap. Charles Reid had vowed that the Hiltons would be "buried in style," and the entire roster of Park-N-Shop employees turned out for their funeral that day, along with several longtime customers. It was the first time a crowd had gathered around the Hilton sisters without regard for their money or their fame or their physical bond, but in plain, unadorned affection for the women they had known best as Violet Hilton and Daisy Hilton. Nearly two dozen floral arrangements banked the casket.

A handful of curiosity-seekers were bold enough to infiltrate the ranks of mourners, but the casket, large enough to accommodate a three-hundred-pound man, remained closed, denying the opportunity for one last look. "I wonder which one died first?" one woman asked. Her question went unanswered. Both Charles Reid and Reverend Sills were impressed by how few gawkers attended, but that did not stop the clergyman from singling them out. "How many of you came here to grieve?" he admonished during the service.

At Forest Lawn Cemetery, the mourners gathered at the headstone of twenty-one-year-old Private First Class Troy Miller Thompson Jr., who'd given his life in Vietnam four years earlier. His mother, Dot, had grown fond of Violet and Daisy during her weekly trips to Park-N-Shop and had donated the empty plot beside her son so that the Hiltons could be laid to rest in "Charlotte's prestige cemetery." The sisters' fellow employees served as pallbearers, gently carrying the extra-wide casket to the grave.

The bonds Violet and Daisy had forged in Charlotte may not have been deep, but they were genuine—more genuine, perhaps, than any they had known before. "I didn't really know them," said a young man from the grocery store who came to pay his respects. "They came to work every day, and they were awfully nice." The marker placed above them reads:

DAISY AND VIOLET HILTON

1908–1969

Beloved Siamese Twins

VIOLET AND DAISY EACH LEFT $1,400 BEHIND—ESTATES WORTH just under $10,000 apiece today. All but $200 of it had come from the employee profit-sharing program at Park-N-Shop. As far as anyone in Charlotte knew, the Hiltons had no living relatives. What happened to their savings was not revealed to the press; perhaps Charles and LaRue Reid shepherded the money to a worthy cause in the same quiet way they had stepped in to help Violet and Daisy.

In the sisters' dresser, the Reids found Violet's pocketbook collection—four or five drawers full. Every one of them contained a few dollar bills. "The only thing I can figure," Charles Reid said, "is that they took lots of taxicabs, and they could just grab a pocketbook on the way out and know there was cab fare in it." Their collection of newspaper clippings and publicity photos, on the other hand, had been packed away, out of sight. The Hiltons' little house bore not one hint of their glamorous past.

At the end of January 1969, the Fox Drive-In paid tribute to Violet and Daisy with one final showing of *Chained for Life*. "They Lived and Died in Charlotte," the advertisements boasted, touting the Fox's connection as the site of "their last theatrical appearance."

. . .

Twenty years later, the show business world tried to nudge the Hilton sisters back into the spotlight. In 1989 a musical based on their lives, called *Twenty Fingers and Twenty Toes,* debuted at New York City's WPA Theatre. The show closed within a month, marred by what the *Chicago Tribune* called its "frantic tastelessness."

Another Hilton-themed musical entitled *Side Show* followed on Broadway in 1997, lighting up theater marquees with Violet's and Daisy's faces once again. Despite earning four Tony nominations, including a dual nomination for the actresses who played the Hiltons, *Side Show* closed after just ninety-one performances. In trying to maintain "a respectful, compassionate tone," *Variety*'s review suggested, the creators had played it too safe. A story that revolved around a carnival freak show demanded more grit—perhaps more grit than a modern audience was prepared to stomach. A reimagined version premiered in 2014, to last for only fifty-six performances.

Nevertheless, renewed interest in the Hiltons' story prompted the city of Brighton, the sisters' hometown in England, to adorn a double-decker bus (number 316 as of December 2019) with Violet's and Daisy's names. Thanks to the efforts of local historian Alf Le Flohic, a commemorative plaque will be placed at their birthplace on Riley Road in May 2021. "Fundraising for the plaque was quite an experience," Alf said. "I had phone calls from the UK tabloids after sensational details on one hand, and on the other, people who were touched by the story of the Hilton twins sending me their hard-earned money with no agenda." He was especially touched by a benefit performance of *Side Show* by the Old Joint Stock Musical Theatre Company. "They chose the plaque fund as their charity and raised several hundred pounds, which was incredible. It was very emotional seeing Violet and Daisy come to life before our very eyes, the closest any of us were ever going to get."

. . .

The greatest surprise came in 2014, when a genealogist who'd been researching the Skinner family contacted a sixty-nine-year-old British woman named Shelagh Childs. He'd discovered that Shelagh's mother, Ethel, who had been adopted as an infant, was Kate Skinner's youngest daughter—the baby whose birth had resulted in Kate's death in 1912. Shelagh's mother, therefore, had been Violet and Daisy's sister.

The news was a double bombshell. Ethel had gone to her own grave knowing nothing of her biological family. "All I knew was my mother was adopted at birth because of her mother's death," Shelagh said.

Troubled upon learning that none of the Skinner family had acknowledged their connection to Violet and Daisy, much less shown them any hospitality during their 1933 tour of England, Shelagh and her husband decided to travel to North Carolina to pay their respects. "I want people to know that someone cared about the twins," she explained. "That's why I went to their grave. I know my mother would have." Shelagh brightened the plot with poppies and crocuses for her aunts. The moment was bittersweet, for Shelagh understood instinctively what a family connection would have meant to her mother, and how thrilled Ethel would have been to discover her long-lost sisters while they were still living. "If anybody would have loved them just the way they were, it was my mum," Shelagh said.

AUTHOR'S NOTE

A story like Violet and Daisy Hilton's is by its very nature filled with exaggeration and grandiose claims to fame. I have approached each of these claims with a healthy dose of skepticism, whether they originated with Mary Hilton, Ike Rose, Myer Myers, Terry Turner, or the Hilton sisters themselves. Violet and Daisy, it turns out, are one of the most consistent sources of misinformation. Consequently, their story has never been told without embellishment—not by the sisters themselves, or by anyone since. My aim has been to brush aside the metaphoric sequins and greasepaint, to explore the unvarnished reality beneath. I cannot promise that I've stripped the truth entirely bare, however. In some cases, decades of deliberately crafted ballyhoo and melodrama have no doubt permanently obscured what actually occurred.

Thankfully, the advent of searchable digital media archives has allowed me to trace the Hiltons' whereabouts with far greater precision than has previously been possible. The national libraries of Australia and New Zealand, as well as the digital archives of *Billboard* and *Variety,* have been indispensable in reconstructing Violet and Daisy's routes around the globe. These sources have given me the distinct advantage of relying on verifiable information, rather than conjecture or the occasionally faulty memories of the Hiltons' show business contemporaries. (Readers who go on to learn more about Violet and Daisy may therefore notice contradictions between my account and others—notably, Dean Jensen's. This newly accessible wealth of digital information is part of the reason why.) Nevertheless, the Hiltons' story remains pocked with gaps where information simply wasn't preserved. Rather than fill in those gaps with suppositions and dramatized scenes, as previous accounts have done, I've left the uncertainty in place.

. . .

Transcripts of the Hilton sisters' emancipation hearing are missing from the records of the Bexar County District Court. The folder that once contained them exists but is empty. This left me nothing but newspaper reports, which present a number of challenges.

While the courtroom dialogue reported by both the *San Antonio Express* and the *San Antonio Light* is reassuringly similar, it is not identical. One source did not seem more or less accurate than the other, so choosing which version to quote has been largely a matter of taste. In some cases I favored clarity of phrasing, in others, drama. (However, in no cases have I taken dramatic license by inventing or altering dialogue spoken in or out of the courtroom. Every word in quotation marks has been written in print or spoken on film.)

Neither the *San Antonio Express* nor the *San Antonio Light* reported the testimony chronologically. Instead they relayed the most dramatic highlights first and filled in less exciting details toward the end of each article. Therefore, it's difficult to determine who testified when. I pieced the order together as best I could, making a few guesses along the way.

Also, two different lines of questioning revolved around two separate but similar dollar amounts: $36,000 from an Orpheum theater contract and $36,142 from the final guardianship report. In the newspapers' abridged accounts of the trial, it's not always 100 percent clear which of these figures is being referred to. Should the official court transcripts ever resurface, it could very well turn out that despite my best efforts I've inadvertently mismatched some of the questions and answers that revolve around those numbers.

• • •

None of the dialogue in this book is my own invention. Even so, a variety of factors makes it difficult to be sure that the Hiltons' words are always their own or reflect their true thoughts and feelings.

In particular, words attributed to Violet and Daisy in newspaper articles before 1931 are worthy of scrutiny. Those early quotes could just as easily have been fed to the press by Myer Myers as spoken by the sisters themselves. Whenever possible, I favored interviews with reporters who described meeting Violet and Daisy in person. However, because they were so rigorously chaperoned at interviews, it's impossible to be sure whether what they said in the Myerses' presence was what they truly thought and felt, or was what they had been instructed to say. On some topics, such as their feelings about separation, the Hiltons remained consistent throughout their lives. On other topics— their views of love and marriage, for instance—their feelings varied. I relied on those threads of consistency as well as my own intuition to sort fact from fiction to the extent that such a task is possible. People can and do change their minds over a lifetime, after all.

Taking the Hiltons' own serialized memoirs at face value is likewise an iffy business. Once free of their guardians, Violet and Daisy regularly embellished and rearranged the events of their lives for dramatic effect. Some of the conversations they recount are no doubt re-creations— they're too stilted and overloaded with detail to pass for normal speech. Nevertheless, I have assumed the risk of judiciously quoting their accounts, even when I could not verify the accuracy of their words.

• • •

Portraying Mary Hilton accurately has perhaps been the most dubious task of all. Verifiable information about the Hiltons' foster mother is scanty, to say the least, leaving a wide chasm between Violet's and Daisy's chilling memories of her abuse and the *Brighton Herald*'s rapturous praise of her kindness. British census records give glimpses of Mary Hilton's whereabouts and circumstances between her birth in 1857 and her departure from England in 1911, but no hints of her personality. No record of Edith's opinion of her mother has come to light. Nor did Myer Myers leave any clues about his mother-in-law's true character or temperament.

And so on the chance that the Hilton sisters villainized Mary further than her own actions warranted, I feel compelled to note that two people did make statements that contradict Violet's and Daisy's claims about their treatment at the hands of Mary Hilton. Mary's daughter Alice said in 1932, "She treated them like her own daughters and everything was done to make them forget their infirmity." Alice's granddaughter, Barbara Hodgson, agrees. "Yes, [Mary] made money, but the money was spent *on* [Violet and Daisy]. They always had beautiful clothes, they had the good education. . . . When they were older and they decided they wanted to run their own affairs . . . that's when they were exploited. . . . I don't know what you call people behind the scenes, producers, and whatever, they were the ones that exploited them. They took all their money, that's where the exploitation came in. Not my great-grandmother who loved them, brought them up, cared for them," she said in a private 2018 interview with Brighton historian Alf Le Flohic.

. . .

Last of all, I should point out that Edith Myers's maiden name was not Hilton. Henry Hilton was in fact Edith's stepfather; in Brighton's birth and census records, her name is listed as Edith Emily Green.

ACKNOWLEDGMENTS

THANKS TO:

Linda Reid Beatty, for sharing photographs and memories of Violet and Daisy Hilton.

John Calhoun, NYPL Performing Arts Library; William S. Fish and Barry Thornton, Mecklenburg County Medical Examiner's Office; Cornelia Pokrzywa; Isabel Schober; Steve Simpson and Naomi Balmer-Simpson; Anne-Marie Varga; and Emily Vuotto, Public Library of Cincinnati and Hamilton County, for providing access to newspaper and magazine articles, and medical reports.

Horst Cawi and Annika Paczkowski, for searching Berlin's newspapers and providing German translations.

Shelagh Childs, for sharing her experience of traveling to North Carolina, and her family history.

Amanda Clay, for granting access to her one-of-a-kind Hilton collection.

Annie Kelley, for making all the toughest phone calls.

Alf Le Flohic, for providing photos, sharing original research, and connecting me with Shelagh Childs.

Olivia Martin, for discussions of conjoined anatomy.

Michael Wilde, for giving up his spare copy of *Intimate Loves and Lives of the Hilton Sisters,* and for his dissertation-quality answers to every Hilton-related question I've thrown at him over the last five years.

NOTES

CHAPTER 2

7 "much more intimate and extreme": James A. Rooth, "The Brighton United Twins," *The British Medical Journal* (September 23, 1911), 654.

7 "a very healthy, lusty young pair" and "to possess an uncommonly vigorous life": "Brighton 'Siamese Twins,'" *Brighton Herald*, February 22, 1908.

8 "double babies": "Double Babies Happy as Most of Singular Kind," *Indianapolis Star*, March 20, 1910.

9 "Take my babies": "Famed Siamese Twins Kept in Bondage Accounting Suit Says," *San Antonio Express*, January 13, 1931.

9 "regain the care, custody, or control" and "at any time hereafter": Jensen, *Lives and Loves.* 14.

CHAPTER 3

10 "motherly lady" and "her emotions were very perturbed": "Brighton 'Siamese Twins,'" *Brighton Herald*, February 22, 1908.

10-12 "tolerably well known" through "Why, I wouldn't part with them for anything": "Brighton's United Twins Christened," *Brighton Herald*, March 28, 1908.

12 "a covering which resembled in shape": "Why Being a Siamese Twin Is Not So Bad," *Louisville Courier-Journal*, January 4, 1925.

12 "The twins are not really on public view" through "the most wonderful little couple in the world": "Brighton's United Twins Christened," *Brighton Herald*, March 28, 1908.

CHAPTER 4

14 "Our earliest and only recollections": Violet and Daisy Hilton, with Michael Lorant, "Life and Loves of the Siamese Twins: Part 1," *The World's News*, September 29, 1937.

14 "The first thing I remember": "Twins Don't Like Nosey [*sic*] Doctors," *Dayton Herald*, September 19, 1925.

15 "convinced that favouritism" through "the more irritable": "Brighton's United Twins. Their First Birthday," *Brighton Herald*, February 13, 1909.

16 "We were never permitted" through "The thought did not take such clear form": Ethelda Bedford, "The Private Life of the Siamese Twins: Chapter I," *San Francisco Examiner*, September 10, 1944.

CHAPTER 5

17 "as good and lovable as they are pretty" and "that they are treated with the utmost fondness": "Brighton's United Twins. Their First Birthday," *Brighton Herald*, February 13, 1909.

17-18 "There was a speech repeated to us daily" through "She'll never hit your faces": Bedford, "Siamese Twins: Chapter I."

19 "We lived in dingy European boarding houses": Ethelda Bedford, "The Private Lives of the Siamese Twins: Chapter II," *San Francisco Examiner*, September 17, 1944.

19 "A lot of the freaks just stood up": Ward Hall in Zemeckis, *Bound by Flesh*.

20 "We were always being looked at": Bedford, "Siamese Twins: Chapter I."

20 "rare novelties": Paul Maloney, *The Britannia Panopticon Music Hall and Cosmopolitan Entertainment Culture* (New York: Palgrave Macmillan, 2016), 176.

22 "enormous crowds daily": Stewart's Waxwork advertisement in *Edinburgh Evening News,* January 11, 1911.

23 "rented": Violet and Daisy Hilton, with Michael Lorant, "Life and Loves of the Siamese Twins: Part 1," *The World's News,* September 29, 1937.

23 "Our earliest lessons" through "We decided early": Bedford, "Siamese Twins: Chapter II."

24 "We soon found": "Appear in 'Freaks,'" *San Diego Evening Tribune,* January 26, 1932.

24 "Mental as well as": Bedford, "Siamese Twins: Chapter II."

25 "ladies' day": "Making the Fairs in Europe," *Billboard,* September 14, 1912.

26 "positively could not make a dollar": "Ike Rose's First Fifty Years in Show Business," *Billboard,* December 8, 1928.

26 "Teach the girls the hard way" through "When Auntie discovered": Bedford, "Siamese Twins: Chapter II."

27 "stuffing candy in our mouths": "Twins Don't Like Nosey [*sic*] Doctors," *Dayton Herald,* September 19, 1925.

27 "the very bedside tone": Bedford, "Siamese Twins: Chapter I."

27 "His voice was": Bedford, "Siamese Twins: Chapter II."

28 "I can hardly imagine": "Freak of Nature," *Launceston Examiner,* February 10, 1913.

29 "We would lie awake" through "We can hold our breaths": Bedford, "Siamese Twins: Chapter I."

CHAPTER 6

30 "The theater thundered": Bedford, "Siamese Twins: Chapter II."

32 "A Fairyland of Palaces of Pleasure by the Sea": Luna Park advertisement, *Melbourne Argus,* November 25, 1912.

32 "horrifying smile": "Luna Park: Successful Opening," *Melbourne Argus,* December 14, 1912.

33 **"walked about"**: Violet and Daisy Hilton with Michael Lorant, "Life and Loves of the Siamese Twins: Part 3," *The World's News*, October 13, 1937.

33 **"No other amusement enterprise"**: Luna Park advertisement, *Melbourne Herald*, February 17, 1913.

33 **"wonderful agility"** through **"not slow at making friends"**: "Freak of Nature," *Launceston Examiner*, February 10, 1913.

33-34 **"Special Engagement of the Modern Siamese Twins"**: Luna Park advertisement, *Melbourne Table Talk*, February 13, 1913.

34 **"Absolute Wonder of a Baffled and Mystified World"** and **"enormous expense"**: Luna Park advertisement, *Melbourne Herald*, February 11, 1913.

34 **"because the best is none too good"**: Luna Park advertisement, *Melbourne Table Talk*, February 13, 1913.

34 **"THE MODERN SIAMESE TWINS"** and **"captivated all who saw them"**: Luna Park advertisement, *Melbourne Herald*, February 15, 1913.

34 **"Here They Are!"** and **"grown-together"**: Luna Park advertisement in *Melbourne Punch*, February 20, 1913.

34 **"principal attraction"** and **"delighting and astonishing"**: "Luna Park," *Melbourne Punch*, February 20, 1913.

34 **"The modern Siamese Twins, Daisy and Violet Hilton"**: "Luna Park," *The Prahran Telegraph*, February 22, 1913.

34 **"a revelation and sensation"** and **"doing 80% of the business"**: *Billboard*, April 19, 1913.

35 **"the greatest attraction at the Sydney Easter Show"**: The Colosseum advertisement in *The Lithgow Mercury*, April 11, 1913.

35 **"Follow the Crowds"**: Showgrounds, Ipswich advertisement in *Queensland Times*, April 22, 1913.

35 **"We were exhibited in different circuses"** through **"wild riders galloped round us"**: Violet and Daisy Hilton with Michael Lorant, "Life and Loves of the Siamese Twins: Part 3," *The World's News*, October 13, 1937.

35 "Lilliputian exhibition": "Ike Rose's First Fifty Years in Show Business," *Billboard*, December 8, 1928.

36 "We were not allowed to have friends": Bedford, "Siamese Twins: Chapter II."

36 "She was fortunate enough": Violet and Daisy Hilton with Michael Lorant, "Life and Love of the Siamese Twins: Part 3," *The World's News*, October 13, 1937.

36 "how a brute had raised him": Bedford, "Siamese Twins: Chapter II."

CHAPTER 7

38 "Daisy and Violet": *Evening Star*, February 24, 1914.

39 "buy a lot of rubbish": "'Knock-down' Affair," *Truth*, August 31, 1912.

39 "Not over one-fifth": Myer Myers, *Souvenir and Life Story*, 4.

39 "fitted up like a nursery" and "chatter away to the audience": "Modern Siamese Twins," *Wanganui Chronicle*, March 27, 1914.

40 "The twins will be 'at home'": "Modern Siamese Twins," *Wanganui Chronicle*, March 26, 1914.

40 "parlour": Modern Siamese Twins advertisement in *Timaru Herald*, March 18, 1914.

40 "hours of reception": Modern Siamese Twins advertisement in *Wanganui Chronicle*, March 25, 1914.

40 "maimed or invalid children": Modern Siamese Twins advertisement in *Wanganui Chronicle*, March 28, 1914.

40 "ALIVE! ALIVE! ALIVE!": Modern Siamese Twins advertisement in *Otago Daily Times*, March 4, 1914.

40 "One would expect to see two imbecile": "Modern Siamese Twins," *New Zealand Free Lance*, August 18, 1914.

41 "The show can be recommended": "Modern 'Siamese' Twins," *Auckland Star*, April 4, 1914.

41 "Fourteen Hundred People have visited": Modern Siamese Twins advertisement in *Otago Daily Times*, March 4, 1914.

41 "with easy grace" and "displayed considerable ability": "Modern Siamese Twins Exhibited at Devonport," *North West Post* (Formby, Tasmania), November 6, 1915.

41 "There is nothing either bashful or forward": "Siamese Twins," *North Western Advocate and the Emu Bay Times*, November 8, 1915.

42 "wit worthy of anyone much older": "The Siamese Twins," *Launceston Daily Telegraph*, October 2, 1915.

41 "The show is a cut above": "Modern Siamese Twins Exhibited at Devonport," *North West Post*, November 6, 1915.

42 "raucous-voiced": "The Siamese Twins. A Revolting Exhibition," *Truth*, December 11, 1915.

42 "They had to lean over" and "That used to just hack the hell out of them": Jim Moore, 1978 interview with Esther MacMillan, 22, digital .utsa.edu/cdm/ref/collection/p15125coll4/id/794.

42 "opportunities for private examination": "Modern Siamese Twins," *Wanganui Chronicle*, March 26, 1914.

43-44 "The Siamese Twins: A Revolting Exhibition" through "In the interest of public decency": "A Revolting Exhibition," *Truth*.

44 "I want to bring under the notice of the Government" and "I understand": Hansard report of the Legislative Assembly of Victoria, 24th Parliament, Volume 142, 4017.

44 "make inquiries": Hansard report of the Legislative Assembly of Victoria, 24th Parliament, Volume 142, 4018, December 14, 1915.

44 "degrading" through "enjoy life in the same way that others do": Hansard report, Volume 142, 4017, December 14, 1915.

45 "poor little kids": "The Siamese Twins," *Truth*, January 1, 1916.

45 "We find life very joyous": "Twins Are Not Freaks," *Washington Post*, August 2, 1925.

46 "The little girls have very sunny dispositions": "Twin Girls Are Bound Together by Fleshy Band," *Honolulu Star-Bulletin*, July 4, 1916.

47 "physically and biologically inferior": Jensen, *Lives and Loves*, 61.

47 "any alien who has" and "This means, sir": Jensen, 58–59.

47 "any convict, lunatic, idiot": Report of the 47th Congress, Session 1, Chapters 376–378, August 3, 1882, www.loc.gov/law/help/statutes-at -large/47th-congress/session-1/c47s1ch376.pdf.

47 "likely public charge": "Record of Aliens Held for Special Inquiry," SS *Sonoma*, July 10, 1916, www.ancestry.com/sharing/15708340?h=d1d925 &utm_campaign=bandido-webparts&utm_source=post-share-modal &utm_medium=share-url.

47 "They're so, so lovely": Jensen, *Lives and Loves*, 64.

48 "No, no, no!": Jensen, 61.

48 "Tie That Binds Them": Jensen, 66.

49 "Daisy and Vilton [*sic*] Hilton, 8 years old": Maritime News, *San Francisco Chronicle*, July 11, 1916.

49 "accompanying alien": "Record of Aliens Held for Special Inquiry," SS Sonoma, July 10, 1916.

50 "Now Booking High-Class Engagements": "The Modern Siamese Twins," *Billboard*, July 22, 1916.

50 "There is not a suspicion of repulsiveness": "Siamese Twins: A Real Pair Just Over from Australia," *Billboard*, July 22, 1916.

50 "Little Girls, Modern Siamese Twins, Enjoying Tour of World": "Little Girls, Modern Siamese Twins, Enjoying Tour of World," *Ottumwa (IA) Review*, July 19, 1916.

51 "store show": "San Francisco Facts," *Billboard*, August 5, 1916.

51 "a dignified presentation": "This Is the Birthday House San Antonio's Siamese Twins Gave Aunt Who Mothered Them," *San Antonio Express*, October 2, 1927.

51 "Carnival King of the World": "Clarence A. Wortham: Carnival King of the World," *National Magazine*, August 1920, 235.

51 "the Little Giant" and "Decency first": "Wortham Framing Another Caravan," *Billboard*, July 29, 1916.

51-52 "For years the object" through "new and meritorious attractions": Rubin Gruberg, "The Carnival: America's Traveling Playground," *Billboard*, December 10, 1921.

52 "Something new": "The Wortham Shows," *Anaconda Standard*, August 12, 1916.

53 "Something Doing Every Minute" through "25 Carloads of Glittering Equipment": *Butte Miner*, August 13, 1916.

53 "Gladway": "Carnival Gets Great Crowd," *Great Falls Tribune*, August 22, 1916.

53 "freak museum": "Carnival Tents Rise Quickly After the Big Train Pulls In," *Great Falls Tribune*, August 21, 1916.

53 "Not one of them a bad one": "Great Wortham Shows," *Billboard*, December 23, 1916.

53 "marine spectacle": Great Wortham Shows advertisement, *Colorado Springs Gazette*, July 14, 1916.

53 "honest-to-goodness water": "Great Wortham Shows Coming," *Evening Kansan Republican*, May 31, 1916.

53 "aquatic extravaganza": "Moose Carnival Is Opened to Big Crowd," *Butte Miner*, August 14, 1916.

53 "to the caverns deep": "Wortham Carnival Pleases Big Crowd," *Anaconda Standard*, August 8, 1916.

54 "The most thrilling and blood-curdling sensation": "Great Wortham Shows Coming," *Evening Kansan Republican*, May 31, 1916.

54 "It may be said and without exaggeration": "Carnival Gets Great Crowd," *Great Falls Tribune*, August 22, 1916.

54 "Those were the people": Ward Hall in Zemeckis, *Bound by Flesh*.

55 "Two English Girls" and "The World's Greatest": www.sideshow world.com/81-SSPAlbumcover/Hilton-Sisters/HS-Front-1.jpg.

55 "A new feature, which will not be ready": "Carnival Gets Great Crowd," *Great Falls Tribune*, August 22, 1916.

55 "Big Attention" and "one of the most interesting human phenomena": "Odd Twins Get Big Attention," *Great Falls Tribune*, August 23, 1916.

55–56 "Well, that is a hard question to answer": "Carnival's Manager Fearing Strike, to Decamp," *Daily Inter Lake*, August 31, 1916.

56 "top money": "Great Wortham Shows More Than Making Up for Bloomers in Utah—Two Big Additions Made," *Billboard*, September 23, 1916.

56 "especial favorites and their little tent": "Twenty Side Shows on 'Gladway' Help to Keep Fair Crowds Happy," *Spokane Daily Chronicle*, September 5, 1916.

56 "breaking all pit show records" and "Newcomer": "Great Wortham Shows More Than Making Up for Bloomers in Utah—Two Big Additions Made," *Billboard*, September 23, 1916.

57 "Captain Hilton": Bedford, "Siamese Twins: Chapter I."

57 "a famous Australian physician": "English Twins of Siamese Variety Coming to Fair," *Riverside Independent Enterprise*, October 7, 1916.

58 "These Freaks Are White": *Billboard*, April 19, 1913.

59 "She set about making us" and "read, recite, and sing": Bedford, "Siamese Twins: Chapter II."

59 "These little girls are as bright as a dollar": "Special Show Train Will Leave City Early Saturday," *Daily Inter Lake*, September 1, 1916.

59 "born entertainers": "English Twins Popular at Fair," *Spokane Daily Chronicle*, September 4, 1916.

59 "We learned to listen" and "We learned to say": Bedford, "Siamese Twins: Chapter I."

60 " 'Speak when you're spoken to' ": "Food Seems to Be Only Matter on Which Twins, Showing Here, Agree," *Dayton Daily News*, October 8, 1925.

60 "Because of our bond" and "Two good friends": Bedford, "Siamese Twins: Chapter I."

60-61 "to avoid a fuss" and "Sometimes I wish": "Say Neither Is 'Boss,'" *Omaha World-Herald*, February 3, 1926.

61 "to read books and to look at nice pictures": Violet and Daisy Hilton, with Michael Lorant, "Life and Loves of the Siamese Twins: Part 2," *The World's News*, October 6, 1937.

61 "It is as though some Power" and "just as amiably": Bedford, "Siamese Twins: Chapter I."

CHAPTER 9

63 "Worthamville": "C.A. Wortham Shows," *Billboard*, February 17, 1917.

63 "dollhouse": "This Is the Birthday House San Antonio's Siamese Twins Gave Aunt Who Mothered Them," *San Antonio Express*, October 2, 1927.

63 "No neighborhood children": Jensen, *Lives and Loves*, 92.

64 "Porter, naturally, was bragging": Jim Moore, 1978 interview with Esther MacMillan, 11, digital.utsa.edu/cdm/ref/collection/p15125coll4/id/794.

64 "the next prominent corner": "C.A. Wortham Shows Have Official Opening," *Billboard*, April 28, 1917.

64 "The girls seemed to be glowing": Jensen, *Lives and Loves*, 87.

64 "It was almost impossible" through "I really wanted": Jensen, *Lives and Loves*, 88.

65 "We did not know how to play": Bedford, "Siamese Twins: Chapter II."

65 "They liked people": Jim Moore, 1978 interview with Esther MacMillan, 15.

65 "unearthly": Jensen, *Lives and Loves*, 89.

66 "to the little playhouse": "Joy, Confetti, Samson Opens Fall Festival," *Omaha World-Herald*, September 27, 1917.

66 "The way the show is framed": "C.A. Wortham Shows Have Official Opening," *Billboard*, April 28, 1917.

66 "unprecedented business": "C.A. Wortham Shows Experience Another Big Week at South Dakota Fair," *Billboard*, September 29, 1917.

66 **"Johnny J. Jones Exposition"** through **"Mr. Jones is to be"**: "Johnny J. Jones Exposition Makes Another Scoop; Engagement of English Siamese Twins," *Orlando Sentinel*, February 10, 1918.

67 **"big show"**: "Johnny Jones' Exposition First Big Show to Open," *Billboard*, February 16, 1918.

67 **"Throughout all the shows"**: "Johnny J. Jones Shows Providing Good Attractions," *Calgary Herald*, June 29, 1918.

67 **"high class engagements"**: "The Modern Siamese Twins," *Billboard*, July 22, 1916.

67 **"Joy Trail"**: "An Old Friend Meets Johnny Jones on 'Joy Trail,'" *Winston-Salem Journal*, March 28, 1918.

67 **"Funshine Alley"**: "Johnny J. Jones Shows Providing Good Attractions," *Calgary Herald*, June 29, 1918.

67 **"jaded amusement seekers"**: "Johnny J. Jones Shows Amused Crowds on Monday," *Edmonton Journal*, July 9, 1918.

68 **Lilliputian "city"**: "Johnny Jones' Exposition First Big Show to Open," *Billboard*, February 16, 1918.

68 **"mechanical attractions"**: "Johnny J. Jones Shows Providing Good Attractions," *Calgary Herald*, June 29, 1918.

68 **"There is not a platform"**: "Johnny Jones' Exposition First Big Show to Open," *Billboard*, February 16, 1918.

69 **"inlaid"**: Ed R. Salter, "Johnny J. Jones' Exposition; Salter Details Activities at Birmingham Winter Quarters," *Billboard*, December 28, 1918.

69 **"what is going to be a most unique and fascinating front"**: Ed R. Salter, "Johnny J. Jones' Exposition Attracts Tremendous Attendance at Orlando (Fla.) Mid-Winter Fair," *Billboard*, March 2, 1918.

69 **a "theater" performance**: "An Old Friend Meets Johnny Jones on 'Joy Trail,'" *Winston-Salem Journal*, March 28, 1918.

69 **"most elaborate"**: Ed R. Salter, "Johnny J. Jones' Exhibition," *Billboard*, June 1, 1918.

69 **"entirely blown away"**: "Jones Expo. in Tornado," *Billboard*, August 3, 1918.

69 "The busy boy": Ed R. Salter, "Johnny J. Jones' Exposition; Salter Details Activities at Birmingham Winter Quarters," *Billboard*, December 28, 1918.

69 "his new front and entire equipment": Ed R. Salter, "Johnny J. Jones' Exposition Winter Quarters Notes from Birmingham, Ala.," *Billboard*, November 23, 1918.

69 "resplendent with an abundance of gilt": "Johnny J. Jones Starts 1919 Season at the Orlando (Fla.) Mid-Winter Exhibition," *Billboard*, February 15, 1919.

70 "positively the most gorgeous": Ed R. Salter, "Johnny J. Jones Exhibition," *Orlando Sentinel*, February 2, 1919.

CHAPTER 10

71–72 "Why cry?" through "You girls belong to us now!": Bedford, "Siamese Twins: Chapter II."

73 "During the ten years following": Bedford, "Siamese Twins: Chapter III."

74 "rag banners" through "hats off": Ed R. Salter, "Johnny J. Jones' Exposition," *Billboard*, March 22, 1919.

74 "a tremendous aggregation": "Johnny J. Jones Exposition Plays First of 1921 Fairs," *Billboard*, February 12, 1921.

75 "inseparable" through "the sophistication of age with the charm of girlhood": "Twins of English Parents, Joined by Spinal Cord, Residents of Alamo City," *San Antonio Evening News*, April 5, 1922.

75 "much sought after as playmates" through "will not permit the two girls to become 'public freaks'": "Violet and Daisy: Successors to Siamese Twins," *New York Herald*, May 7, 1922.

76 "American, and proud of it": "Don't Like to Be Called San Antonio Siamese Twins," *Harrisburg Telegraph*, April 18, 1922.

76 "It seems the fair would not be the fair" and "remarkable memories": "Twins Interest Fair Visitors," *Sioux City Journal*, September 24, 1923.

76 "Except for the people": Jensen, *Lives and Loves,* 92.

77 "Carl Lauther, my manager": Jensen, *Lives and Loves,* 94.

77–78 "something never before done" through "Violet and Daisy Hilton, San Antonio's famous grown-together girls": "Fats to Put on Minstrel Performance," *Lake County Times* July 2, 1924.

CHAPTER 11

79 "the biggest attraction on the ground" and "traveling home": Beverly White, "Wortham's World's Best Shows," *Billboard,* May 12, 1923.

79 "Big-time": Bedford, "Siamese Twins: Chapter III."

80 "the first 'Siamese twins' of an English-speaking race": "Two Beauties Linked for Life," *Asbury Park Press,* December 2, 1924.

80 "having the time of their lives": *New York Daily News,* November 28, 1924.

80 "Gotham": "Female Siamese Twins in New York," *Battle Creek Enquirer,* December 23, 1924.

81 "take them back to a carnival" and "to ferret out novelties": Terry Turner, "Owner of Box Office Record-Breaking Attraction Tells Meaning of 'Siamese Twins,'" *Vancouver Sun,* August 23, 1929.

81 "dowdy New York boarding house": Theodore Strauss, "Tricks Without Mirrors," *New York Times,* November 24, 1940.

82 "I found them a rather dejected lot" through "Now that they were ready": Terry Turner, "Owner of Box Office Record-Breaking Attraction Tells Meaning of 'Siamese Twins,'" *Vancouver Sun,* August 23, 1929.

82 "monstrosities" and "Well, God made the Siamese twins": Theodore Strauss, "Tricks Without Mirrors," *New York Times,* November 24, 1940.

82 "too soft hearted" through "to thresh the matter out": Terry Turner, "Owner of Box Office Record-Breaking Attraction Tells Meaning of 'Siamese Twins,'" *Vancouver Sun,* August 23, 1929.

82 "a great listener" and "weighs both sides": Terry Turner, "The President of Loew's, Inc. Nicholas M. Schenck," *Variety,* October 19, 1927.

82 "came to my rescue": Terry Turner, "Owner of Box Office Record-Breaking Attraction Tells Meaning of 'Siamese Twins'," *Vancouver Sun*, August 23, 1929.

83 "get over": "Inside Stuff on Vaudeville," *Variety*, March 11, 1925.

CHAPTER 12

84 "Siamese Twin Ill": "Siamese Twin Ill, Other Is O.K.," *Hanover Evening Sun*, February 9, 1925.

84-85 "as a lark" and "could not be persuaded": "Siamese Twins Will Play, Sing and Dance," *Hackensack Record*, February 14, 1925.

85 "clean-cut youth" and "isn't presented for sympathetic approval": "Siamese Twins," *Variety*, February 25, 1925.

85 "flecked with as many attempts": "Vaudeville Reviews: State," *Variety*, March 25, 1925.

85 "as easy and natural as two people strolling arm in arm": "Siamese Twins," *Variety*, February 25, 1925.

85 "a drawing room gracefully arranged": Grace Kingsley, "Great Show," *Los Angeles Times*, April 27, 1926.

85 "dotted with bits of crossfire": "Siamese Twins," *Variety*, February 25, 1925.

85 "The comedy angle is a corking stand-off": "Vaudeville Reviews: State," *Variety*, March 25, 1925.

85-86 "The finish is a wow" through "very fair": "Siamese Twins," *Variety*, February 25, 1925.

86 "somewhat weak": "Vaudeville Reviews: State," *Variety*, March 25, 1925.

86 "Daisy and Violet Hilton cannot be truthfully" and "the most appealing personalities": "The San Antonio Siamese Twins; Violet and Daisy Hilton," *Billboard*, April 4, 1925.

86 "Each show had the house packed": "Siamese Twins Break Records," *Billboard*, February 28, 1925.

87 "practically every performance": "Siamese Twins' $34,000 Marks Buffalo Film House Record," *Variety*, March 25, 1925.

87 "bent the walls of the theater": "Siamese Twins Draw $32,500 In Cleveland; Break Record by $6,500," *Variety*, March 18, 1925.

87 "held over": Phil Selznick, "Cleveland," *Variety*, March 18, 1925.

87 "like a report from the Director of the Mint": "Vaudeville's Drawing Card," *Variety*, March 18, 1925.

88 "The 'big time' vaudeville bookers": "Freak Twins Break Records in Vaudeville," *Sioux City Journal*, March 8, 1925.

88 "Never in the history": "Expect Siamese Twins to Make New Record for Loew," *Billboard*, March 28, 1925.

88 "too cute to describe": Twins coloring contest advertisement, *New York Mirror*, March 16, 1925.

89 "The Loew circuit officials state": "Expect Siamese Twins to Make New Record for Loew," *Billboard*, March 28, 1925.

90 "'Weather-Proof' and a Sure-Fire Draw": San Antonio's Siamese Twins advertisement in *Variety*, March 18, 1925.

90 "all attendance records in Milwaukee's theatrical annals": "Wisconsin Theater Breaks Record in Milwaukee," *Variety*, October 17, 1925.

90 "At that time": "Siamese Twins, Orpheum Act," *Variety*, December 9, 1925.

90 "the sensation of vaudeville": Earle Theatre advertisement in *Philadelphia Inquirer*, February 20, 1927.

CHAPTER 13

91 "the greatest campaign in the history of the circuit": "Siamese Twins for Orpheum," *Billboard*, December 12, 1925.

92 "remarkable contrast" and "hardly a point": "Siamese Twins—Alike in Everything Except Their Finger Print Types," *Houston Post*, July 8, 1923.

92 "absolutely identical" and "an amazing feature": "Handwriting Reveals Character," *New York Daily News*, July 12, 1936. (See also Robert Saudek and Ernest Seeman, "The Self-Expression of Identical Twins in Handwriting and Drawing," *Character and Personality* (Vol. 1, No. 2, December 1932), 120.)

92 "It was lots of fun": "Siamese Twins Arrive for Act at Croswell," *Adrian Daily Telegram*, September 14, 1928.

93 "Daisy and Violet Hilton Internationally known" and "Siamese Twin Special": retail advertisements in *Wisconsin State Journal*, February 20, 1929.

93 "Why Are Daisy and Violet Hilton Happy": Midway Lunch advertisement in *Marion Star*, October 20, 1928.

93 "Brother died this winter": "Twins at the Grand Theater," *Circleville Herald*, May 8, 1930.

93 "interesting, and showing kindness of heart": " 'Siamese' Twins Seek Twin Dogs," *San Francisco Chronicle*, April 22, 1926.

93-94 "We would much more prefer": "Siamese Twins Alone," *Oregonian*, March 9, 1926.

94 "We have traveled through many lands": " 'Siamese' Twins Seek Twin Dogs," *San Francisco Chronicle*, April 22, 1926.

94 "The Right Hand Lady" and "The Twin on the Left": "Right and Left," *Brooklyn Daily Eagle*, March 29, 1925.

94 "Tactful and bright little creatures": "Greatest Event of Season; Siamese Twins at Orpheum," *Calgary Herald*, March 1, 1926.

94 "We don't get in each other's way": "Twin Beauties, 16, Linked by Physical Tie, Find Joy in Life," *Buffalo Enquirer*, November 29, 1924.

95-96 "Until we learned" and "When I notice the draft": "Likeness of Siamese Twins Ends at Fingertips, Says Reading Bertillon Expert," *Reading Times*, January 25, 1927.

96-97 "She seemed to take more of a fancy to me": "Twins Found to Be Bright and Attractive," *Beatrice Daily Sun*, July 8, 1929.

97 **"barrel roll"**: "Left Siamese Twin Bride Because Three's a Crowd," *San Francisco Examiner*, February 6, 1944.

97 **"I'm afraid I don't like that"**: "Siamese Twins Back Each Other Up During Interview Granted to Two Reporters," *Reading Times*, January 24, 1927.

97 **"Then they are sure"** through **"When you are talking to Daisy"**: "Likeness of Siamese Twins Ends at Fingertips, Says Reading Bertillon Expert," *Reading Times*, January 25, 1927.

98 **"It is surprising how they captivate you"**: "Greatest Event of Season; Siamese Twins at Orpheum," *Calgary Herald*, March 1, 1926.

98 **"I had thought that a variety of amazing adjectives"**: Gladys Hall and Adele Whitely Fletcher, "We Interview the Siamese Twins," *Movie Weekly*, July 18, 1925.

CHAPTER 14

99-100 **"Life Story and Facts"** through **"little girls"**: Myers, *Souvenir and Life Story*, 3–4.

100 **"around the corner"**: Myers, *Souvenir and Life Story*, 8.

101 **"Twins Tell Why"** through **"It is no wonder"**: Myers, *Souvenir and Life Story*, 12–14.

102 **"nearly all the time"**: "San Antonio Twins Star," *Washington Post*, August 9, 1925.

102 **"So much had happened"**: Bedford, "Siamese Twins: Chapter III."

102 **"Naturally, even as children"**: "Fairy Story on Siamese Twins Deals with More Modern Magic, at State," *Harrisburg Evening News*, February 14, 1927.

103 **"In our work we could be natural"**: Bess Carroll, "Twins Unfold Details of 'Bondage,'" *San Antonio Light*, January 13, 1931.

103-104 **"There was so much love"**: Jensen, *Lives and Loves*, 291.

104 **"The art of being happy"**: Tivoli Theatre advertisement in *Richmond Item*, May 9, 1928.

104 "They inspire an emotion of affection": Sam M'Kee, "Throngs Flock to the State," *New York Morning Telegraph*, March 26, 1925.

104-105 "I can get rid of you" and "By saying it aloud to each other": Bedford, "Siamese Twins: Chapter III."

106 "disability of minority": "Minority Disabilities of Twins Removed," *San Antonio Express*, April 2, 1927.

CHAPTER 15

107 "They are not flappers": "Siamese Twins Fight Removal of Disabilities," *San Antonio Express*, January 18, 1931.

107-108 "We could have signed a contract" through "If by any chance he skimmed": Violet and Daisy Hilton, with Michael Lorant, "Life and Loves of the Siamese Twins: Part 3," *The World's News*, October 13, 1937.

108 "When we hesitated to sign": Ethelda Bedford, "The Private Life of the Siamese Twins: Chapter V," *San Francisco Examiner*, October 8, 1944.

108 "They didn't know what the word exploited meant": Camille Rosengren in Zemeckis, *Bound by Flesh*.

108-109 "This Is the Birthday House" through "The castle so long pictured": "This Is the Birthday House San Antonio's Siamese Twins Gave Aunt Who Mothered Them," *San Antonio Express*, October 2, 1927.

109 "That was just a big publicity splash": "Twins Unfold Story of Bondage," *San Antonio Light*, January 20, 1931.

110-111 "the very latest in modern refrigeration" through "probably cost as much": "This Is the Birthday House San Antonio's Siamese Twins Gave Aunt Who Mothered Them," *San Antonio Express*, October 2, 1927.

111-112 "We could never enjoy" through "any friend of Sir": Bedford, "Siamese Twins: Chapter III."

113 **"When we were twenty-one"** through **"matters got worse"**: Bess Carroll, "Twins Unfold Details of 'Bondage,'" *San Antonio Light*, January 13, 1931.

113 **"The Hilton twins . . . are looking forward to the time"**: "Keith-Albee Girl Twins Confide Individual Tastes Often Clash As to Colors, Friends," *Akron Beacon Journal*, May 20, 1929.

114 **"I asked them if they really wished to know"** through **"They told me"**: "Injunction Is Granted and Receiver Named," *San Antonio Light*, January 21, 1931.

115 **"At times they were affectionate"** and **"They grew very unkind"**: "Decision in Siamese Twins Receivership Case Due Today," *San Antonio Express*, January 21, 1931.

115 **"Why can't we go out and have some fun?"** and **"You are not"**: Bedford, "Siamese Twins: Chapter III."

116 **"We can hate"**: Violet and Daisy Hilton, with Michael Lorant, "Life and Loves of the Siamese Twins: Part 2," *The World's News*, October 6, 1937.

116–118 **"In the wings of theaters"** through **"After all"**: Bedford, "Siamese Twins: Chapter III."

118 **"When we went shopping"**: "Daisy, Violet Look to Future," *San Antonio Express*, January 13, 1931.

118 **"Just look at this!"**: Bedford, "Siamese Twins: Chapter III."

118 **"Says Her Husband"**: "Says Her Husband Fell in Love with Both Siamese Twins," *San Antonio Light*, December 7, 1930.

118 **"What have you done?"**: Bedford, "Siamese Twins: Chapter III."

119 **"They both loved him"**: "This Triangle 4-Sided," *Kansas City Times*, March 26, 1931.

119 **"We don't love Bill Oliver!"** through **"I often tell her about you"**: Bedford, "Siamese Twins: Chapter III."

119 **"To our pal, Bill"**: "Says Her Husband Fell in Love with Both Siamese Twins," *San Antonio Light*, December 7, 1930.

119 "'With love' didn't mean that we loved Bill Oliver": Bedford, "Siamese Twins: Chapter III."

119-120 "keeping one jump ahead" through "Mrs. Oliver asserts": "Says Her Husband Fell in Love with Both Siamese Twins," *San Antonio Light*, December 7, 1930.

120 "We didn't even buy our own clothes": "Siamese Twins Scoff at Love Theft Charge," *El Paso Evening Post*, March 30, 1931.

120 "he was not in love": "Says Her Husband Fell in Love with Both Siamese Twins," *San Antonio Light*, December 7, 1930.

120 "a 'shakedown' attempt": "This Triangle 4-Sided," *Kansas City Times*, March 26, 1931.

120-121 "The girls have got to fight this" through "Slavery hasn't been practiced in this country": Bedford, "Siamese Twins: Chapter III." (Violet and Daisy were in fact a few weeks short of their twenty-third birthday at this meeting, but would persist in giving their age as twenty-three in media coverage surrounding their emancipation.)

121 "No one will believe our story" through "Just talk to me": Bedford, "Siamese Twins: Chapter III."

121 "Walk up and down": Ehelda Bedford, "The Private Life of the Siamese Twins: Chapter IV," *San Francisco Examiner*, October 1, 1944.

122 "ever since they were old enough": "Apologies and More Apologies," *Carbondale Daily Free Press*, September 2, 1930.

122 "We want to be our own masters" through "It is only": Violet and Daisy Hilton, with Michael Lorant, "Life and Loves of the Siamese Twins: Part 4," *The World's News*, October 20, 1937.

123-124 "You don't have to go home with this man" through "We could dress and act our age": Bedford, "Siamese Twins: Chapter IV."

124 "We were put under protective custody": Juan M. Vasquez, "Siamese Twins 'Bondage' Trial Packed Courtroom," *San Antonio Express*, January 8, 1969.

124 "sold": "Hilton Twins Ask Freedom," *San Antonio Light*, January 13, 1931.

124 **"Bondage"**: "'Siamese Twins' File Suit to End 'Bondage,'" *San Francisco Examiner*, January 13, 1931.

124 **"Owners"**: "Siamese Twins, 'Sold' by Their Mother After Birth, Sue 'Owners' for Freedom," *Indianapolis Star*, January 13, 1931.

124 **"Slavery"**: "Siamese Twins Say They Were Held in Slavery," *Houston Chronicle*, January 13, 1931.

124-125 **"The girls must have had the idea"** and **"the sweet side of life"**: "Suit Blamed on Love of Gaiety," *San Antonio Light*, January 13, 1931.

125 **"left alone in the house frequently"** and **"call for aid at any time"**: "Famed Siamese Twins Kept in Bondage, Accounting Suit Says," *San Antonio Express*, January 13, 1931.

125 **"The girls are easily led"** through **"They don't seem to be making any allowances"**: "Suit Blamed on Love of Gaiety," *San Antonio Light*, January 13, 1931.

125 **"shattered"**: "Siamese Twins Await Hearing," *San Antonio Express*, January 14, 1931.

126 **"explaining each part of it"**: "Suit Blamed on Love of Gaiety," *San Antonio Light*, January 13, 1931.

126 **"We did everything for them"**: "Famed Siamese Twins Kept in Bondage, Accounting Suit Says," *San Antonio Express*, January 13, 1931.

126 **"toy apartment"** through **"the utmost contentment"**: Bess Carroll, "Twins Unfold Details of 'Bondage,'" *San Antonio Light*, January 13, 1931.

126 **"Always we have had someone prompting us"** through **"Then we will build a little house"**: "Daisy, Violet Look to Future," *San Antonio Express*, January 13, 1931.

126-127 **"Their high pitched laughter"**: "Siamese Twins Await Hearing," *San Antonio Express*, January 14, 1931.

127 **"except the things we had on when we left"** and **"Boy was the only thing I hated to leave"**: Bess Carroll, "Twins Unfold Details of 'Bondage,'" *San Antonio Light*, January 13, 1931.

127 "We actually seemed to grow in stature": Bess Carroll, "Twins Unfold Details of 'Bondage,'" *San Antonio Light*, January 13, 1931.

CHAPTER 17

128 "Court attachés dusted off" and "They can hang on the rafters": "S.R.O. Expected in Hilton Case," *San Antonio Express*, January 16, 1931.

129 "from flippant high school girls to staid grandmothers" and "chattering, tittering, giggling": "Siamese Twins Trial Delayed," *Lubbock Morning Avalanche*, January 17, 1931.

129 "This is the biggest crowd": "Siamese Twins Seek Freedom from Bondage," *Brownwood Bulletin*, January 16, 1931.

129 "crisp exchange": "Hilton Case Delayed 3 Days," *San Antonio Light*, January 16, 1931.

129 "Is Myers in the court?" through "I see no reason": "Lawyers Clash in Hilton Hearing," *San Antonio Express*, January 17, 1931.

129 "We are here to represent them" through "They're not trying to dodge anything": "Hilton Case Delayed 3 Days," *San Antonio Light*, January 16, 1931.

129-130 "Have you seen Myers this morning?" through "I do not know": "Lawyers Clash in Hilton Hearing," *San Antonio Express*, January 17, 1931.

130 "wait[ing] for the curtain to go up" and "that left people with the impression": Viola Brennan, "Twins Find Many Friends," *San Antonio Light*, January 16, 1931.

130-131 "We've always been regarded as freaks": "Siamese Twins Seek Freedom from Bondage," *Brownwood Bulletin*, January 16, 1931.

131 "How are you enjoying it?" through "I am sorry it was over so soon": "Lawyers Clash in Hilton Hearing," *San Antonio Express*, January 17, 1931.

131 "We didn't know what to expect": Viola Brennan, "Twins Find Many Friends," *San Antonio Light*, January 16, 1931.

131 "There in the court-house": Violet and Daisy Hilton, with Michael Lorant, "Life and Loves of the Siamese Twins: Part 3," *The World's News*, October 20, 1937.

131 "to do anything that they might want" and "Friendliness, awe, wonder": Viola Brennan, "Twins Find Many Friends," *San Antonio Light*, January 16, 1931.

132 "Hello, dear" and "occasionally casting a queer glance at the twins": Felix M'Knight, "Twins Anxious That People Understand," *San Antonio Light*, January 20, 1931.

132 "The crowd, quite open in its sentiment": "Twins Give Receipt for Missing Money," *San Antonio Light*, January 19, 1931.

132 "Outbursts of laughter and sighs of disgust": "Twins Unfold Story of Bondage," *San Antonio Light*, January 20, 1931.

133-134 "All this property was bought" through "Every time I would mention business": "Myers Says He Spent $213,000 of Cash Made by Hilton Twins," *San Antonio Express*, January 20, 1931.

134 "Were you under the impression" and "No, I wasn't": "Twins Give Receipt for Missing Money," *San Antonio Light*, January 19, 1931.

134 "They always told me they did not need money" through "I considered it my money": "Myers Says He Spent $213,000 of Cash Made by Hilton Twins," *San Antonio Express*, January 20, 1931.

134 "had no reason to consider it anything else": "Siamese Twins of Texas Seeking Money Alleged Due," *Corsicana Semi-Weekly Light*, January 20, 1931.

134 "It all went into one lump" through "If this man makes another remark": "Myers Says He Spent $213,000 of Cash Made by Hilton Twins," *San Antonio Express*, January 20, 1931.

134 "sneering remarks": "Twins Give Receipt for Missing Money," *San Antonio Light*, January 19, 1931.

134-135 "ceaseless hammering" through "Do you claim to be a businessman?": "Myers Says He Spent $213,000 of Cash Made by Hilton Twins," *San Antonio Express*, January 20, 1931.

136 "word war" through "Once in Nebraska": "Twins Unfold Story of Bondage," *San Antonio Light*, January 20, 1931.

137 "quiet subdued little woman" through "Show people—that's what we are": Felix M'Knight, "Twins Anxious That People Understand," *San Antonio Light*, January 20, 1931.

CHAPTER 18

138 "rushed pellmell" and "loud talking": "Decision in Siamese Twins Receivership Case Due Today," *San Antonio Express*, January 21, 1931.

138 "make neighborly calls" and "she was met at the gate": "Twins Unfold Story of Bondage," *San Antonio Light*, January 20, 1931.

139 "This is no show": "Decision in Siamese Twins Receivership Case Due Today," *San Antonio Express*, January 21, 1931.

139 "Would the judge believe the story" through "Then I began to talk": Bedford, "Siamese Twins: Chapter IV."

140 "There are, you see" and "stimulated and strengthened": Bedford, "Siamese Twins: Chapter V."

140-41 "Is that your signature?" through "He told us we were born in England": "Decision in Siamese Twins Receivership Case Due Today," *San Antonio Express*, January 21, 1931.

141 "there were no locks on the windows or doors": "Twins Unfold Story of Bondage," *San Antonio Light*, January 20, 1931.

141-43 "But he always told us" through "I never swore at him": "Decision in Siamese Twins Receivership Case Due Today," *San Antonio Express*, January 21, 1931.

143 "sobbed out": "Injunction Is Granted and Receiver Named," *San Antonio Light*, January 21, 1931.

144-145 "In the twenty-three years" through "big time": "Decision in Siamese Twins Receivership Case Due Today," *San Antonio Express*, January 21, 1931.

145-146 "I knew that my client" through "The Hilton twins would not": "Injunction Is Granted and Receiver Named," *San Antonio Light*, January 21, 1931.

146-147 "For the first time in their lives" and "where they reign as queens": "Twins Lay Plans for Wider Travel," *San Antonio Express*, January 22, 1931.

147 "Attorney and Mrs. Arnold" and "The 'don'ts' of our childhood": Bedford, "Siamese Twins: Chapter V."

147 "glowing with the thrill" and "Although we have been in vaudeville": "Twins Sign First Contract," *San Antonio Light*, January 29, 1931.

148 "You don't mean it!" and "Is it really true?": "Siamese Twins Given $100,000," *San Antonio Express*, April 25, 1931.

CHAPTER 19

152 "a hummingbird's life": "Hilton Twins Die at 60," *Greensboro Record*, January 6, 1969. (Paraphrased from Dot Jackson, "The Only Bargain We Get Is Our Weight for a Penny," *Charlotte Observer*, January 6, 1969.)

152 "They loved to go": Juan M. Vasquez, "Siamese Twins 'Bondage' Trial Packed Courtroom," *San Antonio Express*, January 8, 1969.

152 "frilly" and "sophisticated": Eric Gibbs, "Siamese Twins Evolve Technique for 'Dates,'" *Windsor Star*, May 14, 1937.

152 "I remember that very well": Juan M. Vasquez, "Siamese Twins 'Bondage' Trial Packed Courtroom," *San Antonio Express*, January 8, 1969.

152 "We love to go walking": "'It Pays to Be Twins,' Hilton Sisters Declare; San Antonio Girls Enjoy Life on Stage," *Houston Chronicle*, March 29, 1931.

153 "Only by a hard inner struggle": Robert Saudek and Ernest Seeman. "The Self-Expression of Identical Twins in Handwriting and Drawing," *Character and Personality* (Vol. 1, No. 2, December 1932), 121.

153 "There was a kind of desperate 'I'm OK-ness'": Camille Rosengren in Zemeckis, *Bound by Flesh*.

153-154 "More than anything else" through "You were not conscious of it": Juan M. Vasquez, "Siamese Twins 'Bondage' Trial Packed Courtroom," *San Antonio Express*, January 8, 1969.

154-155 "Under the Myerses they were taken care of": Camille Rosengren in Zemeckis, *Bound by Flesh*.

155 "They were just so generous with their money": Jim Moore, 1978 interview with Esther MacMillan, 31, digital.utsa.edu/cdm/ref/collection /p15125coll4/id/794.

155 "In almost all human relationships": Bedford, "Siamese Twins: Chapter I."

155 "When we were eight years old": Michael Naver, "Two Together Half Century," *Baltimore Sun*, September 20, 1960.

156 "We just saw that tolerance": Daisy Hilton, "One Siamese Twin's Engagement Was Big Surprise to Other," *Franklin Evening Star*, July 21, 1936.

156 "Having once given her my word": Bedford, "Siamese Twins: Chapter I."

156 "All this talk about 'identical' twins is just bosh": "Siamese Pair in Atlanta for Few Hours," *Atlanta Constitution*, January 30, 1946.

156 "horrible brown": Eric Gibbs, "Siamese Twins Evolve Technique for 'Dates,'" *Windsor Star*, May 14, 1937.

156 "each of us has an individual personality": Glenn C. Pullen, "Swinging Down the Avenue," *Cleveland Plain Dealer*, May 14, 1941.

156 "sweet romantic stories" through "sophisticated literature": Eric Gibbs, "Siamese Twins Evolve Technique for 'Dates,'" *Windsor Star*, May 14, 1937.

156 "It's a big bore": "Siamese Twins Joined, but Go Separate Ways," *Miami News*, December 29, 1954.

156 "So we decided early on": Daisy Hilton, "One Siamese Twin's Engagement Was Big Surprise to Other," *Franklin Evening Star*, July 21, 1936.

156-157 "If Daisy wants to give her money away": Wheeler W. Dixon and Audrey Brown Fraser, eds. *I Went That-a-Way: The Memoirs of a Western Film Director, Harry L. Fraser* (Metuchen, NJ: Scarecrow Press, 1990), 132.

157 "**She did not help me**": Violet and Daisy Hilton with Michael Lorant, "Life and Loves of the Siamese Twins: Part 3," *The World's News*, October 13, 1937.

157 "**One of us just goes along**" and "**not to act the mother-in-law**": Daisy Hilton, "One Siamese Twin's Engagement Was Big Surprise to Other," *Franklin Evening Star*, July 21, 1936.

157 "**I just read**": "Can't Afford Grudges Say Siamese Twins," *Victoria Daily Times*, February 7, 1940.

157 "**healthy tempers**": Daisy Hilton, "One Siamese Twin's Engagement Was Big Surprise to Other," *Franklin Evening Star*, July 21, 1936.

157 "**When I get mad**" and "**That's right**": Michael Naver, "Two Together Half Century," *Baltimore Sun*, September 20, 1960.

157-158 "**It's lucky that neither of us holds a grudge**" and "**But we never**": Daisy Hilton, "One Siamese Twin's Engagement Was Big Surprise to Other," *Franklin Evening Star*, July 21, 1936.

158 "**And we do not magnify or minimize**": Bedford, "Siamese Twins: Chapter I."

158 "**high-strung, quick-tempered, and jealous**" and "**quiet and broad-minded**": Lady Terrington, "Twin Still Plans Early Marriage," *New York Daily Mirror*, July 7, 1934.

158 "**the diplomat**": Tom Vinciguerra, "Twins Parting with the Stage," *Miami Herald*, April 17, 1955.

158 "**irate and hard to please theater managers**": Lindy Wilder, "Case of Give and Take with Siamese Sisters," *Newport News Daily Press*, October 15, 1960.

158 "**We settled that by deciding**" and "**When we see married couples**": Daisy Hilton, "One Siamese Twin's Engagement Was Big Surprise to Other," *Franklin Evening Star*, July 21, 1936.

158 "**We try to extend the same courtesies**": Lindy Wilder, "Case of Give and Take with Siamese Sisters," *Newport News Daily Press*, October 15, 1960.

158 "**If we can get along, anyone can do it**": Michael Naver, "Two Together Half Century," *Baltimore Sun*, September 20, 1960.

158 "They were very congenial": Juan M. Vasquez, "Siamese Twins 'Bondage' Trial Packed Courtroom," *San Antonio Express,* January 8, 1969.

159 "thought messages": Bedford, "Siamese Twins: Chapter IV."

159 "Marry me, Daisy": Bedford, "Siamese Twins: Chapter V."

159-160 "Actually confronted with this odd situation" through "This way: You will be my wife": Bedford, "Siamese Twins: Chapter IV."

160 "Even as he asked me he took the cigarette" through "Should she be subjected to such restraint?": Bedford, "Siamese Twins: Chapter V."

161 "It is the only life we know": "Why the Siamese Twins Left Home," *Idaho Falls Daily Post,* March 1, 1931.

161 "Why should I submit both of us": Bedford, "Siamese Twins: Chapter V."

161 "Could either of us marry?": Bedford, "Siamese Twins: Chapter IV."

161-162 "Those stories were entirely wrong" through "I told them they should stop having parties": "Don Juan a Headache to Don Galvan," *San Francisco Examiner,* March 18, 1945.

CHAPTER 20

163 "a horror story more horrible than all the rest": David J. Skal and Elias Savada, *Dark Carnival: The Secret World of Tod Browning, Hollywood's Master of the Macabre* (New York: Anchor Books, 1995), 164.

164 "three times as many freaks as a Ringling show": "Film Reviews: Freaks," *Variety,* July 12, 1932.

164 "Half Boy" and "snapped off": Faith Service, "The Amazing Life Stories of the Freaks," *Motion Picture,* April 1932.

165 "58 pounds soaking wet": "Living Skeleton Weds Fat Lady of Barnum and Bailey," *Indiana (PA) Evening Gazette,* November 26, 1924.

165 "Half man, half woman. Brother and sister in one body.": Estelle, "Man-Woman a Woman Now, 1937," The Skittish Library, January 25, 2015, skittishlibrary.co.uk/man-woman-a-woman-now-1937.

167 "could get to eat in the commissary without throwing up": Skal and Savada, *Dark Carnival,* 168.

167 "astonishingly variable results": "Film Reviews: Freaks," *Variety,* July 12, 1932.

167–168 "some horrified spectators" and "smashed all house records": Muriel Babcock, "'Freaks' Rouse Ire and Wonder," *Los Angeles Times,* February 14, 1932.

168 "His theme is never permitted to bloom": Harold W. Cohen, "Todd [sic] Browning Tries Something Different in 'Freaks' at the Penn," *Pittsburgh Post-Gazette,* February 22, 1932.

168 "as human beings rather than curiosities": "Loew's: 'Freaks,'" *Louisville Courier-Journal,* February 20, 1932.

168 "it is impossible for the normal man or woman" : "Film Reviews: Freaks," *Variety,* July 12, 1932.

168 "upon your own reaction": Philip K. Scheuer, "'Freaks' File Side Show," *Los Angeles Times,* February 15, 1932.

168 "To put such creatures in a picture": Muriel Babcock, "'Freaks' Rouse Ire and Wonder," *Los Angeles Times,* February 14, 1932.

169 "an uproar": untitled squib, *New York Daily News,* February 21, 1932.

169 "Are you afraid to see Freaks?": Loew's Theatre advertisement in *Rochester Democrat & Chronicle,* February 16, 1932.

169 "Slimy . . . Gibbering Creatures of Nature": Aztec Theatre advertisement in *San Antonio Light,* May 16, 1932.

169 "reaches the very pinnacle of bad taste": Cecelia Ager, "Going Places: Stars Shun Freaks," *Variety,* July 12, 1932.

169 "happily are not in the repugnant sequences of the film": "San Antonio's Siamese Twins on Aztec Screen," *San Antonio Express,* May 15, 1932.

169 "We thought it was wonderful": "Siamese Twins Give Interview," *Idaho Falls Post Register,* May 1, 1932.

169 "We most certainly do not consider ourselves freaks" and "We, however, are not in carnivals": Clyde Gilmour, "Dignity Vital, Say 'Inseparable' Pair," *Vancouver Sun,* February 5, 1951.

170 "For instance": "Music Halls: Leeds Empire," *Yorkshire Post and Leeds Intelligencer,* January 10, 1933.

170 "still good vaudeville": "Vaude House Reviews: State-Lake," *Variety,* September 27, 1932.

170 "Applause was mild": "Vaude House Reviews: RKO, L.A.," *Variety,* March 8, 1932.

171 "Hilton Sisters not a good draw": "Picture Grosses: 'Consent,' Kate Smith Top Boston, $22,000," *Variety,* August 16, 1932.

CHAPTER 21

173 "the subject of a great deal of controversial talk" and "there is nothing distasteful about their act": "Music Halls: Leeds Empire," *Yorkshire Post and Leeds Intelligencer,* January 10, 1933.

173 "primarily due to the British": "Vaudeville: British Vaude Has Hope," *Variety,* February 20, 1934.

173 "Act sustains interest throughout": "Vaudeville House Reviews: Finsbury Park Empire (London)," *Variety,* January 31, 1933.

173 "crazy on attending boxing matches": "Inseparable Twins with Many Differing Views," *Derby Daily Telegraph,* July 11, 1933.

173 "Hilton sisters create a sensation": "Chatter: London," *Variety,* February 14, 1933.

173 "more warm-hearted": "British 'Siamese Twins,'" *Portsmouth Evening News,* May 23, 1933.

174 "mild scuffle": "Twin Stars Arrive," *Sheffield Independent,* January 31, 1933.

174 "Do I mind": "'Siamese' Twins for Hull," *Hull Daily Mail,* April 6, 1933.

174 "He's a charming boy": "Britain's Siamese Twins; Daisy and Violet Hilton Talk of Themselves," *Hull Daily Mail,* April 12, 1933.

175 "Both of the girls are swell": "One of the Hilton 'Siamese Twins' to Be Married," *San Francisco Examiner*, April 23, 1933.

175 "Now I don't think he'll be able to get here": "British 'Siamese Twins,'" *Portsmouth Evening News*, May 23, 1933.

175 "Enjoyable and meeting with approval": "Edinburgh: Royal," *The Stage*, March 2, 1933.

175 "a hit" and "an enthusiastic reception": "Siamese Twins at the Tivoli," *Aberdeen Press and Journal*, February 21, 1933.

176 "a warm welcome to their natal town": "The Provinces: Brighton Hippodrome," *The Stage*, April 6, 1933.

176 "whole-time attention": "Rush to See Twins," *Hull Daily Mail*, April 15, 1933.

176 "that Siamese twins were in our family tree": Jensen, *Lives and Loves*, 228.

176 "a cinch": "Vaudeville House Reviews: Finsbury Park Empire (London)," *Variety*, January 31, 1933.

176 "brodie" and "Many a good attraction out of town": "Vaudeville: British Vaude Has Hope," *Variety*, February 20, 1934.

177 "The Best of This Week's Shows": "The Best of This Week's Shows," *Western Mail and South Wales News*, May 30, 1933.

177 "Dancing Siamese Twins to Double in Matrimony": "Dancing Siamese Twins to Double in Matrimony," *Brooklyn Daily Eagle*, October 6, 1933.

177 "a prominent English boxer": "Hilton Twins, Back from Abroad, Both to Marry," *San Antonio Light*, October 6, 1933.

177 "the dearest boy in the world": "Siamese Twins to Wed—One a Boxer; The Other a Leader of an Orchestra," *Austin American*, October 7, 1933.

178-179 "a gay foursome" and "After a while": Ethelda Bedford, "The Private Life of the Siamese Twins: Chapter VI," *San Francisco Examiner*, October 15, 1944.

180 "colorful, melodious, fast-moving" and "a large chorus of well-trained Broadway beauties": "Siamese Twins in Revue at Capitol," *Trenton Evening Times,* May 19, 1934.

180 "folded": "Hilton Unit Folds," *Variety,* May 22, 1934.

180 "good business": "Burlesque-Tabloid: Tab Tattles," *Billboard,* April 21, 1934.

181 "Financial security": Jensen, *Lives and Loves,* 287–288.

181 "That's where their hundred thousand dollars went": Jim Moore, 1978 interview with Esther MacMillan, 37, digital.utsa.edu/cdm/ref/collection/p15125coll4/id/794.

181 "They were making the best of their world": Camille Rosengren in Zemeckis, *Bound by Flesh.*

181 "Siamese Twins Denied Right": "Siamese Twins Denied Right to Get Married," *Wilkes-Barre Evening News,* July 5, 1934.

181 "Double Trouble": "Double Trouble for Siamese Twins Seeking Wedding License," *San Francisco Examiner,* July 6, 1934.

182 "rather vague" and "moral grounds": "City Bars Wedding of Siamese Twin," *New York Times,* July 6, 1934.

182 "The whole thing shattered the aplomb": "Marriage License Refused to One of 'Siamese Twins,'" *Charlotte News,* July 5, 1934.

182 "not in the least dismayed": "Siamese Twin Fights for License to Wed," *Charlotte Observer,* July 6, 1934.

182 *"Application is denied"* and "was vested with discretionary powers": "City Bars Wedding of Siamese Twin," *New York Times,* July 6, 1934.

182 "The very idea of such a marriage": "Pygopagus Marriage," *Time,* July 16, 1934.

182 "Nothing doing": "Double Trouble for Siamese Twins Seeking Wedding License," *San Francisco Examiner,* July 6, 1934.

183 "I don't see any reason in the world" through "I think my sister's marriage": "Siamese Twins Refused Right to Marry—Outtakes,"

Fox Movietone News Story 22-604, July 6, 1934, https://mirc.sc.edu/islandora/object/usc%3A41249.

183 "Are Twins People, or a Person?": "Are Twins People, or a Person? Science Ponders the Question as Siamese Pair Enter New Battle," *Jersey Journal,* July 9, 1934.

183 "It's a shame" through "I wish I were": Lady Terrington, "Twin Still Plans Early Marriage," *New York Daily Mirror,* July 7, 1934.

183 "more than twenty states": "Siamese Twin in Plea," *New York Times,* July 14, 1934.

184 "Violet-&-Daisy Hilton" and "a double-monster joined at the buttocks": "Pygopagus Marriage," *Time,* July 16, 1934.

184 "recurrent booms of a dozen flashlight cameras": "It's Immoral; Not Just Two's Company, Three's a Crowd," *Murphysboro Daily Independent,* August 23, 1934.

184 "Owensboro is the only city": "Hilton Sisters Present Attractive Program Here," *Messenger-Inquirer,* July 31, 1934.

184 "goofus dance" and "Chief Eagle Feather, full blooded Cherokee": Barney, "Hilton Sisters," *Variety,* October 30, 1934.

184 "one of the nation's most sensational marriage marts": "Crown Point Again," *Indianapolis News,* August 25, 1934.

185 "vetoed": Hazel Canning, "Should Siamese Twins Be Prohibited from Marrying?" *Ogden Examiner,* September 2, 1934.

185 "We're going to have a showdown": "Twin Invited to Marry in Marion, Ark.," *Charlotte News,* July 6, 1934.

185 "Our pride makes us insist": Lady Terrington, "Twin Still Plans Early Marriage," *New York Daily Mirror,* July 7, 1934.

185 "Write! Wire! Phone! For Open Dates": Hilton Sisters advertisement in *Billboard,* July 14, 1934.

185 "Weep for These Poor Girls!" through "Shades of Myer-Myers": "Weep for These Poor Girls!" *Billboard,* July 14, 1934.

185–186 "if you are really getting married" through "I doubt both statements": W. H. Rice, "Carnivals: Chop Suey," *Billboard,* July 21, 1934.

186 "With the reams of newspaper publicity": Barney, "Hilton Sisters," *Variety*, October 30, 1934

186 "The 40-minute show built around them is sad": Barney, "Hilton Sisters Revue," *Variety*, January 8, 1936.

CHAPTER 23

187 "a complete stage show": "Texas Siamese to Wed at Centennial Saturday Night," *Wellington Leader*, July 16, 1936.

187-188 "If I can get a license" through "Jim smiled good-naturedly": Bedford, "Siamese Twins: Chapter VI."

188 "bucked": "Annulment Suit Halted by Judge," *Clarion Ledger*, October 15, 1936.

188 "Well, my family" and "If I was smart": Jim Moore, 1978 interview with Esther MacMillan, 41, digital.utsa.edu/cdm/ref/collection/p15125 coll4/id/794.

188 "No, we didn't want public attention": "Siamese Twin Violet Hilton's Problems as a Wife," *San Francisco Examiner*, August 23, 1936.

188 "I think every girl": Daisy Hilton, "Siamese Twin Will Be Married at Dallas Cotton Bowl Tonight," *Franklin Evening Star*, July 18, 1936.

189 "We had learned how not to know": "Siamese Twin Violet Hilton's Problems as a Wife," *San Francisco Examiner*, August 23, 1936.

189 "Daisy would have a date": Juan M. Vasquez, "Siamese Twins 'Bondage' Trial Packed Courtroom," *San Antonio Express*, January 8, 1969.

189-190 "I was right in the middle" through "I have known the girls": "Siamese Twin Violet Hilton's Problems as a Wife," *San Francisco Examiner*, August 23, 1936.

191 "Houdini wanted to make us self-reliant": Daisy Hilton, "Hilton Sisters Credit Houdini for Happiness," *Hammond Times*, July 23, 1936.

192 "but that does not mean anything": "Siamese Twin Violet Hilton's Problems as a Wife," *San Francisco Examiner*, August 23, 1936.

193 "convulsed with mirth": Bedford, "Siamese Twins: Chapter I."

193 "Come on down and congratulate the bride!": "5000 Cheer as Twin Is Married," *San Antonio Light,* July 19, 1936.

193 "glided along behind": "Violet Hilton of Siamese Twins Weds," *Des Moines Register,* July 19, 1936.

193 "It's swell": "5000 Cheer as Twin Is Married," *San Antonio Light,* July 19, 1936.

193 "I've been in love with Jimmy": "Siamese Twin Becomes Bride," *Miami Herald,* July 20, 1936. (See also "Violet Hilton of Siamese Twins Weds," *Des Moines Register,* July 19, 1936.)

193 "Because the twins endured" through "was one of those": Jensen, *Lives and Loves,* 279.

193-194 "A crowd pursued us" and "We went to Hollywood": Bedford, "Siamese Twins: Chapter VI."

194 "unimpeachable source": "Siamese Twin's Marriage on Rocks," *San Antonio Express,* September 5, 1936.

194 "forced on them by booking agents": "Annulment Suit Halted by Judge," *Clarion Ledger,* October 15, 1936.

194 "Jimmy and I are" and "I think the world of the girls": Jim Moore, newsreel footage in Zemeckis, *Bound by Flesh.*

194 "never gone through the formalities of a divorce": Bedford, "Siamese Twins: Chapter VI."

194-195 "Two Lovely Girls!": Atlas Theater advertisement, *Victoria Times-Colonist,* February 6, 1940.

195 "Maybe the poor little Siamese twins" and "Vi and Daisy put their careers at risk": Jensen, *Lives and Loves,* 280.

195-196 "after all that fuss and fume" through "they turned their joint backs": "Marriage Was Just a Gag, 'Siamese' Twins Say Here," *Minneapolis Tribune,* October 2, 1936.

196 "They were joined together physically": Jensen, *Lives and Loves,* 280.

197 "Well, maybe there is someone": Lady Terrington, "Twin Still Plans Early Marriage," *New York Daily Mirror,* July 7, 1934.

198 "They wanted to have it done right" through "This young lady is perfectly capable": Jim Moore, 1978 interview with Esther MacMillan, 28, digital.utsa.edu/cdm/ref/collection/p15125coll4/id/794.

198 "I don't want children": Lady Terrington, "Twin Still Plans Early Marriage," *New York Daily Mirror,* July 7, 1934.

198 "We could have children": Clyde Gilmour, "Dignity Vital, Say 'Inseparable' Pair," *Vancouver Sun,* February 5, 1951.

198-199 "quite noticeable, almost" through "And she would give me no information": Jim Moore, 1978 interview with Esther MacMillan, 29–30.

199 "Her illness was at first": "Siamese Twin, Appearing at Tomah, Is Ill," *La Crosse Tribune,* November 29, 1940.

200 "We had to turn our thoughts": Bedford, "Siamese Twins: Chapter VI."

200 "impertinent questions about Violet's marriage" and "The Hilton Sisters grow older": "Reviews of Acts: Hilton Sisters," *Billboard,* December 25, 1937.

200 "dying to know": Barney, "Hilton Sisters Revue," *Variety,* January 8, 1936.

200 "intimate questions": Capitol Theater advertisement, *Nanaimo Daily News,* February 3, 1940.

201 "Freak Acts" and "usually get the theater publicity": "Problems of Vaudeville Booking Today," *Billboard,* April 9, 1938.

202 "friends who attended the wedding" and "she had not been aware of her son's plans": "Elmiran Weds Siamese Twin in Buffalo," *Elmira Star-Gazette,* September 17, 1941.

202 "I felt then that her marriage": Bedford, "Siamese Twins: Chapter VI."

202 "We never consult or advise": Bedford, "Siamese Twins: Chapter I."

203 **"Then one morning when we looked across"**: Bedford, "Siamese Twins: Chapter VI."

203 **"Daisy is a lovely girl"**: "Left His Siamese Twin Bride Because Three's a Crowd," *San Francisco Examiner,* February 6, 1944.

203 **"The marriage was just totally"** and **"Marry one of us"**: Philip Morris in Zemeckis, *Bound by Flesh.*

203 **"Some people thought"**: Jensen, *Lives and Loves,* 299.

CHAPTER 25

204 **"They really could not understand"**: Philip Morris in Zemeckis, *Bound by Flesh.*

204 **"I worked with them"**: Val Valentine in Zemeckis, *Bound by Flesh.*

205 **"When we saw them onstage"** and **"We were embarrassed for them"**: Jensen, *Lives and Loves,* 306–307.

205-206 **"Actually, we hate doing something"** through **"They still love us"**: Dale Huffman, "Hecklers Don't Worry Exotic Siamese Twins," *Cincinnati Post,* June 13, 1958.

206 **"Adults only"**: "Notice," *Franklin (PA) News-Herald,* December 3, 1943.

206 **"It didn't matter to them"**: Jensen, *Lives and Loves,* 317.

206 **"The Hilton Sisters, Siamese twins"**: Vincent Johnson, "Siamese Twins in Trance Thrill Canteen Audience," *Pittsburgh Post-Gazette,* November 20, 1943.

207 **"turnaway business"**: Jack Kofoed, "Let's Have No Sloppy GIs," *Miami Herald,* December 17, 1954.

207 **"The famous Hilton Sisters"**: Bob Fredericks, "On with the Show: Olympia Vaudeville, a Review," *Miami Herald,* November 23, 1944.

207 **"People didn't care what the Hiltons did"**: "Did You Wonder What Happened To: Daisy and Violet Hilton," *Miami Herald,* December 17, 1967.

208 **"In case you care":** Danton Walker, "Broadway," *New York Daily News,* November 2, 1945.

208 **"those old standbys of show business":** George Bourke, "On with the Show: Olympia Vaudeville," *Miami Herald,* November 29, 1945.

208 **"try hard with their harmonies":** "House Review: Olympia, Miami," *Variety,* December 5, 1945.

208 **"Like monkeys in the zoo":** "Hilton Siamese Twins Plan Comeback; Tire of Inactivity," *Quad-City Times,* June 25, 1947.

208-209 **"That is what we"** and **"middle-aged":** "Hilton Sisters Stay Over Night in City; Famed Siamese Twins," *Jacksonville (IL) Daily Journal,* July 30, 1947.

209 **"I don't know why some people think":** Glenn C. Pullen, "Swinging Down the Avenue," *Cleveland Plain Dealer,* May 14, 1941.

209 **"girl show":** "JJJ Contracts Hilton Sisters; Ward Org into Aberdeen, S.D.," *Billboard,* January 17, 1948.

209 **"vacationing"** and **"diversified weather":** "Famous Hilton Twins Rest at Highland Tourist Court," *Hammond Times,* November 29, 1948.

209 **"I wouldn't like to go":** "No Sob Story," *Detroit Free Press,* September 16, 1959.

CHAPTER 26

211 **"The stage had real talent":** Hayden R. Palmer, "Death of Joe Weber Recalls Early Days," *Lansing State Journal,* May 17, 1942.

211 **"they were used by guys who took their money":** Camille Rosengren in Zemeckis, *Bound by Flesh.*

211 **"I'm fascinated by *Chained for Life*":** Hedda Hopper, "Hollywood," *Boston Traveler,* August 10, 1951.

211-212 **"I was assigned"** through **"cheery and happy":** Dixon and Fraser, *I Went That-a-Way,* 131–132.

212 **"We were able to be the puppets":** Judi Green, "Touring Siamese Twins Scan Problems, Accomplishments," *Lowell Sun,* August 19, 1960.

212 "It was not a production in which I took much pride": Dixon and Fraser, *I Went That-a-Way*, 131.

212 "Their hopes for": Jensen, *Lives and Loves*, 338.

212-213 "we decided that our physical" through "Except happiness": Harry L. Fraser, dir., *Chained for Life*, Spera Productions, Inc., 1952.

213 "tied up in litigation shortly after its completion": Dixon and Fraser, *I Went That-a-Way*, 131.

214 "the exploitation would have capitalized": Dixon and Fraser, *I Went That-a-Way*, 133.

214 "a full length feature musical": Hilton Sisters advertisement in *Variety*, August 22, 1951.

214 "'Chained for Life' Chained to Dullness": George Bourke, "Night Life," *Miami Herald*, August 1, 1952.

214-215 "is being dreadfully pompous" through "matched in horror": "Siamese Twins in Film Now at Center Theater," *Boston Traveler*, February 11, 1955.

215 "Never-before-told stories": "Lyric Siamese Twins," *Cincinnati Enquirer*, May 18, 1953.

215 "We don't discuss that": Kenneth Nichols, "Hilton Twins Feature 'I,' Not 'We,'" *Akron Beacon Journal*, September 5, 1952.

215 "The Hilton sisters were well aware": Dixon and Fraser, *I Went That-a-Way*, 133.

215 "simply gushed": Kenneth Nichols, "Hilton Twins Feature 'I,' Not 'We,'" *Akron Beacon Journal*, September 5, 1952.

216 "There's no courtesy" through "last fling": Tom Vinciguerra, "Twins Parting with the Stage," *Miami Herald*, April 17, 1955.

216 "open-air snackery": Damon Runyon Jr., "Famed Siamese Twins Run Miami Snack Bar," *Miami News*, June 8, 1955.

217 "I don't think that I've ever had": Daisy Hilton, newsreel footage in Zemeckis, *Bound by Flesh*.

217 "We intend to make Miami our home": Damon Runyon Jr., "Famed Siamese Twins Run Miami Snack Bar," *Miami News,* June 8, 1955.

CHAPTER 27

218 "Girlie Show": Five O'Clock Club advertisement in *Miami Herald,* May 17, 1956. (See also Dale Huffman, "Hecklers Don't Worry Exotic Siamese Twins," *Cincinnati Post,* June 13, 1958.)

218 "the first time on a fun zone in years": "Carnival Confab," *Billboard,* August 3, 1959.

219 "We don't talk to carnie people": "No Sob Story," *Detroit Free Press,* September 16, 1959.

219 "Siamese Twin Has an Operation—While Sister Sweats": "Siamese Twin Has an Operation—While Sister Sweats," *Detroit Free Press,* September 8, 1959.

219 "People in show business don't run to a doctor": "No Sob Story," *Detroit Free Press,* September 16, 1959.

220 "I'm not the patient": "Siamese Twins Daisy and Violet Have Surgery," *San Francisco Examiner,* October 10, 1959.

220 "We don't feel a thing": "Siamese Twin's Condition Is 'Fair' After Operation," *Oklahoma City Oklahoman,* September 8, 1959.

220 "It was a tense situation": "Siamese Twins Daisy and Violet Have Surgery," *San Francisco Examiner,* October 10, 1959.

220 "Naturally, I was worried": "Siamese Twin Has an Operation—While Sister Sweats," *Detroit Free Press,* September 8, 1959.

220 "successful in every way": "Siamese Twins Daisy and Violet Have Surgery," *San Francisco Examiner,* October 10, 1959.

220-221 "They didn't act like we were a clinical experiment" through "We've got our agent": "No Sob Story," *Detroit Free Press,* September 16, 1959.

221 "Do you know who I am?" through "And there in the backseat of the cab": Phillip Morris in Zemeckis, *Bound by Flesh.*

221 "They were coming up": "An Update to the Legend of Joined Twins," *Charlotte Observer*, May 25, 2014.

221-222 "Well, we're ready to work" through "Is there a theatrical hotel in town": Phillip Morris in Zemeckis, *Bound by Flesh*.

222 "They were like a couple of scared, shaking and hungry little puppies": Jensen, *Lives and Loves*, 358.

223 "time warp": Jensen, *Lives and Loves*, 358.

223 "They said an agent brought them": Dot Jackson, "The Only Bargain We Get Is Our Weight for a Penny," *Charlotte Observer*, January 7, 1969.

223 "We tried to suggest": Jensen, *Lives and Loves*, 360.

223 "They still imagined themselves to be stars": Jensen, *Lives and Loves*, 361.

224 "the sisters were constantly being duped": Henry Woodhead, "Twins Get Simple Funeral," *Charlotte News*, January 10, 1969.

224 "very delightful": Lynn Keziah in Zemeckis, *Bound by Flesh*.

224 "We laid their career to rest right here": Dot Jackson, "The Only Bargain We Get Is Our Weight for a Penny," *Charlotte Observer*, January 7, 1969.

CHAPTER 28

225 "They looked so sad": Jensen, *Lives and Loves*, 365.

226 "Now, that's a good sport": Rosemary Land in Zemeckis, *Bound by Flesh*.

226 "We want to see Mr. Reid" through "They sat down on one chair": Linda Reid Beatty in Zemeckis, *Bound by Flesh*.

226-227 "They told me they could mop my floors": David A. Moore, "A Tale of Two Sisters," *Charlotte Magazine*, July 2008.

227 "They caused quite a stir" through "And he prayed and prayed": Linda Reid Beatty in Zemeckis, *Bound by Flesh*.

227 *"Lord, I know you"*: Tommy Tomlinson, "Twins Had Quiet Life in Charlotte," *Charlotte Observer*, December 7, 1997.

227-228 **"I wanted to help them"** and **"I told them their hair had to be the same color"**: David A. Moore, "A Tale of Two Sisters," *Charlotte Magazine*, July 2008.

228 **"I don't know if they had ever done any manual labor"** and **"a-fussin' and a-gabbin' every minute"**: Jensen, *Lives and Loves*, 373.

228-229 **"They are perfectly charming people"**: "Action Line," *San Antonio Light*, December 2, 1967.

229 **"fanny-to-fanny"**: Jensen, *Lives and Loves*, 374.

229 **"They never said, 'Let's go over yonder'"**: Tommy Tomlinson, "Twins Had Quiet Life in Charlotte," *Charlotte Observer*, December 7, 1997.

229 **"Some even tried"** through **"but I could still"**: David A. Moore, "A Tale of Two Sisters," *Charlotte Magazine*, July 2008.

229 **"the diplomat"**: Tom Vinciguerra, "Twins Parting with the Stage," *Miami Herald*, April 17, 1955.

229 **"they all became meanies"**: Jensen, *Lives and Loves*, 377.

230 **"irresponsible parents"** and **"stormed into the store's office"**: Jensen, *Lives and Loves*, 378.

230 **"We want no part of the press"**: "Did You Wonder What Happened To: Daisy and Violet Hilton," *Miami Herald*, December 17, 1967.

230 **"They were model employees"**: Jensen, *Lives and Loves*, 379.

231 **"Nothing big and fancy"**: "Daisy, Violet Look to Future," *San Antonio Express*, January 13, 1931.

231 **"We never had a home"**: Alan Frazer, "My Boston," *Boston American*, August 10, 1960.

231 **"I would say they weren't unfriendly"**: Robert Tanzy in Zemeckis, *Bound by Flesh*.

231 **"The twins are a little haughty"**: Kenneth Nichols, "Hilton Siamese Twins Feature 'I,' Not "We,'" *Akron Beacon Journal*, September 5, 1952.

231-232 "We never allow people to get too close to us": Lindy Wilder, "Case of Give and Take with Siamese Sisters," *Newport News Daily Press,* October 15, 1960.

232 "We never get close to any woman": Michael Naver, "Two Together Half Century," *Baltimore Sun,* September 20, 1960.

232 "all sorts of questions": "Britain's Siamese Twins; Daisy and Violet Hilton Talk of Themselves," *Hull Daily Mail,* April 12, 1933.

232 "I think the first reaction": Tommy Tomlinson in Zemeckis, *Bound by Flesh.*

232 "Being stared at doesn't hurt you": Gladys Hall and Adele Whitely Fletcher, "We Interview the Siamese Twins," *Movie Weekly,* July 18, 1925.

232 "Daisy's the one that did most of the talking": Tommy Tomlinson, "Twins Had Quiet Life in Charlotte," *Charlotte Observer,* December 7, 1997.

233 "Housewives are the dullest people on earth": "Hilton Siamese Twins Keep Separate Interests Although Joined Together," *Burlington Free Press,* November 11, 1952.

233 "We don't like homes, families, and kids": Michael Naver, "Two Together Half Century," *Baltimore Sun,* September 20, 1960.

233 "He lived close to them": Linda Reid Beatty in Zemeckis, *Bound by Flesh.*

233 "They were always giving things away": Henry Woodhead, "Twins Get Simple Funeral," *Charlotte News,* January 10, 1969.

233 "Whatever became of the Hilton Sisters?": "The Hilton Sisters," *Philadelphia Enquirer,* January 5, 1964. (See also "Action Line," *San Antonio Light,* December 2, 1967.)

234 "I guess they felt": Jim Moore, 1978 interview with Esther MacMillan, 39, digital.utsa.edu/cdm/ref/collection/p15125coll4/id/794.

234 "I asked them not long ago": Dot Jackson, "The Only Bargain We Get Is Our Weight for a Penny," *Charlotte Observer,* January 7, 1969.

234 "They were eager to appear" and "I think the sisters were happiest": Henry Woodhead, "City's Siamese Twins Buried Simply," *Charlotte Observer,* January 9, 1969.

234 "I remember them telling me": Jensen, *Lives and Loves*, 376.

235 "be good" and "I don't know how many" through "They were still": Linda Reid Beatty in Zemeckis, *Bound by Flesh*.

CHAPTER 29

236 "mean stuff": Linda Reid Beatty in Zemeckis, *Bound by Flesh*.

236 "They were very rarely sick" and "just about every day": David A. Moore, "A Tale of Two Sisters," *Charlotte Magazine*, July 2008.

237 "tried to talk with them": "Funeral Set for Siamese Twins," *Charlotte Observer*, January 7, 1969.

237 "We are firmly convinced that" through "There is no doubt": Violet and Daisy Hilton with Michael Lorant, "Life and Loves of the Siamese Twins: Part 2," *The World's News*, October 6, 1937.

238 "Violet and I have always been together in life": "Why Being a Siamese Twin Is Not So Bad," *Louisville Courier-Journal*, January 4, 1925.

238 "half dead": Hussein Salih in David Cohen, "Separated but Still as One," *London Evening Standard*, February 6, 2003.

238 "I knew they hadn't gone": David A. Moore, "A Tale of Two Sisters," *Charlotte Magazine*, July 2008.

239-240 "Other girls may be able to do things we cannot": "Twin Beauties, 16, Linked by Physical Tie, Find Joy in Life," *Buffalo Enquirer*, November 29, 1924.

240 "*We were born this way*": "Hilton Siamese Twins Plan Comeback; Tire of Inactivity," *Quad City Times*, June 25, 1947.

240 "*This is the way*": "Siamese Twins, in City, Are Strong for Compromise," *Syracuse Post-Standard*, February 25, 1948.

240 "When the time comes to die": "Casper to Have Sight of Two 'Grown-Together' Girls Soon," *Casper Star*, June 17, 1923.

240 "No autopsy was performed": "Siamese Twins Buried Together," *Miami Herald*, January 13, 1969.

240 "They said to me, *Mr. Reid*": Tommy Tomlinson, "Twins Had Quiet Life in Charlotte," *Charlotte Observer*, December 7, 1997.

241 **"Perhaps the only normal thing"**: Henry Woodhead, "City's Siamese Twins Buried Simply," *Charlotte Observer*, January 9, 1969.

241 **"buried in style"**: "Hilton Twins Die at 60," *Greensboro Record*, January 6, 1969.

241 **"I wonder which one died first?"** and **"How many of you came here to grieve?"**: Henry Woodhead, "Twins Get Simple Funeral," *Charlotte News*, January 10, 1969.

241 **"Charlotte's prestige cemetery"**: Forest Lawn funeral notice, *Charlotte Observer*, January 8, 1969.

241-242 **"I didn't really know them"**: Henry Woodhead, "City's Siamese Twins Buried Simply," *Charlotte Observer*, January 9, 1969.

EPILOGUE

243 **"The only thing I can figure"**: Tommy Tomlinson, "Twins Had Quiet Life in Charlotte," *Charlotte Observer*, December 7, 1997.

243 **"They Lived and Died"** and **"their last theatrical appearance"**: Fox Drive-In Theatre advertisement in *Charlotte Observer*, January 31, 1969.

244 **"frantic tastelessness"**: Michael Kurchawa, "Millions of Reasons to Avoid Musical 'Twenty Fingers,'" *Chicago Tribune*, January 12, 1990.

244 **"a respectful"**: Greg Evans, "Side Show," *Variety*, October 20, 1997.

244 **"Fundraising for"** through **"They chose the"**: Alf Le Flohic, email to the author, March 5, 2019.

245 **"All I knew was my mother was adopted"** and **"I want people to know that someone cared"**: Mark Washburn, "An Update to the Legend of Joined Twins," *Charlotte Observer*, May 25, 2014.

245 **"If anybody would have loved them"**: Shelagh Childs, telephone interview with the author, January 12, 2020.

250 **"She treated them"**: "Siamese Twins' Luxury," *The People*, March 6, 1932.

250 **"Yes, [Mary] made"**: Barbara Hodgson, interview with Alf Le Flohic, July 28, 2018. Transcript deposited in the Keep, Brighton, England.

SOURCES

PRINT

Bogdan, Robert. *Freak Show: Presenting Human Oddities for Amusement and Profit.* Chicago: University of Chicago Press, 1988.

Dixon, Wheeler W., and Audrey Brown Fraser, eds. *I Went That-a-Way: The Memoirs of a Western Film Director, Harry L. Fraser.* Metuchen, NJ: Scarecrow Press, 1990.

Dreger, Alice Domurat. *One of Us: Conjoined Twins and the Future of Normal.* Cambridge, MA: Harvard University Press, 2004.

Frost, Linda. *Conjoined Twins in Black and White: The Lives of Millie-Christine McKoy and Daisy and Violet Hilton.* Madison: University of Wisconsin Press, 2009.

Jensen, Dean. *The Lives and Loves of Daisy and Violet Hilton: A True Story of Conjoined Twins.* Berkeley: Ten Speed Press, 2006.

Koch, Helen Lois. "Some Measurements of a Pair of Siamese Twins." *Journal of Comparative Psychology* 7, no. 4, (August 1927): 313–333.

Myers, Myer. *Souvenir and Life Story of San Antonio's Siamese Twins.* San Antonio: Naylor Printing Co., circa 1925.

Quigley, Christine. *Conjoined Twins: An Historical, Biological, and Ethical Issues Encyclopedia.* Jefferson, NC: McFarland & Co., Inc., 2003.

Saudek, Robert, and Ernest Seeman. "The Self-Expression of Identical Twins in Handwriting and Drawing." *Character and Personality* 1, no. 2, (December 1932): 91–128.

Skal, David J., and Elias Savada. *Dark Carnival: The Secret World of Tod Browning, Hollywood's Master of the Macabre.* New York: Anchor Books, 1995.

Thomson, Rosemarie Garland. *Freakery: Cultural Spectacles of the Extraordinary Body.* New York: New York University Press, 1996.

FILM

Zemeckis, Leslie, dir. *Bound by Flesh.* IFC Films, 2012.

Browning, Tod, dir. *Freaks.* Metro-Goldwyn-Mayer, 1932.

INDEX